Doing Task-based Teaching

Also published in
Oxford Handbooks for Language Teachers

Doing Task-based Teaching

Dave Willis and Jane Willis

OXFORD
UNIVERSITY PRESS

Great Clarendon Street, Oxford OX2 6DP

Oxford University Press is a department of the University of Oxford.
It furthers the University's objective of excellence in research, scholarship,
and education by publishing worldwide in

Oxford New York

Auckland Cape Town Dar es Salaam Hong Kong Karachi
Kuala Lumpur Madrid Melbourne Mexico City Nairobi
New Delhi Shanghai Taipei Toronto

With offices in

Argentina Austria Brazil Chile Czech Republic France Greece
Guatemala Hungary Italy Japan Poland Portugal Singapore
South Korea Switzerland Thailand Turkey Ukraine Vietnam

OXFORD and OXFORD ENGLISH are registered trade marks of
Oxford University Press in the UK and in certain other countries

© Oxford University Press 2007

ISBN: 978 0 19 442210 9

Printed in China

CONTENTS

ACKNOWLEDGEMENTS

When we began planning this book, we sent out a request to language teachers worldwide who were involved in TBT. We asked them to send us tasks which had worked well with their learners together with outline lesson plans to go with them. We also asked them what advice they would give to other teachers hoping to implement TBT, and to report difficulties and problems they had encountered themselves and had heard of from colleagues in connection with TBT. The response was magnificent. So first, and most importantly, we would like to thank the contributors listed at the end of this book, not only for sending us their tasks and ideas, but also for responding so willingly to our follow-up requests for more details. Sadly we were unable to find space for all the tasks sent in—we received well over 100—but everyone's advice has been collated and incorporated at relevant stages in the book, and especially in the final chapter. It is their co-operation that makes this book truly worthy of its title: *Doing Task-based Teaching*.

We'd also like to thank the large number of teachers and trainers whom we have met and talked to over the past ten years at conferences, workshops, and talks in Argentina, Brazil, Canada, Chile, Germany, Greece, Ireland, Italy, Japan, New Zealand, Pakistan, Portugal, South Korea, Spain, Switzerland, Taiwan, Thailand, Turkey, UAE, UK, and more recently at IATEFL conferences. We would also like to include participants in the TBLT 2005 conference at Leuven who sent us feedback through Steve Mann, who attended that conference. By asking questions and filling in slips of paper in workshop sessions, teachers have, sometimes unwittingly, contributed advice and ideas that have helped to shape this book We should also thank Masters students at Birmingham and Aston Universities who, through their assignments and research, have given us useful insights into classrooms all over the world and demonstrated how TBT can work in practice.

Several people—whose names we do not know—read various early outlines and drafts of chapters and commented thoughtfully and constructively on many aspects, helping us to reshape and fine-tune the contents. Steve Mann gave us detailed feedback on the last four chapters, which certainly clarified a few issues for us, and helped to make the final version more readable. Roger Hawkey kindly wrote a short section on testing for our final chapter. We are very grateful to you all and just hope that we have done justice to your suggestions.

Many other people, including former colleagues from Aston University and the University of Birmingham, have helped and encouraged us in many ways. Thanks to all of you, too.

INTRODUCTION

Doing Task-based Teaching has been written for language teachers who want to gain a better understanding of how task-based teaching (TBT) works in practice. It aims to give beginner teachers the confidence to start using tasks in their lessons, and help experienced teachers to widen their repertoire of tasks and task sequences. It draws on the classroom experiences not only of the writers themselves, but of over 30 teachers in twelve different countries. These committed teachers have sent in examples of tasks they have designed and used successfully in their lessons. In the book we take further account of the realities of the classroom by looking at ways of combining a task-based approach with current coursebooks.

Chapter 1 begins by exploring some commonly held views on TBT and addressing some common misconceptions. It distinguishes between approaches that begin with a focus on grammatical form and those that begin with a focus on meaning, and looks at the principles that underpin them. It explores the meaning of the term 'task' and argues that a teacher-controlled focus on grammar should come at the end of a task cycle.

From Chapter 2 onwards, the emphasis is very much on *doing* task-based teaching.

Chapter 2 describes four practical sequences of meaning-focused activities leading to a focus on form. These sequences are used to illustrate a coherent and accessible explanation of some basic theories and principles behind TBT.

The next three chapters (3, 4, and 5) focus on designing tasks. They illustrate a variety of different task types, and look at ways of grading, appraising, and evaluating tasks. For each task type, there are examples of specific tasks used in classrooms round the world, as described by the teachers who used them. There is detailed advice on generating effective tasks for different levels of learner and on integrating reading and writing activities.

Chapter 6 distinguishes between a focus on language in use and a focus on form in isolation. It explores stages in a task cycle where learners are naturally concerned with improving their language and becoming more accurate (language focus). Turning to a focus on form, the chapter illustrates how different items can be identified and taken from the language of the spoken or written texts associated with a task sequence and used as the basis for form-focused exercises. Many examples are given and there is advice on finding and creating texts and preparing for examinations.

Chapter 7 looks at typical classroom discourse and explores how far it can be extended to reflect the language used in the discourse arenas of the world outside. The use of tasks opens up a far wider potential for real-world language use, especially when teaching students with specific needs. This chapter describes 'real-world' tasks that incorporate everyday English and electronic communication. It lists typical features of spontaneous spoken English, examples of which can be brought into the classroom. It acknowledges the difficulties in dealing with variable social dimensions and illustrates task sequences leading to role-plays designed to highlight the social dimension. Finally, it explores the roles of a TBT teacher—as a manager of discourse as well as a purveyor of knowledge.

Chapter 8 illustrates ways of adapting and refining tasks to tailor them more precisely to the needs of specific classes, to make them more engaging and to guard against minimal participation by less motivated learners. Planning a task-based lesson involves making decisions about pre- and post-task activities, the outcome, interim goals and structure of the task, interaction patterns and the degree of accuracy, and/or spontaneity. The chapter also illustrates the need to devise very clear instructions. Each of the seven broad parameters in task design is further broken down into specific aspects that can be adjusted or 'tweaked' in different ways. Readers are encouraged to experiment by changing one such aspect to see what difference it makes in their lessons and to plan a small-scale action research project.

Chapter 9, on task-based syllabus design, outlines the problems with starting from an itemized language-based syllabus and looks at different meaning-based approaches to syllabus design. It discusses task-based syllabuses for the design of ESP, general, examination, and coursebook based courses, as well as courses based on learner outcomes or 'can do' statements. Starting with topic lexis is essential to facilitate task-based interactions, and the problem of integrating systematic language coverage in TBT can be solved through use of a pedagogic corpus. Finally, there is an explanation and summary of a set of procedures for syllabus design.

Chapter 10 takes up the most frequently asked questions about TBT that have not already been answered in the first nine chapters. It begins with a summary of the most commonly reported problems with TBT, and then responds to questions that arise out of these problems, such as integrating TBT into the prescribed coursebook. It looks at ways of turning textbook activities into tasks, making time to do tasks in class, dealing with large classes, stimulating unmotivated and unwilling learners, combating overuse of L1, and handling mixed ability classes. The chapter includes much advice from the teachers who contributed tasks and it ends with their most useful tips for teachers who hope to implement TBT in the future.

Reader activities are included at intervals throughout the book and follow-up activities and further reading appear at the end of most chapters. These activities aim to help readers to reflect constructively on what has gone before or to prepare for what is coming in the next section. There are also activities of a more practical nature, applying the ideas in the preceding section to the reader's own teaching context, for example, designing a specific task and writing task instructions for a class of their own, planning a task-based sequence, identifying useful language features in a text, and designing form-focused exercises for those features. Many activities could be used to promote constructive discussion or provide the basis for written assignments on teacher training programmes.

The Appendices include lesson plans and commentaries for tasks, projects and scenarios, tape-scripts, a sample course outline, and a sample handout that can be used in a workshop on task design. The aim is to supply teachers with enough data so they can adapt and try these tasks out with their own classes and plan their own form-focused materials.

Note on terminology

The book is entitled *Doing Task-based Teaching* and we have on the whole used TBT as the short form to refer to task-based teaching. Of course, where teaching goes on, learning does, too—or so we hope! The reader will, therefore, find TBL used from time to time, particularly when we are quoting from the work of others.

Dave Willis and Jane Willis, Kendal, Cumbria, February 2006

1 THE BASIS OF A TASK-BASED APPROACH

1.1 *What do you think about task-based teaching?*

Proponents of task-based teaching (TBT) argue that the most effective way to teach a language is by engaging learners in real language use in the classroom. This is done by designing tasks—discussions, problems, games, and so on—which require learners to use the language for themselves. But TBT is not the same the world over. Teachers who begin with the notion that tasks should be central to teaching then go on to refine an approach which fits their own classrooms and their own students. (See Edwards and J. Willis 2005.) Before going on to discuss TBT in greater detail it is necessary to look carefully at some of the things which are important in a task-based approach.

READER ACTIVITY 1A

The essentials of a task-based approach

Think about what you have heard about TBT and say how far you agree with the following statements:

1 Many people can operate effectively in a foreign language even though their grammar is limited and they make a lot of mistakes.
2 Learners will not be able to do a task unless they have the right grammar.
3 TBT accepts the importance of grammar.
4 TBT is not suitable for learners who are preparing for an examination.
5 You do not have to be a highly experienced teacher to use TBT effectively.
6 You cannot do TBT unless your own English is completely fluent and accurate.
7 TBT can be used to teach both the spoken and the written language.
8 Tasks are always done in pairs or groups.

Commentary

Here is a commentary on these eight statements:

1 Most of us know someone who fits this description. Some years ago we were shown round the city of Prague by a Czech friend whose English was very limited. He was rarely able to produce a full sentence without at least one or

two mistakes. He rarely used a past tense form, yet he managed to tell us all about the Prague Spring of 1970 using present tense forms with appropriate past adverbials. Even with his severely limited English he was fluent and entertaining. The important thing was that he was willing to make the most of the English he had. This is one of the most valuable things we can give a learner: the confidence and willingness to have a go, even if their language resources are limited. Many of us fall into this category ourselves with respect to at least one foreign language which we use occasionally but have never mastered.

2 This depends what you mean by 'the right grammar'. Learners talk about the past long before they have control of the past tense: they say things like 'Yesterday I play tennis'. Long before they have proper control of question forms they can make questions using intonation and interrogative words:

Where you live?
What you want?

In commenting on the previous question we pointed out that learners can be highly resourceful language users, creating complex meanings even with a limited grammar. One of the most important things about TBT is that it promotes learners' confidence by providing them with plenty of opportunities to use language in the classroom without being constantly afraid of making mistakes. Once they have a stock of words they can begin to communicate. And, once they begin to communicate, we can help them shape their language so that it becomes more complex and more grammatical.

3 Most current approaches to TBT certainly recognize the importance of grammar. Today task-based activities are almost always followed by one or more form-focused activity. Many traditional methodologies begin by teaching grammatical forms and then go on to set communicative activities in which they believe learners will be able to use those forms. The initial aim of TBT is to encourage learners to engage in meaning with the language resources they already have. This makes learners acutely aware of what they need to learn. They are then given form-focused activities to help them develop that language. They may later do a repeat task which gives them the opportunity to incorporate some of the language they have focused on at an earlier stage.

4 TBT is certainly not designed with examinations in mind. It is designed to produce learners who can use their English in the real world outside the classroom, even if that language is grammatically inaccurate. If an examination genuinely tests learners' ability to use the language, then TBT will prepare them for this very effectively. Unfortunately some examinations set a much higher premium on grammatical accuracy than on the ability to use the language. But TBT can be adapted to prepare learners for examinations of this kind. In Chapter 6 we will look at form-focused activities within the context of a TBT programme. The form-focused activities which follow a task can be designed or

supplemented to reflect the sort of question that learners will face in the examination.

5 Any teacher will need basic classroom skills—the ability to motivate learners and organize activities in the classroom. They will also need to be able to demonstrate and explain important language features. So an experienced teacher who already has these skills will start with an advantage. But the most important thing in TBT is the willingness to engage with learners in communication, and to allow learners the freedom to use the language. Some experienced teachers find this very difficult because they are used to controlling learner language in order to avoid mistakes. TBT requires a willingness to surrender some of that control. Teachers who come to the classroom with an open mind, whether they are experienced or inexperienced, will learn to use TBT effectively if they have the confidence to trust the learners and give them every opportunity to use the language for themselves.

6 Sometimes teachers who don't have confidence in their own English respond by controlling learners very strictly, so that they can predict almost everything that will happen in the classroom. But if learners are always controlled, they will never learn to use language freely. They need an English-speaking model, and the best model they can get is a teacher whom they respect. So try to use English freely in the classroom even if you do make some mistakes. Mistakes are a natural part of spontaneous use. Once learners are involved in a task which engages their interest, they won't even notice them. So use your English to talk freely to learners: don't deprive them of the best learning aid they could possibly have. You are much more valuable as a model than the cassette recorder, or CD, or video screen.

7 Many people believe that TBT focuses almost entirely on the spoken language. There is certainly a lot of talking in the TBT classroom, from both teachers and learners, but TBT can also be used to teach reading (see Chapter 3) and to provide valuable writing practice as illustrated in later chapters.

8 It is true that many task-based teachers like learners to work in pairs or groups. This is generally because this gives learners more opportunities to use the language for themselves. But TBT can certainly be accommodated within a teacher-led classroom (see Chapter 7), and one of the most successful practitioners of TBT, N. S. Prabhu, used a teacher-fronted methodology (Prabhu 1987), working always with the class as a whole.

1.2 *Starting with form and starting with meaning: alternative approaches to teaching*

Some approaches to language teaching, which we will call form-based approaches, are based on the belief that we need to take great care, at each stage of learning, that learners produce the language accurately. Usually this involves a focus on form at the very beginning of a teaching sequence. By a focus on form we mean that teachers isolate one or two specific forms, specific grammatical structures or functional realizations, and identify these as the target forms. Learners know that by the end of the teaching sequence, often contained in a single lesson, they will be expected to produce these forms with an acceptable level of accuracy.

A well known form-focused approach is often known as PPP (Presentation → Practice → Production). This begins by highlighting one or two new forms and illustrating their meaning. It then goes on to practise that form under careful teacher control. This control is gradually relaxed until finally learners are offered the opportunity to produce the target form(s) in a communicative activity. This approach has four main characteristics:

1 A focus on one or two forms, specified by the teacher, which are later to be incorporated in the performance of a communicative activity.
2 This focus on form comes *before* learners engage in communicative activity.
3 Teacher control of learner language. This is imposed strictly in the early stages of the cycle and gradually relaxed.
4 The success of the procedure is judged in terms of whether or not learners do produce the target forms with an acceptable level of accuracy.

Other approaches, which we will call meaning-based approaches, are based on the belief that it is more effective to encourage learners to use the language as much as possible, even if this means that some of the language they produce is inaccurate. Teachers provide learners with opportunities in the classroom to use the language for genuine communication. This involves a focus on *meaning*. Inevitably, in the course of a meaning-focused activity, learners will sometimes naturally focus on language for themselves. They will, for example, stop for a moment to think 'How do I best express this next idea?', 'What's the word for X?', or 'Should I be using the past tense here?' When this happens learners are not simply thinking about forms specified by the teacher and how best to incorporate these forms in their output. They are thinking about language in general and searching their own language repertoire to decide how best to express themselves in a given communicative situation. We will call this a focus on *language*. Sometimes this focus on language involves teacher participation too. Teachers repeat learner utterances, reshaping them to make them clearer, or supply words or phrases to help learners shape their message. When teachers do this they are acting as participants in the interaction. As long as teachers are doing this in order to help learners with communication we regard it as a focus on language.

Finally, teachers direct learners' attention to specific forms which occur in the course of a task or an associated text. They may exemplify, explain and practice these forms. This we will call a focus on *form*. Teachers should take care that this focus on form does not detract from a focus on meaning. The simplest way to do this is to withhold this focus on form until after a task has been completed. Sometimes this focus on form is incidental. The teacher stops a learner and offers correction. This correction is aimed primarily at ensuring that the learner is aware of the correct form. It is not offered to help with meaning. When teachers do this they are standing outside the interaction and commenting on learners' performance with regard to accuracy.

We are, then, looking at a three-way distinction:
- A focus on *meaning*, in which participants are concerned with communication.
- A focus on *language*, in which learners pause in the course of a meaning-focused activity to think for themselves how best to express what they want to say, or a teacher takes part in the interaction and acts as a facilitator by rephrasing or clarifying learner language.
- A focus on *form* in which one or more lexical or grammatical forms are isolated and specified for study, or in which the teacher comments on student language by drawing attention to problems.

Long (1988) makes a similar distinction, but uses different terminology, contrasting a focus on *form* (singular) with a focus on *forms* (plural). Roughly speaking, what he refers to as a focus on *form,* we have referred to as a focus on *language*; and what he refers to as a focus on *forms* (plural), we have referred to as a focus on *form* (singular).

A meaning-focused approach normally involves a focus on meaning and a focus on language *before* a focus on form. Meaning-based approaches have the following characteristics:

1 The teacher does not attempt to control learner language.
2 The success of the procedure is judged on whether or not learners communicate successfully.
3 At some stages during a meaning-focused cycle of activities learners and teachers will focus on language. Learners will pause to think how best to express themselves and may discuss different options with fellow students or look for help in a dictionary or grammar book. Teachers will participate in the interaction by helping learners to shape and clarify what they want to say.

4 Focus on form comes after focus on meaning. Advocates of a meaning-based approach will spend most of the time in the classroom on activities which promote communicative language use, but will supplement these with activities designed to promote accuracy. Course books which take a form-based approach encourage teachers to devote a lot of time in the classroom to form-focused activities, presenting specific forms of the language to their students and practising those forms. They will, however, almost certainly reinforce these activities with opportunities for communicative language use.

1.3 Language as meaning

When children begin to use their first language they communicate without using sentences. Early utterances may simply consist of pairs of nouns like 'book table'. Depending on the context and intonation and the accompanying gestures this may be interpreted as 'The book is on the table', or 'Please put the book on the table', or 'Shall I put the book on the table?' Relying on a shared context, children manage to convey meanings quite effectively without using grammatical sentences. Much the same is true of learners at the elementary level.

Taking this observation as a starting point, one might argue that early communication is primarily lexical and that grammar plays a subsidiary function. Let us put this to the test by looking at a text which has minimal grammar:

> Mother little girl. Mother say little girl go see grandmother. Mother give little girl big basket food. Mother say 'You take food grandmother ...'.[1]

We feel reasonably confident that many of you will have identified the opening of the story of *Little Red Riding Hood*. It is not true to say, however, that we have simply a string of words to tell this story. If we had offered you the sequence:

> Mother girl little. Say mother grandmother go see girl little. Basket big food girl little mother give. Say 'Grandmother food take you ...' mother.

You would certainly have found this much more difficult, perhaps impossible, to interpret. What, then, is the important difference between the first and the second versions of the story?

You might answer this by saying that the word order in the first version makes sense. More precisely, you might say the first version follows the conventions of English clause and phrase structure. Each clause has the

---

[1] We are indebted to Andrew Wright for this striking example.

structure 'subject + verb + ...'. In the phrases 'little girl' and 'big basket' the adjective comes in front of the noun. So the first version does conform to some of the rules of English grammar. It follows the rules of English word order, the rules of English clause and phrase structure.

So, it is possible to tell a story quite adequately with a string of words and a very limited grammar of structure. There are no definite articles or indefinite articles in the first version of the story, and no other determiners such as 'this/that' or 'his/her'. There are no verb tenses. This raises an interesting question. If things like articles and tenses are unnecessary why do we bother with them at all? The answer, of course, is that articles and tenses are far from unnecessary. Even in the telling of a simple story we can make things much easier for our listener by using the full resources of the grammar:

> Once upon a time there was a mother who had a little girl. The little girl was going to see her grandmother. Her mother gave her a big basket of food and said 'Take this food to your grandmother'.

So grammar is vital if we want to make things reasonably easy for listeners or readers.

It is also difficult to express complex abstract meanings without grammar. One day our daughter, Jenny, was playing in the garden with her two-year-old son. He was filling a bottle with water from an outside tap, pouring the water in a hole he had dug and watching it disappear. Jenny was thirsty and asked him for the bottle. When he gave it to her she drank some of the water. He was horrified. 'No,' he said, 'that water not for drinking. It for putting in hole.' He used the form 'for + -ing' to express purpose, and it is difficult to see how he could have got his message across efficiently without that complex little bit of grammar.

It is, then, possible to make meanings with a very limited grammar. Many of us go through life as foreign language users with a very limited grammar, and most of us know people who can manage quite effectively in English even though they do not have command of basic grammar like the past tense and question forms. But if we want to express meanings in an efficient, listener/reader friendly manner we need more than vocabulary and word order. We also need a grammar that identifies things clearly and relates them to one another: articles and determiners. We need a grammar that places things in a temporal setting: a tense system. And we need a grammar that is capable of expressing abstract relations, phrases like 'for + -ing' to express purpose.

This suggests two possible starting points for language teaching. One possibility would be to see meaning as the starting point for language development, and to see form as developing from meaning. If we take this line we would encourage learners to use the language as much as possible to communicate. As we have seen, vocabulary is central to communication, so it would be necessary to introduce learners to the basic vocabulary for a given topic, but it would not be necessary in the same way to provide complex grammatical input for the task. This does not mean that we would ignore grammar in a task-based approach. But it would not be the initial aim of instruction. We would still provide learners with guidance to help them develop an acceptable grammar of the language. And we would still provide sample sentences to illustrate the target grammar. But this would be subordinated to encouraging learners to use the language freely, without worrying too much about formal accuracy. The success of a teaching programme would be judged in terms of the learners' growing ability to use the language for communication.

The second possibility is to see form as primary. If we take this view, we seek first to introduce acceptable forms in the target language and then to provide learners with opportunities to associate these forms with appropriate meanings. Teaching procedures are designed to teach learners to produce a range of grammatical sentences. This does not mean that vocabulary is ignored and that there is no focus on meaning. Vocabulary is taught, but it is secondary to grammar. The aim of teaching is to introduce acceptable sentences. We can think of these sentences as grammatical frames. Vocabulary simply provides items to fill out these frames.

This approach does not ignore meaning and communication. Once the grammar has been taught learners are provided with opportunities to use it in meaningful situations. The primary focus, however, is on grammatical accuracy. The success of a lesson is judged in terms of the learners' growing ability to produce formally accurate sentences in the target language.

Of course most approaches to language teaching seek to provide a balance between form and meaning. Teachers will provide a variety of lessons, with some of them offering a primary focus on form, and others, often called *skills lessons*, providing a primary focus on meaning. TBT has a good deal in common with skills lessons.

1.4 *Meaning and tasks in the classroom*

Some of the most successful activities in the classroom involve a *spontaneous* exchange of meanings. Perhaps the teacher starts by telling a personal story which immediately engages the learners' interest. They respond with stories of their own. Learners who are not telling stories are listening with interest, working hard to understand what is going on. The teacher helps by providing the odd vocabulary item and by occasionally stepping in and rephrasing a learner's contribution. The same kind of thing might happen with a discussion. The teacher begins by stating an opinion. Learners respond with their own opinions and a useful discussion ensues.

These are golden moments in a language classroom. There is real personal involvement, with an accompanying increase in confidence and fluency. Almost certainly learners will experience some language development. They will pick up the odd useful phrase or vocabulary item from the language they are exposed to. They may find the answer to some grammatical problem which has been worrying them for some time. They may suddenly find, for example, that the question forms which have been so elusive begin to come spontaneously and fluently. A gifted teacher may be quick enough to analyse some of the language used in this sort of classroom exchange and use it for form-focused work in this or a subsequent lesson.

But it is impossible to guarantee this kind of spontaneous activity in the classroom. Spontaneity cannot, by definition, be produced to order. There are also questions to be raised about such spontaneous activities. Can we be sure that a given topic will engage learners' interest? How do we know that all of the class will be genuinely involved in discussion or story telling? Can we be sure what language will occur to provide opportunities for form-focused work? It is very difficult to provide language support on the spur of the moment. Will the teacher be able to take immediate advantage of form-focused opportunities which do occur? Let us look at a brief sequence of activities which might help us meet some of these possible shortcomings of a reliance on spontaneous engagement.

There are a number of burning social issues in the modern world which concern almost all societies. One of these is the use of addictive drugs. Many people have firm opinions on the subject. It is quite possible that a teacher with an adult class at a reasonably advanced level could introduce a successful and spontaneous activity simply by referring to a recent newspaper article and expressing an opinion. The class might well respond to this by expressing their own opinions and engaging in argument and discussion.

Let us imagine however that the teacher decides to take a rather more structured approach. For example, if you want to promote discussion of any controversial topic you can prepare students by offering a series of statements and asking learners as individuals to say how far they agree with each statement and to give reasons for their opinions. The following sample activity demonstrates how this may be done.

SAMPLE ACTIVITY SEQUENCE

Drug abuse

Here are some statements about the problem of addictive drugs. Look at these statements and give each one a mark from 1 to 4, according to the following scale:

1 = strongly agree   3 = disagree
2 = agree   4 = strongly disagree

1 All drugs should be legalized.
2 So-called soft drugs, like cannabis, should be legalized, but hard drugs should never be legalized.
3 All convicted drug dealers should be given long prison sentences.
4 The property of convicted drug dealers should be confiscated.
5 Profits made from drug dealing should be confiscated.
6 It is pointless to send drug addicts to prison. In most cases this will simply reinforce the habit.

This opinion survey could be central to a sequence of activities:

1 The teacher introduces the topic and highlights one or two issues.
2 The teacher introduces the survey, asking for a brief statement of opinions on one or two issues, drawing attention to some of the lexis related to the topic.
3 Learners work as individuals to set down their opinions on the 1–4 scale, and to think of supporting arguments.
4 Learners work in groups to compare opinions and decide on a group rating on the 1–4 scale.
5 Teacher chairs a general class discussion.
6 Learners read a text on the issues and compare the author's views with their own.
7 Teacher chairs a discussion in which learners compare the author's views with their own.

These procedures are designed to provide a focus for discussion and reading by providing a clear outcome. The survey provides a very clear outcome. Individual learners express their opinions in the form of a 1–4 rating. They are then required to justify their opinions in a group discussion. The teacher then elicits the outcome of the group discussion with questions like 'Ramon, in your group, how many people agreed that soft drugs should be legalized?', and follow up questions like 'What about your group, Maria? Did you all agree or were there disagreements?'

When learners go on to read the text, they have a clear purpose. They want to find the writer's opinion on a number of specific issues. They are probably interested by now to find out how far the writer supports their own particular views.

What we have done here is provide a formal framework to promote discussion and to provide a reason for reading.

READER ACTIVITY 1B

Why should we structure a discussion?

What do you think is to be gained from formalizing a discussion in this way?

Commentary

There are at least six possible advantages to be gained from formalizing the discussion:

1 It gives the teacher the opportunity to introduce in a meaningful context some of the vocabulary—words and phrases—which will be useful in the discussion. The vocabulary will be introduced as the teacher goes through the opinion survey, explaining what is involved in the statements.

2 Learners are given the opportunity to gather their thoughts as they work with the opinion survey, before they go into the group discussion.

3 It is much easier to express an opinion on a very specific issue than on a general topic. If you say to someone 'Do you agree that all drug dealers should get long prison sentences?', you are more likely to get a response than if you simply say 'What do you think about dangerous drugs?'

4 All learners are required to form an opinion and to engage with the topic. Some will do so with lively interest. Others may find this particular topic less interesting. But they will all be engaged at some level.

5 If learners have no real opinion on the issue, they may stand apart from the discussion. But once they have committed themselves to an opinion by entering it as a 1–4, they are more likely to defend that opinion.

6 The questionnaire and the text will provide material for form-focused activities at a later stage in the teaching sequence. It is possible to identify before the lesson those language items which are worth focusing on. This means that the teacher will have time to prepare form-focused activities before the lesson.

When we offer the learners formalized activities of the kind described above to facilitate their participation in meaningful activities we are engaging in task-based learning. Instead of relying on the learners' spontaneous interest and reaction, we are designing activities which will help promote interest and interaction. It is activities of this kind which we call *tasks*. Task-based learning and teaching is a development on CLT (communicative language teaching) in that it lays emphasis on the design of tasks and the development of task-based teaching.

So we create tasks to facilitate meaningful activities in the classroom. Tasks are not a substitute for interesting topics which engage learners' interest, but they can enhance that engagement and interest.

1.5 *Characterizing tasks*

If you ask the question 'What is a task?' in the context of language teaching, you will get different answers from different researchers and practitioners. Some would call almost any classroom activity a task:

> Task is therefore assumed to refer to a range of work-plans which have the overall purpose of facilitating language learning—from the brief and simple exercise type to more complex and lengthy activities such as group problem-solving or simulations and decision-making. (Breen 1987)

Unfortunately this definition includes anything that might happen in a language classroom, so it is not very useful if we are trying to characterize task-based teaching in order to distinguish it from other kinds of teaching. Let us look at some more sharply focused definitions:

READER ACTIVITY 1C:

Characterizing tasks

Here are four definitions of task taken from the literature on task-based teaching. Make a list of the features of a task these writers refer to. Which do you think is the most complete definition?

1 'A piece of classroom work which involves learners in comprehending, manipulating, producing, or interacting in the target language while their attention is principally focused on meaning rather than form.' (Nunan 1989)
2 '[Tasks are] activities where the target language is used by the learner for a communicative purpose (goal) in order to achieve an outcome.' (J. Willis 1996)
3 'A task is an activity in which
   • meaning is primary
   • learners are not given other people's meanings to regurgitate
   • there is some sort of relationship to comparable real world activities
   • task completion has some sort of priority
   • the assessment of the task is in terms of outcome.' (Skehan 1998)
4 '… we define a *language use task* as an activity that involves individuals in using language for the purpose of achieving a particular goal or outcome in a particular situation.' (Bachman and Palmer 1996)

Commentary

In the light of our earlier discussion it is not surprising that meaning plays a large part in these attempts to characterize a task. The first definition (Nunan) highlights *meaning*. Definitions 2 (Willis) and 4 (Bachman and Palmer) highlight *outcome* or *goal*. We have shown how a task can provide a formal framework for meaningful discussion by providing an explicit outcome or goal. The most complete definition is 3 (Skehan). Skehan includes meaning, and suggests that learners should be producing their own meanings, not simply regurgitating or repeating something that they have been told by someone else; it includes outcome by suggesting that task *completion* has priority, in other words that it is important to achieve an outcome; and it says that the assessment of the activity should be seen in terms of outcome. Finally, Skehan suggests that a classroom task should relate in some way to an activity in the *real world*.

We can, then, determine how task-like a given activity is by asking the following questions. The more confidently we can answer *yes* to each of these questions the more task-like the activity.

1 Does the activity engage learners' interest?
2 Is there a primary focus on meaning?
3 Is there an outcome?
4 Is success judged in terms of outcome?
5 Is completion a priority?
6 Does the activity relate to real world activities?

The first of these introduces as an additional feature: the notion of engagement. This is because without engagement, without genuine interest, there can be no focus on meaning or outcome. Learners have to want to achieve an outcome, they have to want to engage in meaning.

Figure 1.1 Does the activity engage the learners?

These criteria will not provide us with a watertight *definition* of what constitutes a task, but they will provide us with guidelines for the design of activities which are task-like in that they involve real language use. This is very much in line with Skehan's conclusion:

… some of the time it may be difficult to decide whether an activity merits the label 'task' since the two underlying characteristics of tasks, avoidance of specific structures and engagement in worthwhile meanings, are matters of degree, rather than being categorical. (1998: 96)

READER ACTIVITY 1D

Evaluating a task

Look back to the opinion survey about drugs above. How does it meet the criteria set out above?

Commentary

1 The topic is probably intrinsically engaging for many learners. The task seeks to secure engagement from *all* learners.

2 If the activity is introduced without any preceding language study then it is almost certain that there will be a focus on meaning, on the exchange of opinions and supporting arguments. On the other hand, it would detract from the activity as a task if there was an introductory activity practising passive modal verbs with sentences like:

> I think soft drugs should be legalized.
> Drug traffickers should be sent to gaol.

After an introduction like this, there would be a stronger tendency for learners to focus on specific forms. This tendency would probably be even stronger if students were given explicit instructions such as:

> Try to use the following forms in your discussion:
> 'should be punished', 'should be confiscated'

So the more we try to control the language that learners produce, the more learners are likely to be concerned with form rather than meaning, and the less task-like the activity becomes.

Since communication depends crucially on vocabulary, it may well be necessary to introduce a number of vocabulary items to enable students to complete the activity. This is the purpose of the teacher explaining the opinion survey and initiating a brief preliminary discussion. But there is no need to focus on grammar before beginning the task.

3 The purpose of the opinion survey is precisely this: to provide an outcome. Instead of just having a general discussion without any definite conclusion, learners are asked to commit themselves to a rating for each statement.

4 This will depend on how the teacher handles the activity. If, for example, a teacher moves round the groups correcting their language this moves the criteria for success towards accuracy, and the focus of the activity towards form rather than outcome and meaning. If, on the other hand, the teacher

leaves the groups to get on with the discussion or, while moving round the groups, facilitates the discussion, clarifying learner language, expressing opinions and agreement or disagreement, then this reinforces the importance of outcome.

If the teacher provides a follow-up activity which values the student discussion, this enhances the importance of outcome. So if groups are given a chance to express their opinions to the class as a whole and if this leads on to a serious class discussion, then this again enhances the importance of outcome. If, on the other hand, the teacher gives little value to the conclusions that students have reached and moves on rapidly to another activity, this will detract from the importance of outcome.

As with meaning, the focus on outcome depends on the way a teacher handles the activity. The more a teacher values students' opinions and encourages them to express their opinions, the more task-like the activity becomes.

5 Students should be given reasonable time to complete the activity and should be encouraged to do so.

6 This activity relates to real-world activities on three levels:

Level 1: On a very general level it gives learners the opportunity to engage in producing meanings which will be useful in the real world. They will be using vocabulary to do with a topic of general interest. They will also be expressing opinions on how the world ought to be rather than simply on how it is. In some cases they will be using language that is already familiar to them. In other cases they will be stretching their language resources to enable them to express new meanings. We might call level 1 the level of *meaning*.

Level 2: At another level they will be practising a kind of discourse which is very common in everyday life. They will be expressing opinions and constructing arguments to support those opinions. They will be agreeing and disagreeing; explaining, elaborating, and organizing their arguments; relating to arguments produced by others; and so on. We might call this the level of *discourse*.

Level 3: At yet another level they will be engaging in an activity which could quite easily occur in the real world. It is quite conceivable that they might, on some future occasion, be engaged in a discussion on this very topic. We might call this the level of *activity*.

So the relationship with real-world activity is a complex one. Some activities engage with the real world on all three of the levels we have listed. Other activities may engage only on the first two levels.

Not all tasks meet the real-world criterion so satisfactorily. There are, for example, a lot of games-playing activities which do not relate precisely to the use of language outside the classroom. Our learners are not learning English so that they can play games outside the classroom. But in playing the game they are using lots of language and language skills which will be useful outside. But an activity should relate to the real world at least on levels 1 and 2 if it is to be a useful and motivating task.

1.6 *Why not start with grammar?*

Many lessons begin by isolating one or two forms for study. These forms are then presented and practised in various ways so that they become foremost in the learners' minds. The teacher then moves on to a communicative activity—a task, if you like. But learners have already been primed to focus on particular forms. Let us imagine that the teacher wants to teach verbs of liking and disliking followed by the –ing form. Learners are exposed to sentences like: 'I like playing tennis', 'I don't like skiing', 'I love listening to music', 'I hate cooking'. These forms are practised intensively. The teacher then asks learners to work in groups and find out what group members like and dislike. They are told to use the forms they have practised.

It may seem that this group activity focuses on both form and meaning. But this is very difficult for learners to think about both form and meaning at the same time, particularly at the elementary level. This is difficult even for accomplished language users. Some years ago there was a radio quiz programme in which contestants were asked to face the YES/NO challenge. All they had to do to win a handsome prize was answer questions for one minute without saying 'yes' or 'no'. This may sound easy, but the contestants always found it extremely difficult. Indeed it was very unusual for anyone to win the YES/NO challenge. And the audience took great delight in the fact that something which seemed so easy turned out to be so difficult. They roared with laughter when a contestant said 'yes' or 'no' and the quizmaster banged his gong. The quizmaster would start off with a few opening questions like 'What's your name?' and 'Where do you live?' Very often he would repeat the answer so you would get a sequence like:

A   What's your name?
B   John.
A   John?
B   Yes.
GONG!

The better contestants would be looking out for this trick, so they would answer 'That's right', or 'Correct', or something like that. Then the questioning might go on for some time until a sequence like this occurred:

A You live in Manchester?
B That is correct.
A And your name is Joe?
B No, John.
GONG!

Some contestants would concentrate so hard on what they were saying that their words became very hesitant and unnatural. But they were nearly always caught out in the end:

A Time's nearly up. You're doing really well, aren't you?
B Yes.
GONG!

This simple game seems to us to show that it is extremely difficult to concentrate on what we are going to say and at the same time on *how* we are going to say it, in the sense of what words or forms we are going to use. The contestants found it almost impossible to take part in a question and answer session and, at the same time, to think about the form of their answers, *how* they were answering questions, so as to avoid saying 'yes' or 'no'.

How much more will this apply to learners? If they have been asked to concentrate on producing forms of the language which they have only just been presented and practised—for example, the –ing form of the verb—will they be able at the same time to think about what it is they want to say? It seems to us that learners will be obliged to follow one of two possible strategies:

- They might try conscientiously to produce the target form. As a result their language will be halting and stilted. They will be unable to concern themselves with real-time communication because their attention is taken up with thinking about form. If this happens they are only getting practice in making sentences. There is not a primary focus on meaning.
- They will engage with meaning and will ignore the fact that they are supposed to be producing a particular form. They will engage in a meaning-focused activity, in spite of the teacher's intentions and wishes. If this happens then learners have transformed the activity into a task with a focus on meaning, but from the teacher's point of view the lesson has failed in its declared aim of helping learners incorporate the target form in their spontaneous language use.

They may of course switch between these two strategies, first focusing on meaning, then, possibly in response to teacher correction, focusing on the target form.

So if we begin with a pronounced focus on form it is almost impossible for learners to switch immediately to a focus on meaning. The benefits of a focus on meaning will be lost. Learners will not make the most of all the other language they have if their efforts are directed to reproducing the target forms. They will be less likely to grow in fluency and confidence. They will be less equipped to use the language outside the classroom.

But there is an even more important reason for rejecting an initial and continuing focus on form: the procedure is likely to end in failure. We will look at language acquisition research in the next chapter (Chapter 2 (2.4)). This research shows that it is very rare for learners to be exposed to a new form and, within the space of a single lesson incorporate it into their spontaneous language production. We all know from our experience as teachers that it takes a long time before learners have spontaneous command of 'do-questions'. For a long time after forms like 'What do you want?' or 'What does X mean?' have been presented and intensively practised, learners go on producing questions like 'What you want?' and 'What mean X?' The same is true of past tense forms, question tags, the distinction between present continuous and present simple, and almost any learning item you care to mention. This apparent failure comes about not because learners are careless or teachers are incompetent. It comes about because learning is a developmental process which is not subject to the learner's conscious control.

It takes time for language to develop. The first treatment of a new form or forms will not lead to mastery. It may aid development in that the learner will be more likely to *notice* the new form (see Schmidt 1990) in future once it has been highlighted. But the form will not become a part of the learners' spontaneous repertoire until they have had time to assimilate it. This has been a part of the consensus on language learning since the interlanguage studies of the late 1960s and early 1970s. (See Corder 1967; Selinker 1972.) These studies described the learner as operating a set of strategies for second language development which are influenced, but not driven by a concern with language form. There is certainly a place for a focus on specified forms in a task-based approach. But form should be subordinate to meaning and, for this reason, should come after rather than before a task. We will discuss this in more detail in the next chapter and again in Chapter 6.

Further reading

Ellis, R. 2003. *Task-based Language Learning and Teaching.* Oxford: Oxford University Press.
Chapter 1 gives an overview of tasks used in SLA research and in the language classroom.

Skehan, P. 1998. *A Cognitive Approach to Language Learning.* Oxford: Oxford University Press.
Chapter 5 evaluates the second language acquisition research relating to task-based instruction.

Willis, D. and **J. Willis.** 2001. 'Task-based language learning' in **R. Carter** and **D. Nunan** (eds.). *The Cambridge Guide to Teaching English to Speakers of Other Languages.* Cambridge: Cambridge University Press.
This paper offers a brief summary of the rationale behind task-based learning and teaching.

Willis, D. 2003. *Rules, Patterns and Words: Grammar and Lexis in English Language Teaching.* Cambridge: Cambridge University Press.
Chapters 1 and 2 look in more detail at the relationship between grammar and lexis.

Willis, J. 2004. 'Perspectives on task-based instruction' in **B. Leaver** and **J. R. Willis** (eds.). *Task-based Instruction in Foreign Language Education: Practices and Programs.* Washington, D.C.: Georgetown University Press.
Chapter 1 (pp. 3–44) gives an overview of the origins of TBT, explores its relationship with CLT and other perspectives on task-based practices.

2 TASK-BASED SEQUENCES IN THE CLASSROOM

2.1 Task sequences

In Chapter 1 (1.4) we gave an example of a task-based sequence which began with a teacher-led introduction to an opinion survey about drugs. This was followed by the class working on the opinion survey as individuals. The next stage was a group discussion, which led into a teacher-led class discussion. Next there was a reading activity, which would again be followed by a discussion and evaluation of the writer's arguments. What we have here is a sequence of tasks; each of the stages above could be described as a task. This task sequence prepares the way for a number of form-focused activities which could then follow. Learners have been concerned with meanings which involve, for example, the passive form of the modal 'should', as in 'should be punished', 'should be confiscated'. They are, therefore, ready to go on to look in detail at the structure and use of the passive with 'should' and, by extension, with other modals.

So a task-based lesson would probably involve not a single task, but a sequence of tasks. These tasks relate to one another. The teacher-led introduction is a task in itself. It involves a genuine exchange of meaning, in which learners are required to process language for meaning. It also serves a *priming* function. It prepares or *primes* learners for the coming reading in two useful ways:

- It helps learners focus on the topic and engage their own knowledge and opinions on the subject.
- It affords an opportunity to introduce the vocabulary associated with the topic, in this case words like 'legalize' and 'addicts' and phrases like 'hard drugs'. This is done both in the written statements which provide the basis for discussion, and also in the subsequent teacher-led discussion.

Responding to the statements on the opinion survey as individuals is again a task in itself. Learners will be working on their own to make decisions and construct arguments, even though they do not voice those arguments at this stage. But this task is also *preparation* for the next stage. Learners are preparing to take part in a discussion. This involves a focus on meaning as they get their ideas together and decide how to express those ideas in English. At this stage learners will inevitably focus on language to some extent. They might, for example, take note of the passive modals 'should be legalized' and 'should be punished', and wonder how these might be used in the coming discussion. This process, whereby learners scan input for language which might be useful as output at a later stage, is often known as 'mining'. But this is quite different from a teacher-imposed focus on form. First there is no isolation of a particular form which learners will then feel obliged to use in the discussion which follows. If they believe the form is useful and they can indeed use it, then they may choose to do so. By the time learners have reached a stage at which they are capable of handling a discussion at this level they may be able to produce modal passives fluently and accurately. If, on the other hand, learners do not have this confidence, they may choose to avoid the form. Secondly, their success in the discussion will not be judged by whether or not they incorporate any particular form in their arguments. So preparation may involve a concern with language, but it does not involve a teacher-controlled focus on form and assessment on the basis of form.

The next task is the class discussion. This is the task that the other activities have been preparing for, but it also leads in to the next task, the reading. This again is a task, a meaning-focused activity, because learners will be reading with purpose. They will be checking their own opinions against those expressed by the author. These two tasks are probably the most important in the sequence. They are the tasks which reflect the real world most closely. They were also probably the starting point in planning the sequence. The whole aim was to enable learners to participate in a discussion and to follow this up with a reading task.

We have, then, a series of tasks. One of them, the introduction, is teacher led. (We will look in more detail at teacher-led tasks in Chapter 7.) One task, responding to the opinion survey, is done by learners as individuals. Another task, the group discussion, involves participation by students as both speakers and interested listeners. The next one, the reading, is a purely receptive task. The sequence is punctuated by teacher-led discussion briefly summarizing some of the results of the individual survey, then later of the class discussion and of the reading.

The introduction to the sequence serves the purpose of priming learners for what follows by introducing vocabulary and helping them focus on the topic. The individual response to the opinion survey is preparatory. It allows learners time to prepare for the next class discussion by thinking about the content of the task, in this case their opinions on drugs. In doing so they will inevitably rehearse and prepare some of the language they will use at the next stage.

So we have a sequence of tasks which have different characteristics and purposes. The important thing, however, is that there is a focus on meaning at all stages. As learners progress through the sequence they will be attending to meaning at each stage. The sequence also provides a way of repeating those meanings and the language that is used to express them. By the time they come to the focus on form, learners will have heard the vocabulary and grammar associated with the task several times over.

2.2 *Planning a task sequence*

Obviously it is important to plan a task sequence. The planning starts with identifying a topic, in this case drug abuse. The next stage is to decide on a target task or tasks. In most cases, though not always, these will be tasks which closely reflect activities which learners may engage in the real world. The group discussion and the reading are target tasks. They both reflect language use in the real world. The teacher then has to decide how to prime learners—how to introduce relevant vocabulary, how to focus learners' minds on the content of the task sequence and how to explain or demonstrate what will be expected of them in the target task. In this case there is also the need for a preparatory stage at which learners can think about both topic and language. So the planning process for the teacher begins with the *target* tasks, and then involves building in priming and preparation, which we will call *facilitating* tasks.

So far we have talked as though the sequence is covered in a single lesson. But it may be useful to plan ahead. In the example we have been discussing, for example, it would be possible to go through priming in an earlier lesson and ask learners to do the preparation as part of their homework. So in one lesson the teacher would introduce the topic and the opinion survey (priming) and ask learners to respond to the opinion survey (preparation) for homework. The next lesson would then begin with a brief summary from the teacher followed by the class discussion and the reading.

This approach has the advantage that it affords plenty of time for preparation. Learners will have time to prepare what they want to say. Conscientious learners may well consult a dictionary and a grammar book as part of the preparation. They may even make written notes to help them with the coming discussion. What we have here is a focus on language in the context of meaning. It is not a focus on form as defined in Chapter 1 (1.2). Here we have a focus on language in a search for ways to express the right meaning. The learner begins by asking 'What ideas do I want to express?' and then goes on to say 'How can I best express those meanings?', before going on to consult the dictionary or grammar. Forms will be identified by the learner, and will be as many or as few as the learner feels necessary. There is no teacher control, and the success of the procedure will be judged in terms of how well the learner participates in the coming discussion. So instead of a teacher-initiated focus on form we have learners exploring the language in response to a need to express required meanings.

The reading text may come immediately after the class discussion, or if the discussion goes really well and takes up lot of time, it may be postponed to the next lesson. So instead of being compressed into a single class session the task sequence may begin with the setting of homework one day. This is followed by a class discussion the next day, with a reading task in the following lesson.

READER ACTIVITY 2A

A conversational task

Imagine you want learners to give an account of a very busy day they had recently. This is the kind of thing we often talk about in everyday conversation. Can you plan a sequence of tasks around this target task?

Commentary

Here is one way of building a task sequence:

1 *Priming* You might begin by telling learners about a very busy day of your own or by asking them to listen to a recording of someone talking about a busy day, and encouraging them to ask you questions about it.

2 *Preparation* Ask learners to make a written list of all the things they did on their busy day. They may use dictionaries to help them with this task.

(If you plan ahead, the priming can be done at the end of one class, and the preparation can be done for homework. The target tasks can then be done in the next lesson.)

3 *Target task* Put learners in groups of three or four. They should tell each other about their busy days, and decide which person in the group had the most difficult day.

4 *Planning* Groups are asked to help the person with the most interesting story to prepare to tell the whole class what they have done.

5 *Target task* Two or three learners are asked to give their accounts to the class, who listen and then vote on who had the busiest/hardest day.

You may have thought of other sequences. The important thing is that at each stage there should be a primary focus on meaning, and that by the time learners come to the target tasks they are able to perform effectively.

2.3 Building in focus on form

2.3.1 Focus on form at the end of the sequence

Although we have argued the case against focusing on specific forms before learners engage with a task, there are good arguments for studying specified forms at the end of a task sequence. There are at least three good reasons for a focus on form at the end of the sequence:

- It helps learners to make sense of the language they have experienced. First learners have listened to their teacher using particular forms and seen those forms in a reading passage or heard them as part of a listening activity. After this a form-focused stage offers them the opportunity to look in detail at some of the forms that have been used. Since this focus on form comes after learners have experienced the language in use, they have a context which will help them to make sense of the new language.
- It highlights language they are likely to experience in the future. Once language forms have been studied they become salient. That is to say, they are more likely to be noticed in the future. And if they are noticed, they are more likely to be learned.
- It provides motivation. Learners want to know why they have been studying, and this usually means they want to know what they have learned. We have argued above that it is unlikely that they can learn to use a new form with any consistency over the course of a single lesson. This applies no matter what methodology we use. But we still need to show learners what learning opportunities they have been offered in a given lesson. By putting grammar at the end of the cycle there is every chance that we can increase motivation. While learners have been grappling with tasks, they have been working with meanings and struggling to find the language to express those meanings. When they come to the form-focused phase of the lesson they are likely to be receptive to ways of expressing those meanings. The focus on form provides answers to questions about the language that they have already begun to ask themselves.

Let's look at a task sequence based on an idea from Aurelia García teaching in Santa Rosa, La Pampa, Argentina. The sequence is designed for 11–12 year-olds at the elementary level. It begins with a teacher led discussion about the subjects on the timetable. 'How many subjects are there?' 'How long do you spend on each subject?' 'Which subjects are the most useful?' 'Which subjects do you think need more time?' 'How many maths lessons would you like?' 'Are there any more subjects you would like on the timetable?' And so on. Learners are then asked to work in groups to draw up their ideal timetable. They can work in Spanish if they wish, but when they have finished this stage some of them will be asked to present their timetable in English. After this, there is further teacher-led discussion in English until a final timetable is agreed.

The teacher-led discussion will feature vocabulary covering the subjects on the timetable, the days of the week, and times of the day. There will also be expressions like 'twice a week', 'four times a week', and so on. The teacher will also invite learners to state their opinions as to which subjects are more useful than others, and which are the most useful. They will also be asked if there are any other subjects they would like to see on the timetable. Since the names for subjects are central to the coming work it will be useful to list them in English and in Spanish.

This use of Spanish might worry some teachers. But Aurelia comments:

> Let's not be afraid of L1. One of the barriers that has been hard to break is the idea that using the L1 in the English class is a sin. We start many of the tasks at the elementary level in L1, Spanish, with the intention of activating previous knowledge in our students about the subject matter we are proposing and, little by little, while getting into the task cycle, they gradually turn to English. In all cases the presentation is in English. … Needless to say, intermediate or advanced students can perfectly well work through the whole process in English.

We made the point at the beginning of Chapter 1 that '… TBT is not the same the world over. Teachers who begin with the notion that tasks should be central to teaching then go on to refine an approach which fits their own classrooms and their own students'. Aurelia is working with the realities of her classroom situation. She believes that learners at the elementary level will use the L1 among themselves and will use it for support when things are difficult. It is better to take this and work with it, building it into the task sequence, than to pretend it doesn't happen.

Before the group discussion, the teacher gives them a table to complete with the following headings:

Subject	Lessons per week	Hours per week	Comments

and enough rows for them to enter all their subjects. At first the group discussion may be largely in Spanish, but the teacher reminds them that they must make their presentations in English and gives them time to prepare for this. During the presentations, the teacher asks questions to check the groups intentions: 'So you would like to have maths five times a week?' 'Why is there only one history lesson?' and so on. After the presentations the teacher leads a round-up discussion and produces a table on the blackboard summarizing the views of the class as a whole.

Aurelia was able to round off a sequence like this with a real life encounter. She persuaded the school co-ordinator to come in to class to hear the learners' ideas for their ideal timetable and to comment on them and ask a few questions. This gave the 11–12 year-olds a real sense of achievement.

One of the features of this task sequence, like many others, is that there is a lot of built-in repetition. At each stage there will be talk about subjects and timing. Once the emphasis moves on from the real to the ideal timetable there is a need for expressions like 'we want' and 'we'd like'. At each stage learners may wish to mine the language they have been exposed to in order to find language to help them express their own meanings. But again this is not a focus on form. The primary focus is on meaning and learners are free of teacher control. They can make their own choices as to how they express themselves.

After the ideal timetable task comes a form-focused activity. Learners are asked to fill out sentence frames like this:

> We have four … … lessons a week, but I think we should only have … …
> I'd like to have more … and less …

They could then be asked to memorize five sentences like this for homework and be ready to repeat them to the class in the next lesson. This has all the characteristics of a focus on form. It identifies specific forms which are to be produced in a controlled fashion, and learners' success will be judged to a large extent on how accurately they produce these sentences. But, when it comes at the end of the sequence, this focus on form serves the three functions outlined above: it helps learners to make sense of the language they have experienced; it highlights useful forms for future acquisition; and it provides motivation. But, because it comes at the end of the task sequence, it does not detract from a focus on meaning.

2.3.2 Exploiting written language

Here is another sequence of tasks which could be used at the elementary level:

1 The learners are asked to look at this picture:

Figure 2.1 Objects on a tray

The teacher checks that learners have the necessary vocabulary.

2 The picture is removed and learners are asked to work as individuals to make a list in English of as many things as they can remember.

3 Learners move into pairs to see how many items they can remember between them.

4 The teacher works with the class as a whole to build up a list to see if, between them, they can remember all the things in the picture.

5 The teacher writes up a few sentences on the board:

> There is an exercise book on the left of the coins.
> The keys are between the coins and the banana.
> There are some bananas at the top on the left.
> The ten pound note is in the middle of the tray.
> There is a glass on the left of the ruler.
> There are some keys between the coins and the address book.

6 Learners are asked to say whether these sentences are true or false.

7 The sentences are rubbed off the board and learners are asked to work in pairs to write sentences of their own about the picture—three true sentences and three false.

8 The picture is removed. Learners read out their sentences and the other students are asked to say from memory if each sentence is true or false. The teacher gives feedback after each sentence and corrects the sentences which are false.

9 Learners are asked to work from memory to call out true sentences about the picture. The teacher makes a list of their sentences.

10 For homework they are given four sentences to complete, to make two true and two false sentences:

> There are … keys between the … and the …
> The … is next to the …
> There is a … on the right of the …
> The … are on the left of the …

They are also asked to produce two sentences of their own, one true and one false. This written work is taken in during the next lesson and marked by the teacher.

11 In this next lesson learners produce sentences orally without looking at their written work. Their classmates, without looking at the picture, try to remember if the sentences are true or false. If they are false they must be corrected.

READER ACTIVITY 2B

Tasks and real-world activities

1 Do any of the tasks in this 'Objects on a tray' sequence relate to real-world activities?
2 What are the target tasks in this sequence?
3 What is the purpose of stages 1–4?
4 In stages 5 and 6 learners are working with written language. How do you think this will affect their attitude towards accuracy?
5 What is the purpose of stages 10 and 11?
6 How might you follow up this activity?

Commentary

1 None of these tasks are real-world activities in the sense that they represent things we normally do in the real world. But all the way through learners are concerned with real-world meanings. In this case they are expressing the location of objects relative to one another. In the pair work at stage 7 they will also be involved in real discourse as they evaluate one another's responses. This contrasts with the 'Ideal timetable' activity, which is very much a real-world task involving learners in using English to express feelings and opinions of real concern to them.

2 As we have seen, there are no target tasks in the sense of tasks relating to the real world. But the sequence is working towards the memory game at stages 7 and 8.

3 Stages 1–4 are facilitating tasks, priming, focusing on the topic, and introducing and checking vocabulary.

4 The fact that the sentences in stage 5 are written gives the learners an opportunity for mining, trying to find language which will be useful at later stages. Since stage 6 involves writing, learners have time to recall language forms which they might want to use in their written output. This does not mean that they will necessarily be able to recall these sentences when it comes to the target tasks at stages 7 and 8. Nor will they be judged at any stage on their ability to produce specific forms rather than on their ability to perform the tasks successfully.

5 Stages 10 and 11 provide a focus on form. They fulfil the purposes of a focus on form outlined above.

6 Once learners have been through a sequence like this they can use the experience to play similar games in the future. The teacher could take a tray into the class with familiar objects on it and simply ask learners to remember the objects and where they are. Or she could take in an empty tray and get learners to place objects on it. This could lead into a discussion task in which learners try to produce a drawing of the tray and all the objects on it. This would be a challenging and useful way of reviewing a range of vocabulary items, and also the grammar involved in this task.

2.4 Second language acquisition research and TBT

Research into second language acquisition, into how we learn a language other than our mother tongue, particularly how we learn languages in a classroom setting, is a relatively new branch of enquiry, less than 50 years old. There is still no consensus on how we learn languages, but there is a growing consensus on how we do *not* learn.

Lightbown and Spada (2006) contrast what they call the 'get it right from the beginning' approach and the 'get it right in the end' approach. The 'get it right from the beginning' approach is based on the belief that it is possible to accumulate one grammatical form after another, ensuring mastery of one before moving on to the next. So each stage of instruction specifies one or two forms and seeks to help learners to master these before they move on. Most grammar translation and audiolingual programmes are based on this belief. But it is clear from our experience in classrooms that this simply does not happen. Learners do not achieve mastery of one form before moving on to the next. As a result of this most teaching programmes based on the 'get it right from the beginning' approach build in recycling to ensure that the same items are treated again and again in the syllabus. But at each stage there is a sharp focus on one or two isolated forms.

A few highly motivated and highly gifted learners may learn languages successfully in this way, but Lightbown and Spada comment that '... it was the frequent failure of traditional grammar translation and audiolingual methods to produce fluency and accuracy in second language learners which led to the development of more communicative approaches to teaching in the first place'. Most teaching programmes have advanced beyond grammar translation and audiolingualism, but very many programmes are still based on the belief that we should isolate structures and teach each one intensively before offering learners the opportunity to use it.

The 'get it right in the end' approach is based on the belief that what learners need most of all are exposure to language and opportunities to use language meaningfully. Given this exposure, learners are highly creative problem-solvers. They will develop a language system which works, even though they will make mistakes on the way. Lightbown and Spada say:

> In the 'get it right in the end' position the emphasis is primarily on meaning, but those who hold this position argue that there is a role for form-focused instruction and correction. The research ... has shown that second language learners benefit from form-focused instruction which is provided within communicative contexts. The challenge is to find the right balance between meaning-based and form-focused activities.

We are arguing the case for a task-based programme of this kind, one which also allows for a focus on accuracy and a focus on form. But there is another important reason why meaning must come first.

Corder (1973) argues the case for language teaching programmes with 'high surrender value'. This term is taken from the world of life insurance. If you have a life insurance policy with a *low* surrender value you must pay into it for a very long time before it is worth very much. If you cash in your policy early you get very little return on you investment. But if you have a policy with a *high* surrender value, you can cash it in after a relatively short time and still get a good return on your investment.

Until they reach a very advanced stage, learners' language will display deficiencies at every stage of their development. If they do not have the confidence and fluency to make the most of their limited language they will have gained very little from their course of study: their course has a low surrender value. But if they are confident enough to make the most of their language with all its shortcomings and inaccuracies then they have acquired a valuable skill for life, they have high surrender value. They will have gained a lot from their course of study, even if it finishes before they have achieved anything like a complete command of the grammar of the language. Nor do they simply have a skill they can apply. They also have the basis for language development. Once they can use the language outside the classroom they will go on learning. So they have a skill which will grow in value. If this is the case then one of the most valuable things we can give learners is the ability to make the most of their language in spite of its deficiencies. And the best way to do this is to give them plenty of opportunities to use their language in the classroom in an atmosphere which rewards successful use and does not penalize inevitable failings in accuracy.

Further reading

Lightbown, P. and **N. Spada**. 2006. *How Languages are Learned* (Third Edition). Oxford: Oxford University Press.
Chapter 6 contrasts the 'get it right from the beginning' approach and the 'get it right in the end' approach, which are briefly reviewed above.

Nunan D. 2004. *Task-based Language Teaching*. Cambridge: Cambridge University Press.
Chapters 3 and 8 look at the components of tasks and at the notion of a task sequence.

3 TASKS BASED ON WRITTEN AND SPOKEN TEXTS

3.1 Introduction: reading for a purpose

When we read a text we read for a purpose. We may read a newspaper or magazine article because the topic interests us and we want to learn more about it. Perhaps we have strong opinions on a subject and want to find out what others think about it. Sometimes a headline catches our eye, and we read an article to satisfy our curiosity. When we read a story for enjoyment we begin to speculate on what happens next, and to predict how the story will develop. In all of these activities we engage with a text for a purpose, and purposeful reading means reading for meaning.

Much the same applies to listening. Just as we read newspapers and magazines, so we listen to news programmes and discussions on radio and television. In an academic setting we attend lectures or tutorials. In everyday life we listen to people recounting their experiences and telling anecdotes. So most of the reasons we have for reading also have their counterparts in listening activities.

In the classroom there is a danger that reading or listening takes place in a void, without purpose or challenge. But it is possible to design tasks which will provide a context for written or spoken texts in order to provide the purpose or challenge which is basic to reading or listening in the real world. These tasks are valuable learning activities in themselves and by providing a context they also make the reading or listening into a meaning-focused activity.

In this chapter we will look at a number of ways of designing tasks based on written texts, and go on to see how these texts can be recycled so that they become familiar to learners. Many of these techniques will be familiar to teachers who have already used them as the basis for skills lessons. Indeed almost all of the techniques involved in task-based teaching are already familiar to most experienced teachers. It is the way these techniques are ordered and deployed that makes the difference. Here we will look at how to build activities, many of them already familiar, into a task-based framework. Finally we will go on to apply the same techniques to spoken texts.

3.2 Discussion tasks

In Chapter 1 (1.4) we gave an example of a discussion task based on an opinion survey on the subject of dangerous drugs. This was part of a task sequence leading to a reading text. We made the point there that:

> … we create tasks to facilitate meaningful activities in the classroom. Tasks are not a substitute for interesting topics which engage learners' interest, but they can enhance that engagement and interest. And … group work gives all learners a chance to give their views.

So a discussion based on an opinion survey or questionnaire helps to involve learners, to engage their interest and to provide a reason for reading. When introducing any text on a controversial topic, it is worth going through some procedure to get learners to commit themselves to an opinion on the issue. An opinion survey is the obvious way to do this. Alternatively you could take the same set of statements, give two statements to each group and ask the group to produce one argument for and one argument against each of their statements. They could then read out their arguments and compare their ideas with other groups who had considered the same statements. This would promote discussion in the same way as a survey and would also involve the groups in a short writing activity.

So discussion is a good way of leading into a text dealing with a controversial topic. Other tasks can be designed to lead into texts of other kinds.

3.3 Prediction tasks

All reading involves prediction, but prediction tasks work particularly well with narrative texts. As soon as we see a headline or the title of a story we begin to anticipate what follows; we begin to ask ourselves questions. As we read we find answers to our questions, and these answers prompt other questions, and so on. By setting prediction tasks we help learners by providing a context for reading and by guiding the reading process. Teachers routinely involve learners in some kind of prediction exercise as part of the preparation for reading comprehension. This can be formalized and built into a task which is just as important as the reading itself.

Stage 1: Priming for prediction

Here is a prediction task sequence we have often used. It mirrors the reading process because, as soon as you see the story headline, you begin to speculate on what could have happened and how it could have happened.

Here is the headline from a short newspaper article about a man who jumped off the Empire State Building, one of the highest buildings in New York:

> Hello, I've just jumped off
> the Empire State Building

How could someone who has just jumped off the Empire State Building possibly be alive to tell the tale? Work in groups to think of as many explanations as you can. You can use simple drawings to help with your explanations.

Figure 3.1 The Empire State Building

Students work together for a couple of minutes to come up with possible explanations. After working in groups learners are invited to share their ideas with the class. Explanations we have heard include: 'He was wearing a parachute'; 'He was abseiling'; 'He only jumped from the ground floor'; 'He was bungee-jumping'; 'He had a safety net.' All of these explanations can be expressed very simply by a competent speaker of English, but learners do not have the appropriate vocabulary and have to be quite resourceful, saying things like: 'He have thing on his back, like rubber, like elastic. He jump like this'. This is accompanied by gestures to indicate the effects of a bungee-jump. They will almost certainly accompany their explanations with drawings. This is a valuable exercise in stretching their language resources to meet a communicative need, and if the teacher is encouraging and helpful it can be a lively and enjoyable activity. Obviously at this point you need to be careful not to tell the class which explanations is right or which one is nearest to what happens in the text. This would spoil the prediction task which follows.

Stage 2: Prediction task

Here are some words and phrases taken from the article. They appear in the same order here as in the article:

All alone in New York—decided to kill himself—the 86th floor—held on to the safety fence—over 1,000 feet below—a narrow ledge—the offices of a television station—the strong wind—poured myself a stiff drink—a great Christmas

Work in groups to decide what happened. Try to include information from as many of the clues as possible.

This kind of prediction task involves speculative discussion and can be regarded as a target task since it involves the kind of speculation and discussion which takes place in the real world outside the classroom. Here, to prompt the discussion, we have taken a number of phrases from the text which is to be studied later. With another text it might work better to take the two opening sentences, or perhaps the opening sentence and the final sentence. Another possibility is simply to take a number of key words from the text. There are no hard and fast rules about what is going to work best. There are, however, a few things worth bearing in mind:

- Make sure the task is 'doable'. Give plenty of clues, so that learners have a lot to talk about and also have a good chance of coming up with an acceptable solution to the problem.
- Be prepared to adjust the task for a subsequent class. If you have given too much help the first time so that the task is not very challenging you may choose to withhold some of that help the next time round. If you have given too little help, you may choose to be more helpful the next time. The first time you work with a particular text, however, it is always wise to give too much help rather than too little. This goes back to making the task doable. Students can get very frustrated if they do not have enough to work with.
- You may also vary the clues you give learners. In this case we have suggested giving the headline and a few words and phrases. An alternative would be to give the first and last sentences and a few phrases, or you might simply give a few key phrases.

You might also vary what is required of learners. Here we have asked them to predict the story. Instead you might ask them to list a number of questions, say five questions that will be answered in the text. If you change the demands of the task you will probably have to vary the clues as well. For example, if you ask them to list five questions you might simply give them the headline and the phrases: 'decided to kill himself', 'safety fence', 'narrow ledge', 'television station'. If you do this, they will then list questions like 'Why did he want to kill himself?', 'Which storey did he jump from?', and so on.

The most important feature of the prediction stage is that it involves meaning-focused language use. Learners will be drawing on all their language resources to enable them to work together to put together a satisfactory story or to prepare their questions. But in presenting the task to the learners the teacher will also make use of opportunities for priming and teaching. Learners are going to encounter these phrases in the final text; by going through the phrases, the teacher will be priming learners, introducing the topic and preparing them to tackle lexical difficulties which they will encounter in the text. Priming inevitably involves opportunities for language learning. Some learners, for example, may take note of the reflexive pronoun in 'kill himself', or they may notice the collocation 'strong wind', or the noun modifier in 'safety fence'. They will be seeing these items again, and the items will be salient because the learners' attention has already been caught.

Stage 3: Preparing for report

At this stage you should ask learners to prepare one member of their group to tell the story they have decided on, so that he or she can tell that story to the whole class.

READER ACTIVITY 3A

Language use preparing for a reporting task

What useful language work is taking place at this stage? How does it build on what has gone before?

Commentary

The purpose at this stage is preparation. Learners pool their ideas to produce a polished version of their story. It will build on what has gone before in that they will try to recall and incorporate the phrases which were used to define the task in Stage 1.

Because learners are about to tell their story to the whole class, they will be concerned with both fluency and accuracy. They will want to tell it with some fluency, but they will also want to present it in the best language they can. Their focus on accuracy means that they will propose phrasings which they believe to be acceptable and effective. They will also correct one another and, on occasions, argue about the best version. The teacher should be ready to respond to requests for help at this stage—to comment on acceptability and to resolve disputes.

Stage 4: Report

Members from two or three groups tell their story to the whole class who listen in order to compare stories. This report is itself a target task of the kind identified in Chapter 2 (2.2), because it represents the kind of thing we do with language in the real world, in this case storytelling. But it serves a special function here in that it encourages learners to focus on language as well as meaning.

READER ACTIVITY 3B

Language use in a target task

1 What is happening at this stage in terms of language use?
2 What might the teacher ask the class to do as they are listening to the stories?
3 What might the teacher usefully do to reinforce learning?

Commentary

1 The individuals who have been chosen as storytellers will have valuable speaking practice. They will be trying hard to remember the ideas that were provided at the preparation stage. This is a target task involving storytelling, a common everyday activity.

2 It is important that learners have some reason to listen to the different stories. For the first story the teacher should say 'Listen carefully to X's story. Is it the same as yours? Does X miss anything important out?' For subsequent stories the teacher might say something like 'Now listen carefully to Y as he tells the story. Is it different from X's story in any way? Does it have any more details? Does Y miss anything out?' In this way learners are set a listening task to encourage them to process carefully what they hear. Listening to stories is also a target task.

3 The teacher might retell the story very quickly, reformulating language where the storyteller made mistakes. Occasionally she might comment on these reformulations and draw the class's attention to them. More positively she might draw attention to the storyteller's achievements. She might take notes during the telling so she can comment positively on useful words or phrases which were used appropriately.

4 At this stage, if the task sequence is to be spread over two lessons, you could ask the learners to write up their story for homework and compare it next lesson with the real story.

Stage 5: Reading

Students read the story. Again we have a target task. After the previous stages learners should be curious to read the story to find out if their guesses are accurate. They will approach the story with the same kind of curiosity as a reader who picks up a magazine or newspaper and reads the headline. This means that there is a focus on outcome: the checking of their guesses, or the satisfaction of their curiosity. In order to check their guesses and satisfy their curiosity they will be reading primarily for meaning, so the reading becomes a task within a task.

Jim Burney, aged 24, was out of work and out of money and all alone in New York over Christmas. He decided to kill himself by jumping off the Empire State Building.

He took the lift to the top floor, the 86th, where he held on to the safety fence for a moment. He said a quick prayer, then threw himself off and fell towards the hundreds of cars moving along Fifth Avenue, over 1,000 feet below.

When he woke up half an hour later he found himself on a narrow ledge on the 85th floor, outside the offices of a television station, where the strong wind had blown him. The young man was so relieved that he decided to give up the idea of committing suicide.

He knocked on a window of the offices and crawled in to safety. Mike Wilson was on duty there at the time. 'I couldn't believe my eyes', he said. 'It's not often you see someone coming in through the window of the 85th floor. I poured myself a stiff drink, and one for Jim too.'

Jim Burney himself not only survived. He had a great Christmas—he got a lot of invitations to Christmas dinner!

Although the reading is important in itself it may take relatively little time. As well as providing reading practice and exposure to the target language it fulfils the important function of providing a rationale for all the language work which has gone before. You may, after this reading, ask for learners' reactions to the story. Did they guess everything correctly? Or just some things? Later they will go on to recycle the task so that the lexis and grammar become familiar (see Section 3.8 below) and meanings will become even clearer. Finally they will look in detail at certain lexical and grammatical features of the text. (See Chapter 6.)

Stage 6: Focus on form

The focus on form comes at the end of the task sequence. This text contains a number of expressions of place:

> in New York—off the Empire State Building—to the top floor—where he held on to the safety fence—threw himself off—towards the hundreds of cars—moving along Fifth Avenue— over 1,000 feet below—on a narrow

ledge on the 85th floor—outside the offices of a television station—where the strong wind had blown him—knocked on a window of the offices—crawled in to safety—on duty there—coming in through the window of the 85th floor

It is worth asking learners to go through and underline all the phrases to do with place. The phrase 'took the lift to' is an important one. You could point out that 'took the/a … to …' is a phrase that can be used with any form of public transport, but normally only for shortish journeys. Ask learners how many words or phrases they can fit into the frame:

I took the … from … to ….

The most interesting grammatical feature in this text is the use of reflexives. There is one example of the reflexive used for emphasis or identity: 'Jim Burney himself'. There are three examples of the reflexive used as direct object: 'to kill himself'; 'threw himself off'; 'found himself on a narrow ledge'. The last of these is one of the most frequent of all reflexive phrases. Finally there is a reflexive used as indirect object: 'I poured myself a stiff drink'. You could ask learners to pick out the phrases with '…self' and use these to introduce some work in their grammar books on reflexives. They could then go on to look for reflexives in other texts that they have studied.

Stage 7: Evaluation

Of course you will be monitoring learners' reactions at each stage of the process outlined above. How long does the prediction task take? Do they engage in real discussion? Is there too much use of their mother tongue? Is the storytelling generally successful? You will be looking for answers to these and other questions. They will help you to decide if the task is worth doing again and, if so, how it might be adapted to meet the needs of a similar class more precisely in the future.

It's also a good idea to check learners' reactions at the end of the process. You could ask them to talk about the experience in groups and jot down their feelings. Did they find the prediction task too difficult or too easy? Would they have liked more help? Did they like the story? Did they need more help with vocabulary before the reading stage? Did they feel the language was useful? You could give them a few of these questions to help with their group discussion and evaluation. This kind of class evaluation and discussion serves at least three functions:

- It involves meaning-focused language use. Engaging learners in genuine discussion which has a real outcome is the best kind of language practice they can possibly get.
- Like your critical observation, it will help to adjust the task for future use.

- It helps to motivate learners if you involve them in decision making and really take notice of their reactions.

3.4 *Jigsaw task sequences*

A jigsaw task, sometimes called a split-information task, is one in which one individual or group has some information and another individual or group has quite different information. In order to achieve an outcome they have to put the information together. In the prediction task we have just looked at all the learners were given the same information in the form of a set of clues to the story. It would be possible to give some of the information to some groups of learners and quite different information to other groups. They would then need to pool their information to predict the story. This technique will be familiar to many teachers as a way of providing learners with a purpose for communicating. Let us go on to look at some other ways of providing a jigsaw.

Stage 1: Pre-task

Here are four possible ways of setting up a jigsaw task:

1 Split information, as described above.

2 Jigsaw the text. This would work very well, for example, with a discussion text. Different groups could be given different paragraphs and asked to reconstruct the arguments for and against, before being given the whole text.

3 Crumpled paper. Andrew Wright has demonstrated an intriguing way of jigsawing a text. Type it on one side of a sheet of paper, then screw up the paper into a ball and give one ball to each pair or group. They are not allowed to unfold the paper, but can roll it around. They can read some words, some phrases and some whole sentences, but not the whole text. They then exchange ambassadors, who tell other groups what they have discovered, and bit by bit the class tries to reconstruct the whole text.

4 Jigsaw note-taking. Joann Chernen working in Vancouver Community College offers another kind of jigsaw. On an EAP course with trainee bakers she labels learners as As, Bs, Cs, and Ds. She then asks them all to read the same text but to take notes on different aspects of the text. For example, in a text on making chou paste, the As are responsible for reporting on the main points of chou paste products and ingredients; the Bs are responsible for reporting on the main points of the mixing procedures; the Cs are responsible for reporting on the main points of the piping procedures; and the Ds are responsible for reporting on the main points of the baking and handling procedures. They then come together

as groups, each one with an A, a B, a C and a D, and between them construct a summary of the text. So all the learners read all of the text, but they concentrate on different aspects of the text, and then bring their different perspectives together.

Stage 2: Putting the story together

In this stage the groups prepare their stories. The group work here will involve the role of 'ambassador': a member of the group whose role is to talk to other groups. At Stage 3 each A group is going to send one of their number, as ambassador, to one of the B groups to compare stories with them.

Group A: Here are a few clues to help you predict the story:

> Jim Burney, aged 24—all alone in New York over Christmas—jumping off the Empire State Building—the 85th floor—a television station—decided to give up the idea—poured myself a stiff drink

When you have prepared your story help your ambassador to prepare what he/she is going to tell Group B. Ambassadors may write down ten words to help them work with Group B.

Group B: Here are a few clues to help you predict the story:

> decided to kill himself—the top floor, the 86th—over 1,000 feet below—a narrow ledge—Mike Wilson was on duty at the time—had a great Christmas.

When you have prepared your story help your ambassador to prepare what he/she is going to tell Group A. Ambassadors may write down ten words to help them work with Group A.

In this example it is suggested that ambassadors should be allowed to write down up to ten words. You should choose an appropriate number of words which will enable the ambassadors to do their job, but will not allow them to write down the whole story.

Stage 3: Preparation

This is similar to the Preparation in stage 3 of the prediction task above. An ambassador from each A group goes to work with a B group, and vice versa. They exchange stories without referring to any written instructions. Ambassadors then return to their own groups and the groups put together their final version of the story. This can be done orally or in writing.

The stages then follow the same sequence as in the prediction task above: report—reading—focus on form—evaluation.

3.5 *Student as question master*

The normal procedure in the classroom is for teachers to ask questions and for students to answer them. In many cases the reading lesson consists of a text and a set of questions. The students read the texts and the coursebook or the teacher then asks the questions to assess their comprehension.

A very productive alternative is to ask students to prepare questions for themselves. This can be done by identifying or handing out the text in advance of the lesson and asking one group of about four students to act as questioners. They will work as individuals to prepare a set of questions on the text for homework. When they come together in class they can decide as a group on their final list of questions. Meanwhile the other groups of four are working hard on the text to try to predict the questions that will be asked and to prepare answers. During the reading lesson the groups who answer questions will be expected to do so *without referring to the text.*

Stage 1: Select a text

It would be quite possible to use a story, like the one used above, but it is probably better to use a text which is rich in information, such as the following:

Helping people click

With the stigma of online dating fading, the internet is fast becoming the choice for young professionals writes Emily Dubberley.

In March last year, Ed Miles married Maryam Hussein. They had known each other for three years and spent more than 1,000 hours talking but they'd only spent 12 days together, face to face.

Ed and Maryam met online, via IRC (internet relay chat) dating. Within a few days of meeting they were chatting for four hours each day, but seeing each other posed a problem: Maryam lived in the United Arab Emirates and Ed lived in London.

Over the next three years, the couple spent most evenings in front of their webcams, chatting over Instant Messenger. Ed visited Maryam and, in February 2002, he proposed. After filling in countless visa applications and forms, they married in Maryam's home town and are now living 'happily ever after' in London.

Ed and Maryam's story may be extreme, but the way they met is becoming increasingly common. While dating agencies used to have a stigma attached, the internet has changed people's perceptions. According to Matchcom, the world's biggest dating site, 81% of users are now more comfortable admitting they use a dating service than they were a year ago. And Datingdirect.com found that 68% of people think online dating is better than its offline equivalent.

People like 30-year-old Simon Newman, who has been using dating sites for six months support this. 'I'd never join an agency or place a personal ad, but using a website seems less desperate. It's just a bit of fun.'

Guardian online 22.1.04

Introduce the topic of dating agencies in class. You will almost certainly want to explore the two relevant meanings of 'click': one is what you do with a computer mouse, the other is a slightly old-fashioned term for when two people realize they are going to get on very well together, as in 'We met at the dance and just clicked straight away'. Then ask all students to prepare the text for homework. Ask one group to act as 'question master'. Members of that group should, as homework, prepare a number of questions they can ask about the text. Explain to the other groups that they will be expected to answer detailed questions on the text but without the text in front of them.

Stage 2

In class allow the question-master group time to decide on ten final questions. Meanwhile ask the other groups to anticipate questions and be prepared to answer them.

Stage 3

The question-master group then take turns to read out their questions and the other learners, working as individuals, write down the answers. They then compare answers and decide on a final list. If you adopt some procedure like this, it ensures that all members of the group answer the questions individually. They cannot simply rely on the best members of the group to do all the work. You can take in the individual answer papers to check. Alternatively, the question-master group can come out in front and hear the answers from each small group in turn, with the teacher acting as referee. Points can be allotted to each group for a correct answer and entered in a grid like this one.

Question	Group				
	A	**B**	**C**	**D**	**E**
1					
2					
3					
4					
5					
6					
7					
8					
9					
10					

Figure 3.2 Answer grid

Stage 4

In terms of focus on form, this text provides insights into a range of tense uses. It starts with the marriage of Ed and Maryam in March last year. Then the second sentence shifts back to a time before their marriage. The second paragraph takes us to the time they first met. The third paragraph is about the time between their meeting and their marriage. Paragraphs four and five are about the present time—about how dating services are used now. Given this shifting of the time perspective it is not surprising that there are a lot of time expressions in the text: 'in March last year', 'for three years', 'spent more than 1,000 hours talking', 'spent 12 days together', and so on. Nor is it surprising that an almost bewildering range of tense forms is used. Three form-focused activities suggest themselves:

- Pick out all the expressions of time.
- Pick out all the instances of the –ing form and classify their uses.
- Treat the text as a cloze passage, removing all the tense markers and asking learners to recall the tenses used and fill in the blanks.

This could lead into a review of a number of tense uses.

3.6 *General knowledge tasks*

Teachers are used to engaging learners' knowledge of the world as a way of promoting discussion. You can use this as the basis for a task cycle if you can find appropriate texts, like the one below on whales. One way is to begin with a short quiz. Students answer the quiz, and discuss their answers. This can generate a good deal of class discussion before students turn to the text to confirm whether they were right or wrong. Another way is to ask groups to write seven facts about whales they are sure of. Both these tasks can generate a good deal of class discussion before students actually read the text to confirm whether they were right or wrong. They could then classify the points into categories like physical characteristics, food, habits, life cycle, other.

Here are some questions for a quiz which might be set for a high school class based on a text about whales, downloaded from the web (www.enchanted learning.com/subjects/whales/).

Read these sentences about whales and say if they are TRUE or FALSE.

1 The blue whale is the largest animal in the world.
2 Fish breathe by filtering water, but whales breathe air through their blowholes.
3 Apart from dinosaurs the blue whale is the biggest creature that has ever existed on Earth.
4 Whales are the only mammals that spend their whole life in water.
5 Whales have hair.

6 A blue whale can grow to a length of almost 60 metres.
7 It eats about 4 tons of fish every day.
8 Like fish whales are silent creatures.
9 The smallest whales are less than ten feet long.
10 Whales produce milk to feed their young.

Here is the text which gives you the answers to the questions:

Whales are large, magnificent, intelligent, aquatic <u>mammals</u>. They breathe air through blowhole(s) into lungs (unlike fish who breathe using gills). Whales have sleek, streamlined bodies that move easily through the water. They are the only mammals, other than *manatees* (seacows), that live their entire lives in the water, and the only mammals that have adapted to life in the open oceans.

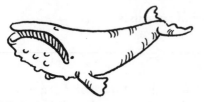

Whales breathe air. They are not fish. They are mammals that spend their entire lives in the water.

Cetaceans are the group of mammals that includes the whales, dolphins, and porpoises.

Like all mammals:
● whales breathe air into lungs,
● whales have hair (although they have a lot less than land mammals, and have almost none as adults),
● whales are warm-blooded (they maintain a high body temperature),
● whales have mammary glands with which they nourish their young,
● whales have a four-chambered heart.

Size

The biggest whale is the blue whale, which grows to be about 94 feet (29 m) long – the height of a 9-storey building. These enormous animals eat about 4 tons of tiny krill each day, obtained by filter feeding through baleen. Adult blue whales have no predators except man.

The smallest whale is the dwarf sperm whale which as an adult is only 8.5 feet (2.6 m) long.
The <u>blue whale</u> is the largest animal that has ever existed on Earth. It is larger than any of the dinosaurs were. They are also the <u>loudest animals</u> on Earth.

READER ACTIVITY 3C
Using questions to generate discussion

1 How might you use the true/false questions to generate class discussion?
2 What other types of question might you use apart from true/false?
3 How do you think these would affect language use?

Commentary

1 The true/false questions can generate a good deal of discussion before the class go on to read the text. You can begin by asking learners to compare their answers with one or two others. You can then ask groups or individuals to read out their answers and ask the rest of the class to say how many they have got right or wrong on the basis of their general knowledge. As teacher you should be careful not to give away the correct answers. The class can then go on to suggest which answers are wrong and to explain why. Finally you can get the consensus view of the class as a whole and write this on the board. Only then do learners go on to check their answers against the text.

2 True/false questions are probably the easiest to prepare, but multiple choice questions are better for promoting discussion. On the subject of whales you might ask questions like:

- Whales are:
  A fish.
  B reptiles.
  C mammals.
- Whales have:
  A a lot of hair.
  B a little hair.
  C no hair.
- A large blue whale will be:
  A about a hundred feet long.
  B about fifty feet long.
  C more than a hundred and fifty feet long.
  etc.

Alternatively you might use open-ended questions like:

How do whales breathe?
How do they feed their young?
What do they eat?
etc.

Open-ended questions clearly require more extended answers than true/false or multiple choice questions. Learners can work in groups to produce written answers to these questions.

You need to select your texts carefully, depending on your students. The text on whales, for example, may not be suitable for a class of adults, but would be ideal for a class of high school students. The same site—'Enchanted Learning' (www.enchantedlearning.com/Home)—has a number of other activities on each topic, with worksheets and quizzes already prepared.

3.7 Corrupted text

'Corrupted text' is simply a label for a text which has been changed in some way and needs to be restored. For example, some elements may be omitted and learners asked to fill the gaps. Alternatively the order of sentences or paragraphs may be changed.

3.7.1 Factual gap filling

You can provide learners with a challenging problem-solving activity based on a written text by omitting factual information from the text and asking the learners to complete the text. This works particularly well with a text which is rich in numerical information. The examples below have been used successfully with low-level elementary learners.

Stage 1: Pre-task

Tell learners they are going to read about the biggest and the most expensive houses in the world, and also about the smallest house in Great Britain. Explain to them a bit about the houses and ask them to guess:

> The most expensive house in the world was built in 1890. How much do you think it cost to build?

> The biggest house in the world is in North Carolina, USA. How many rooms do you think it has?

> The smallest house in Great Britain is a cottage in North Wales. How many rooms do you think it has? How big do you think they are?

Write down their guesses to see later who is closest to the correct figure.

Stage 2: Reading task

Give learners the gapped text and ask them to work first as individuals:

Three houses

Read about the biggest house in the world, the most expensive house in the world and the smallest house in Great Britain. All the numbers have been left out, but they are given below. Can you put them back to complete the text?

The biggest house in the world is Biltmore House in Ashville, North Carolina, USA, belonging to the Vanderbilt family. It was built in 1890 at a cost of US$(**a**). It has (**b**) rooms and stands in an estate of (**c**) hectares.

The most expensive house in the world is the Hearst Ranch at San Simeon, California. It was built for the newspaper owner in (**d**)—(**e**) at a cost of US$ (**f**). It has over (**g**) rooms and a garage for (**h**) cars.

The smallest house in Great Britain is a cottage in North Wales built in the nineteenth century. It is ten feet ((**i**) cms) high and measures only six feet ((**j**) cms) across the front. It has a tiny staircase and two tiny rooms.

Here are the numbers you need:

30 million; 4.1 million; 48,100; 1922; 309; 250; 182; 100; 39; 25

(Texts adapted from *The Guinness Book of Records* for 1986 for use in J. Willis and D. Willis 1988)

Stage 3: Planning and report

Ask learners to share their solution with a group. Finally ask members from one or two groups to read out their answers to the class. See how far they agree. As teacher, it may be a good tactic to hold back from telling them which answers are correct at this point, as holding back engenders discussion and creates a further learning opportunity for the next stage.

Stage 4: Checking the solution

There are a number of ways of giving the solution. You could simply announce the answers as they are shown below. This would give learners practice in listening to numerical expressions. As an alternative you could read out the full texts including the numbers. This would be a useful way of recycling the text for listening as well as giving practice in numbers. Finally you could use an OHT to give the answer, requiring learners to read the text again to check their answers.

The answers are: (a) 4.1 million; (b) 250; (c) 48,100; (d) 1922; (e) 39; (f) 30 million; (g) 100; (h) 25; (i) 309; (j) 182.

3.7.2 Linguistic gap filling

Texts often contain information which is supplementary to the main story, argument or description. This is certainly the case with the Empire State Building text in Section 3.2 and 3.3 above. You can cut out the supplementary information and ask the learners to replace it, as we show below.

Stage 1: Priming

Set up the task by giving the headline and the instructions, and leading a class discussion on their predictions. (See Section 3.3 above.)

Stage 2: Reading task

Here is the story. Nine phrases and sentences have been left out. There are brackets, e.g. (1), in the text to show where they have been removed. The nine phrases and sentences are listed below the text. Can you put them back in the right place?

Hello, I've just jumped off the Empire State Building

Jim Burney (1) was out of work and out of money and all alone (2). He decided to kill himself by jumping off the Empire State Building.

He took the lift to the top floor, (3), where he held on to the safety fence (4). He said a quick prayer, then threw himself off and fell towards the hundreds of cars moving along Fifth Avenue (5).

When he woke up (6) he found himself on a narrow ledge (7), outside the offices of a television station (8). The young man was so relieved that he decided to give up the idea of committing suicide.

He knocked on a window (9) and crawled in to safety. Mike Wilson was on duty there at the time. 'I couldn't believe my eyes,' he said. 'It's not often you see someone coming in through the window of the 85th floor. I poured myself a stiff drink (10).'

Jim Burney himself not only survived. He had a great Christmas. (11)

a half an hour later	g for a moment,
b in New York over Christmas	h aged 24
c the 86th	i on the 85th floor
d of the offices	j and one for Jim too
e where the strong had blown him	k over 1,000 feet below.
f lots of people invited him to Christmas dinner	

This is certainly a task; the outcome, which can be shared, is the completed text and the task requires learners to concentrate on meaning. It should also generate discussion in groups. However, it is much more a language-focused task than the previous prediction task. Whereas the prediction task led into a reading activity which mirrored the way we read in real life, the reading activity here is much more artificial. It is simply a preparation for the gap-filling activity.

Stage 3: Report: checking solutions

A member of one group reads out their version of the story, while the other groups listen and compare. Alternatively the teacher may read out the story or play a recording of it, while the groups listen and check their versions.

Stage 4: Follow-up: memory challenge

Pairs are asked to work together without the text to see how much of the story they can recall and re-tell or write from memory. They can then exchange stories with another pair to compare versions and check the facts. This is a useful consolidation task.

3.7.3 Re-ordering

Here is a different corrupted text exercise, in which sentences and phrases that make up the text have been re-ordered. The learners' task is to restore the original text. This is a very common textbook activity, but it is also one that learners could be asked to prepare for other groups to do. In Appendix 1.2 you will find a sample 'text puzzle' lesson by Craig Johnston based on a text called 'Profit motive and the media' which is suitable for a mixed ability class of adults. Our sample task here is more suitable for children. The text is the first part of a story called 'Franky helps Monty'. The story was written in 1999 by a boy in the United States called Eric Ross Weinberg. We found it on the web at http://home.earthlink.net/~jjweinb/eric/frankyf.html.

Stage 1

Introduce the story. Explain that the story is about a monster called Monty, who is afraid of the dark. You can encourage them to say if they know anyone who is afraid of the dark or if they have ever been afraid of the dark themselves. What did they do about it? The title of the story is 'Franky helps Monty'. How do they think Franky might help Monty? What sort of creature do they think Franky might be?

Stage 2

Give the learners the jumbled story. Ask them first to work as individuals, and later ask them to compare their solution with others in a group. You may need to give them some help with some of the words, or allow them to use dictionaries.

We are going to look at a story called 'Franky helps Monty' by Eric Ross Weinberg. The first sentence of the story is:

Monty was a big monster.

Here are the next seven sentences. Can you put them together to make the first part of the story?

a Monty was big for his age, and should have been able to scare anyone.
b He was afraid of the dark.
c He was yellow with blue spots, and he had big orange ears and a very big, green nose.
d Each night, when he closed his cave with the giant boulder, it got very dark.
e But Monty had a problem.
f One evening, when he just couldn't sleep, he decided to go for a walk and get some berries.
g He used to lie awake, afraid of the dark, listening to a lot of the strange sounds of the night.

Stage 3

Ask the learners to read out what they have written. If there are any discrepancies draw attention to them and ask the class to decide on the best version. Read out the paragraph or put it up on an OHT:

> Monty was a big monster. He was yellow with blue spots, and he had big orange ears and a very big, green nose. Monty was big for his age, and should have been able to scare anyone. But, Monty had a problem. He was afraid of the dark. Each night, when he closed his cave with the giant boulder, it got very dark. He used to lie awake, afraid of the dark, listening to a lot of the strange sounds of the night. One evening, when he just couldn't sleep, he decided to go for a walk and get some berries.

You might simply ask learners to check their answers as they listen or read. Or you could ask them to put their answers away as they listen to or read the correct version. They then go back to their answers and make any changes they want to make.

Stage 4

If the rest of the story is on the web, there are a number of things you might decide to do. You might look up the rest of the story and tell it to the class. Or you might work through the story with a series of tasks using different techniques. You might start by asking the class how they might help Monty solve his problem. For the second part, for example, you can simply tell learners what happens and suggest that those who can read should find and read the story on the web. Alternatively you could use a variety of techniques to work through the other paragraphs. For example, you might give them a number of words and phrases and ask them to predict the second paragraph. Again you might have to give some help with words.

> something shining in the blackberry patch—hid down low—flashlight—person—very small—on and off—caught the shining creature—I am a monster—a firefly—Franky—live with me—your friend

Here is the second paragraph with the last six words omitted; can you guess what they were?

> One evening, when he just couldn't sleep, he decided to go for a walk and get some berries. While picking his favorite berry, the blackberry, he noticed something shining in the blackberry patch. He hid down low thinking that it might be a flashlight with a person behind it. But the light was very small, and it blinked on and off. This was interesting. What was it? He reached out with his claw and caught the shining creature.
>
> 'Well hello there. Who are you? My name is Monty, and I am a monster.'
>
> The little light answered in a small, soft voice, 'I am just a firefly. I didn't mean to disturb you. My name is Franky.'
>
> 'Oh, you are not disturbing me,' replied Monty. 'In fact, I would like to invite you to …

Once learners in pairs have thought of a possible group of six words, you could ask them to continue the story and write a suitable ending, thus leading into a new task cycle, where they end up writing or telling their ending to the class and discussing or voting on the best endings. By the way, the original version of the second paragraph ended with 'live with me in my home', but your learners may have had even better ideas.

3.8 Ways to recycle texts

Once a text has been studied in detail it is a valuable learning resource. It contains language items which will be useful to the learners in a number of ways. There are valuable words and phrases which they will be able to use in a range of contexts. There are good examples of the use of tenses, modal verbs, prepositions, and other grammatical items. These examples can be recalled in grammar lessons so that you can draw on a familiar context to illustrate the grammar, as we will show in Chapter 6. It is, therefore, useful to recycle texts to help learners become familiar with the wordings of the texts studied for comprehension. This makes it more likely that learners will acquire for productive use the useful language they have met in the text. There are a number of possible ways of recycling texts in addition to the 'memory challenge' that we suggested in 3.7.2.

3.8.1 Corrupted text

After a text has been processed for meaning, corrupted text exercises can be used to recycle it. You might choose to do this immediately after the text has been studied or you may choose to do it some time later. If you do it some time later, you might ask learners to read through the relevant text for homework before coming to class.

The text on online dating (3.5), for example, would also make a good gap-filling task for consolidation purposes after a form-focused stage. No prior preparation is needed. There are ten phrases with numbers in the text: '1000 hours', '12 days', 'four hours each *day*' and so on. You simply write all ten number phrases from the text on the board from the lowest number to the highest—the class can help you order them by calling them out in sequence. Then they turn their texts over. Read the text out loud minus the number phrases—saying 'beep' instead of the phrase. Pause while learners write down the missing phrase. Learners can see whether their answers are the same as their partners. Finally, they check by re-reading the original text, to see if they now have the phrases where they occur in the original text.

3.8.2 Quizzes

You can use quiz questions to check learners' recall. Questions may be true/false, multiple choice, or open-ended. Instead of going through the questions from 1–10 or whatever, you can allow learners to take them in any order they like. The idea then is to get as many questions as possible right, before getting one wrong. After learners have processed a number of texts you can have a Grand Quiz and ask them to re-read a number of texts for homework. You can then set a quiz based on these texts, or ask the learners to set a quiz for each other.

3.8.3 Group dictation

This is also a well-established activity used, for example, by Davis and Rinvolucri (1988) and sometimes referred to as 'running dictation'.

Stage 1

Type the text in large, clear, well-spaced type and prepare five or six copies. Put these copies on the walls of the classroom distributed round as evenly as possible. Or they could be pasted on to card and placed face-down round the edges or down the centre of the room.

Stage 2

Divide the class into groups. Provide each group with a blank sheet of paper.

Stage 3

Explain that each group is going to write down the text. The members of the group will take it in turns to go to one of the copies of the text pinned on the wall and try to remember as much as they can. They will then come back to the group and dictate what they have read and remembered. As soon as this is finished the next member of the group goes to read the text. The aim is to reproduce the original text word for word.

Stage 4

As soon as a group believes they have completed the text they must take it to the teacher. The teacher takes a note of the time they have taken and writes it on their paper. When all the papers are in the teacher marks them and adds thirty seconds for each mistake. She then announces the results.

Variation 1

With a short text like the Empire State Building text it is possible to use the full text. With a longer text there is a danger that the activity becomes tedious. It might be better to take only a section, perhaps a couple of paragraphs.

Variation 2

Instead of giving learners a blank paper at stage 2 you can make the task easier by providing them with a heavily gapped version of the text. With a gapped text you might give the groups some time to work on the reconstruction from memory before letting them read the full version posted on the wall.

3.8.4 Communal memory

This works on the same principles as dictogloss reconstruction tasks. All learners will have had access to the same text but not all learners will remember the same things about it. With dictogloss, after a pre-task stage where the text topic is introduced, the teacher reads out the text once only at normal speed, without pausing, and students write as much as they can to jog their memories. They then work together to reconstruct it as near to the original as they can.

With communal memory tasks, you can use a text they have already read for an earlier task. Begin by asking learners to work as individuals to put down in note form as much as they can remember about the text, but without looking at the actual text or their notes on it. Then ask them to work in pairs to pool their ideas. Move from pairs to fours. Finally work with the class as a whole to see how much they can recall between them. You might still be able to identify gaps in their recall. You can ask questions based on these gaps. Finally you can read out the text or ask learners to check their own copies.

If you try these tasks out in class, you will probably find, as we did, that during the reconstruction stages, in pair and group interaction, the learners move from discussing facts and content vocabulary, to discussion of lexical and grammatical patternings and helping each other resolve language problems. (For more discussion on this, see Storch 2002.)

3.8.5 Summaries

Ask learners working in pairs to re-read a text and take up to ten words of notes, then put the text away and summarize it from memory using a set number of words. You might, for example, ask them to summarize the text 'Helping people click' in exactly 44 words to produce something like:

> Ed Miles and Maryam Hussein got to know each other through the internet. After three years of internet chat they finally met. Ed and Maryam are now happily married. Internet dating like this is becoming more and more common and more and more acceptable.

Learners can then read out their summaries to compare with what others have written.

Setting an exact number of words presents learners with a linguistic challenge. To reach the precise number of words, they need to 'juggle' with grammar and wordings. How would you, for example, reduce the words here to 37, without changing any meanings?

A tip to help you here: when deciding how many words to set, write the summary yourself first, then count the words you used. And what did we change to reduce the word count? We used 'became friends' to replace five words in the first line, and left out 'and more' twice in line 4.

3.8.6 Personalizing tasks

Much of the lexis and some of the grammar in a text can be recycled by asking learners to relate the task to their own life in some way. After the Empire State Building text, for example, learners could be asked to talk about their fear of heights or about experiences with high buildings. After the Monty story they could be asked to recall their own childhood and whether they were afraid of the dark, or to recall experiences involving fear of the dark. Tasks like this could be set as homework at the end of a task sequence. This would encourage learners to review the texts and mine them for useful language.

3.9 Spoken texts

3.9.1 The nature of spoken text

Linguists often distinguish between spoken and written language by pointing out that spoken language is generally *interactional,* whereas written language is generally *transactional.* What this means is that spoken language is generally, though not always, used for social purposes—to make friends, to pass the time happily with family and friends and so on. Written language, on the other hand is generally, though not always, used to convey information. Another important difference is that spoken language usually involves two or more active participants in the production of language, whereas writing is normally produced by one participant and received by another.

These are useful distinctions and account for many of the differences between spoken and written language, but it is a mistake to think that the distinction between spoken and written language is entirely clear cut. For example email chat has a lot in common with the spoken language used in everyday conversation, whereas a university lecture has a lot in common with the language of a textbook. Both email chat and everyday conversation involve participants in taking turns in producing language, and they are both used to make friends and to pass the time with friends. On the other hand both university lectures and textbooks involve one participant as the producer of language, and the other participants simply as receivers; and they are both primarily concerned with imparting information.

It is important to take account of this in preparing teaching materials. Some spoken texts, particularly monologues which have information transfer as their primary purpose, are most usefully treated in the same way as written texts. Learners need practice in listening to spoken monologue of this kind and should learn to process them aurally, and the sort of activities used to exploit monologue in the classroom will have a lot in common with the techniques used to exploit written texts.

READING ACTIVITY

Here is the transcript of the first part of a mini-lecture on a dinosaur, the velociraptor, together with two pictures which go with the lecture. Can you think of one or more tasks you might use to exploit this text?

The Velociraptor

OK, so let's take a look at the flesh-eating dinosaurs, the meat eaters. And let's start with the velociraptor. This will be very familiar to a lot of you if you've seen the film Jurassic Park. In the film you see the velociraptors hunting humans. It's really scary. The film shows that the velociraptor was one of the most intelligent dinosaurs and it was also one of the most dangerous. We often think of dinosaurs as being huge animals, like tyrannosaurus rex, but the velociraptor was only about the size of a large dog—about one metre high and two metres long—and it normally weighed between 10 and 15 kilos. They lived about 80 to 85 million years ago. As you can see from the picture they stood on two legs and had a long tail. They could move very fast—up to 60 kilometres per hour—and they used their long tails to help them to turn very quickly. They used them to balance so they could turn really quickly. They used to hunt in packs, in groups of four or more animals together, just like wolves or lions do today. It had a small head—only about 20 centimetres long—but it had incredibly

Figure 3.3 Velociraptor and hadrosaur

powerful jaws with teeth up to 3 centimetres long. They used these teeth to cut up their prey, the animals they killed. They did their killing with their claws. Its main weapon was a claw on its foot, about 10 centimetres long. This claw was retractable—the velociraptor could draw it in, just like cats do, so it was always very sharp. It used this claw to kill the animals it preyed on—mainly defenceless plant-eaters like the hadrosaur.

Commentary

1 This text is rich in information, including numerical information. So you could give the transcript to learners with all the numbers removed and give them a list of the numbers and ask them to put them back in the appropriate places. They could then listen to the text to check their answers. This would certainly be a viable task, but it would have the disadvantage that learners would be exposed to the text first in written rather than spoken form. It is important, remember, to give learners practice in processing this kind of material aurally. So the task suggested above might be better as a memory challenge task for recycling purposes at a later stage in the lesson.

2 An alternative would be to set a prediction exercise. You could give learners the title of the lecture together with the picture of the velociraptor and the opening three sentences of the text. They could then be asked to work in groups to predict five questions which would be answered in the lecture. You could then lead a class discussion leading to a pooling of the questions to make a long list. Finally the class could vote on the most likely ten questions before listening to the lecture to find out if their predictions were correct. This would have three advantages:

- It would mean that their first exposure to the text was in its original spoken form.
- It would reproduce the study context. When we listen to a lecture we do not listen in total ignorance. We have strong expectations as to what information will be contained—what questions will be answered.
- It would provide an opportunity to prime the learners with much of the vocabulary they would need in order to understand the lecture.

3 If you know that learners have some previous knowledge of velociraptors you could give them a quiz before they listened to the lecture. You might then listen to their answers and lead a class discussion to decide how sure they were of the answers before listening to the lecture. If they have no previous knowledge of the subject, but they have access to the internet, you could ask them to prepare the topic for homework before giving them the quiz in class. This would have the same advantages as 2 above.

4 You could summarize the main points of the text very briefly in note form, change their order, and ask learners to predict the sequence they will come in. They then listen and number the main points.

5 You could give the script of the lecture to one group of learners and ask them to prepare a quiz for homework. They could then give their questions to the other groups who would listen to the lecture and try to answer the questions.

3.9.2 Sources of spoken text

The easiest spoken texts to find and adapt for task-based use are recordings from your coursebook; most coursebooks have transcripts of their listening comprehension materials. Radio interviews often contain sustained responses to the interviewer's questions that bear a strong resemblance to transactional monologue and these can easily be found on the web. There are CDs and cassettes of stories, or short TV or film documentaries, and it is always possible to audio record topical BBC World News items (or get several students to do so). Often transcripts for these are available on the BBC website (http://www.bbc. co.uk).

3.10 Review

It is important to give learners a reason for working with texts. There are a number of familiar techniques designed to do this. Ideally the learners should be reading or listening to material which provides its own motivation—topics which they find engaging, stories at an appropriate level and so on—but this is not always possible. Apart from anything else, it is not always possible to select material which will engage everyone in a given class. And it is not always possible to predict with certainty just what topics and texts will engage learners' interest. However, a good task is likely to stimulate motivation, whatever the topic.

Even if a text is intrinsically interesting, it is still worthwhile providing a task-based framework for text processing. There are three possible advantages to be gained:

- The framework will provide a context in which you can prime learners by introducing, in a meaningful context, the vocabulary they will need to process the text.
- The framework will ensure that learners approach the text in the same way as we approach text processing in real life. We rarely approach a text without some expectations as to its nature. By using a task to contextualize a written or spoken text we help create these expectations for learners, providing a real purpose and context for reading or listening.
- A well designed task will help to provide or enhance the motivational challenge involved in processing a text.

Most of the techniques outlined in this chapter involve some sort of prediction. In some cases the prediction is explicit—as when learners were asked to predict the outcome of the Empire State Building story. When asking learners to predict in this way it is important to provide the right level of challenge. They need to be given enough clues to ensure that they have a reasonable chance of making worthwhile predictions. But you need to keep enough hidden to ensure that they still have a reason for reading or listening. This means you will sometimes need to practise restraint and hold back what you know to be the 'right' answers, and not give away too many clues too soon.

In other cases, as when learners begin with a general knowledge quiz, the prediction is less overt, but this activity still has the effect of encouraging learners to speculate on the contents of the text. Here again, you should make sure that there are questions still unanswered as learners move on to the reading or listening. The job of the teacher in setting up and orchestrating a task is to sharpen learners' curiosity and ensure that they will read or listen with interest.

One of the problems of encouraging learners to process text for meaning is that they will not be concerned with the wordings of the text. Good reading and listening strategies depend very much on high level processing, with learners predicting as they read or listen, and checking out and adjusting their predictions as the text unfolds. This means that they will pay attention to the key words in a text, but the minutiae of syntax and phrasing will pass by unnoticed. Given this, it is important to recycle texts in such a way that learners *will* take careful note of the actual wording of the text. This can be done partly by precisely focused language activities which target particular elements of the text. But it is important that by the end of a task cycle, learners have become as familiar as possible with the wording of a text. Once a text has been processed for meaning it represents a valuable learning resource, one which learners can recall for themselves, and one which the teacher can recall for them to provide well contextualized examples of grammatical and lexical features of the language.

Texts can be used for follow-up tasks, either immediately after the initial study of a given text, or some time later. But it is certainly worthwhile to ensure at some stage that learners pay close attention to the precise wording of the texts they have processed. Chapter 6 gives more suggestions for form-focused exercises and for ways of working with spontaneous interactive spoken language. Meanwhile here are some ideas for exploring some of the tasks and ideas contained in this chapter.

3.11 Follow-up activities

1 Try out one or two of the tasks illustrated in this chapter. After the class, while it is fresh in your mind, write down what you did and what you noticed happening. If you can, try the same task again with a different set of students and notice the similarities and differences between the two classes.

2 Try out a set of tasks and ask students for their feed-back after each one (written anonymously by individuals, in the last three or four minutes of class time).

3 Try asking students to find and bring to class one text each on a topic that they are interested in reading. (Sources: internet, library books, library cassettes/CDs, radio, TV recordings, recordings of interviews conducted in English, letters written in English, print-outs of people's biographies from individual websites, comic books (e.g. Asterix), or even textbooks.) Give learners a deadline to produce these, make sure they write the source reference and date on the text, and take note of its copyright status. The first task can be for them each to present a very short summary of their text, persuading the class to choose it for a shortlist of texts to be used in their lessons. You can then select the most popular ones and design a set of tasks for each one.

The next two chapters will provide more ideas for generating different types of task taking topics or themes as starting points.

4 FROM TOPIC TO TASKS: LISTING, SORTING, AND CLASSIFYING

4.1 Introduction

In Chapter 3 we looked at different ways of designing and using text-based tasks, using texts as our starting point. In this chapter, our starting point will be a specific topic or theme, such as 'Families', 'Holidays', or 'Pets', that draws largely on learners' own experiences or world knowledge. For each topic, we can design a sequence of tasks, each one leading into another. Some of these will be target tasks, in the sense that they reproduce discourse activities which we might carry out in the real world. Others will be facilitating tasks in that their function is to help learners to carry out the target tasks. (See Chapter 2 (2.2).)

So, for example, 'Volcanoes' might constitute the topic for one or two lessons. After an initial priming stage, where, for example, the teacher might show some pictures of volcanoes and talk about her experience of them, the subsequent task sequence could include facilitating tasks of listing facts learners know about volcanoes followed by labelling a diagram of a cross-section of a volcano, having first listened to a teacher's explanation; these could then be followed by one or more target tasks: comparing two different kinds of volcanoes; making a quiz about a specific volcano; or recounting their own experience (from TV or other sources) of a volcano erupting.

Note on taxonomies of tasks

In the taxonomy of tasks used in this book, the task types are classified according to cognitive processes such as 'listing' and 'ranking'. This differs from most earlier taxonomies or typologies which often list 'opinion exchange', 'jigsaw', 'information gap', 'decision-making', and 'problem-solving' as separate task types (Pica *et al.* 1993: 18–27). We feel that a cognitive classification, though not watertight, is more specific and more generative as a tool for teachers to use. Tasks generated with particular cognitive processes in mind will often involve the above task types; for example, opinion exchanges and information gaps would naturally occur when listing and discussing, for example, qualities needed by a world leader. Later, agreeing on a particular order of ranking will necessarily involve opinion gaps, evaluation and decision-making.

Another distinction often made is between 'real-world' tasks and pedagogic tasks. Many tasks in this chapter involve activities and topics that one might well do or talk about outside the classroom—choosing holidays, earthquake safety procedures (commonly called 'real-world' tasks), while others, like the picture dictogloss story activity, would certainly rank as 'pedagogic' by nature. Chapter 7 goes into this in more detail.

4.2 Selecting topics

So how can we select suitable topics for tasks? We can choose topics that

- feature in our learners' English textbooks
- typically appear on examination papers or in oral tests
- appear elsewhere on the school curriculum (for example, in geography, history, or current affairs)
- are of topical or seasonal interest
- often figure in casual conversations in social settings (for example, in coffee breaks, with host family, in bars or clubs)
- learners want to be able to talk about outside class with foreigners they might meet, or write about to email pen friends, or 'chat' about in web-based chat sites.

One way to raise motivation is to ask learners to suggest their own topics, or to get them to choose topics they like best from a list of topics that have proved popular with previous learners. In fact getting learners to select and rank topics they like could form an excellent decision-making task at the start of a new term. Many teachers have reported that giving learners a chance to choose their own topics has significantly enhanced learner engagement.

Not all learners will be equally keen on all topics but, if an engaging task is set, any reasonable topic can engender enthusiasm, especially if it is explored from a new or unusual angle.

The choice of potential topics is boundless. For interest, take a look at this map of the world and skim through topics chosen by English teachers in different parts of the world for their task-based lessons.

At this point, we suggest you stop for a moment and note down three or four topics that you feel would be suitable for your classes. In the following sections we will look at ways of designing different types of task and you can design some tasks based on your topics. This is best done together with a fellow language teacher (or two) as ideas often flow more freely. You can then evaluate the tasks you thought of, refine the best of them, and select a set of tasks that you can grade, write instructions for, and use in class.

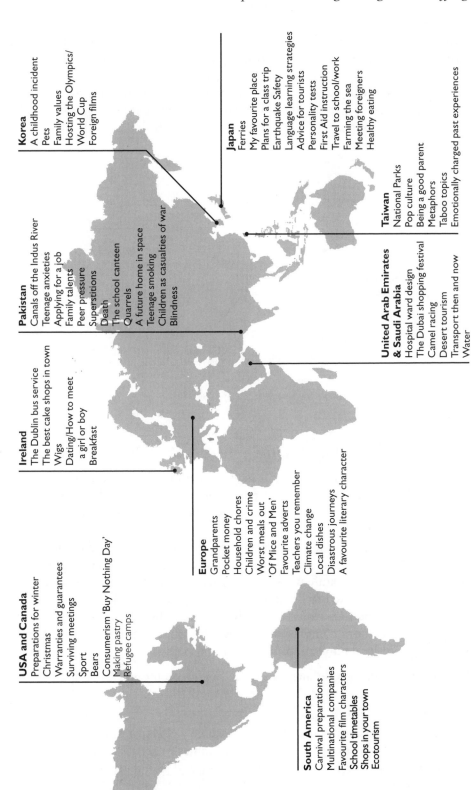

Korea
A childhood incident
Pets
Family values
Hosting the Olympics/
World Cup
Foreign films

Japan
Ferries
My favourite place
Plans for a class trip
Earthquake Safety
Language learning strategies
Advice for tourists
Personality tests
First Aid instruction
Travel to school/work
Farming the sea
Meeting foreigners
Healthy eating

Taiwan
National Parks
Pop culture
Being a good parent
Metaphors
Taboo topics
Emotionally charged past experiences

Pakistan
Canals off the Indus River
Teenage anxieties
Applying for a job
Family talents
Peer pressure
Superstitions
Death
The school canteen
Quarrels
A future home in space
Teenage smoking
Children as casualties of war
Blindness

**United Arab Emirates
& Saudi Arabia**
Hospital ward design
The Dubai shopping festival
Camel racing
Desert tourism
Transport then and now
Water

Ireland
The Dublin bus service
The best cake shops in town
Wigs
Dating/How to meet
a girl or boy
Breakfast

Europe
Grandparents
Pocket money
Household chores
Children and crime
Worst meals out
'Of Mice and Men'
Favourite adverts
Teachers you remember
Climate change
Local dishes
Disastrous journeys
A favourite literary character

USA and Canada
Preparations for winter
Christmas
Warranties and guarantees
Surviving meetings
Sport
Bears
Consumerism 'Buy Nothing Day'
Making pastry
Refugee camps

South America
Carnival preparations
Multinational companies
Favourite film characters
School timetables
Shops in your town
Ecotourism

Figure 4.1 Sample topics from around the world

As noted in the previous section, the task types described in this and the next chapter (see Figure 4.2) are derived from a broad classification of cognitive processes. This has proved to be an effective way of generating a set of different types of task based around one topic area. And once learners are familiar with the basic topic vocabulary, they can explore that topic from a variety of angles, exercising a range of cognitive skills which present different linguistic challenges.

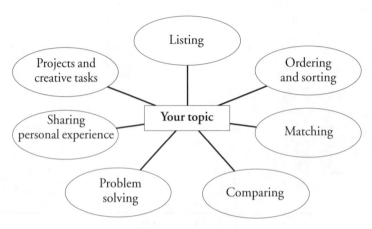

Figure 4.2   Generating tasks from a topic

4.3   Tasks involving listing

The simplest type of task is listing. It may seem at first sight far too simple, but the linguistic challenge can vary according to what you ask learners to list; it could result in a list of words or short phrases or even quite complex sentences. With the topic 'transport' at the elementary level, learners might simply list the kinds of transport available locally—a list of nouns. At a later stage they could be asked to produce a list of the features of an ideal transport system—probably a mixture of phrases and sentences. At a more advanced level they could be asked to list reasons for using (or not using) particular forms of transport. This would probably result in a list of quite complex sentences. Even more complex would be a list of recommendations for improving your local public transport system.

Listing can usefully be split into two kinds: brainstorming and fact-finding.

4.3.1   Brainstorming

Brainstorming has been found to be an extremely effective way of getting even shy learners involved in topics and promotes richer task interaction. (See Cullen 1998 for background, principles, and useful techniques for brainstorming.)

Brainstorming can either be teacher-led involving the whole class, or with learners in pairs or small groups brainstorming among themselves. Or as a combination of both—starting with a teacher-led class brainstorm which learners then continue in pairs.

Here are some ideas for listing tasks that teachers in Japan, New Zealand and Brazil have tried out successfully, often starting with a class brainstorm then going on to complete their list in pairs or groups:

- qualities of a world leader
- criteria for choosing a place to stay for a vacation or weekend
- landmarks typically used when giving directions in your area
- things to mention when describing a specific animal
- items to include in an earthquake kit, with a reason for each one
- things that cats tend to do/like doing
- household chores (and who does them in your home)
- strategies for learning English outside class.

Most teachers advised giving learners a specific number of items to aim for, for example, five qualities for the 'world leader' task. Then learners know when they have completed their task. To judge what number to set, do the task yourself, then deduct one or two—so that learners can achieve the task without frustration. If you time yourself while you are doing the task, you can estimate a suitable time limit to set for your learners. Better still, do this with a colleague.

4.3.2 Fact-finding

Fact-finding involves asking learners to search for specific facts in books or leaflets or on a website, or to ask other people outside class. If you introduce the topic the lesson before and do a 'priming' stage for the task then, you could set a fact-finding task for homework. Then they work out how to express these facts in English and come to class ready prepared with a draft list. Some examples follow:

- Find out five facts about the volcano Mount Etna to share with other students next lesson. Write them down. Also note down three or four useful words or phrases about volcanoes you could teach your partner.
- Find out what three people outside this class think about cats as pets. Do they like cats or not? List the reasons they give. Prepare to report their views in English in your next lesson.
- Find out the birthdays of seven people you or your family know. Write the name of the person, who they are, and the date of their birthday. Bring your list to class.

Listing often forms a starting point for more complex tasks:

- Lorie Wood gave three websites for ecotourism and asked her advanced learners to design a trip that upheld ecotourism principles. They began by identifying those principles and listing them.
- At the beginning of a project on refugee camps, Yvonne Beaudry gave her intermediate students some websites to look at to find out and list the facilities a refugee camp should have. Groups were then asked to design their own camp.

4.3.3 Games based on listing: quizzes, memory challenge, and guessing games

The listing process can form the basis for many simple activities like quizzes, memory games, and guessing games. For example, the volcano lesson could begin with each pair collating and finalizing their list of facts, and then writing a true/false quiz, by changing some of the statements in their list so that they are not true. Or they could write five quiz questions about Mount Etna to give another pair to do, or to ask the class. This could even become a competition, with the class divided in two halves taking turns to respond orally to the true/false statements, or to ask and answer each other's questions, with points being scored by each team for right answers.

Guessing games can also incorporate listing. For example, they can involve

- the class asking the teacher questions (or vice versa) such as 'Guess what I had for breakfast today', or
- students writing five short sentences about their chosen animal and then reading them or saying them for the class, then asking 'Guess what animal this is' (see Appendix 1.4), or
- the well-known game 'Guess what I've got in my bag'.

Here is a brief account of how Sandee Thompson does a version of this last task with her low intermediate learners.

Junk we carry round with us

Sandee gets learners to guess what she has in her book-bag that day. After accepting guesses from the class, Sandee then reveals the objects one at a time and talks about them—a good example of teacher talk forming comprehensible input. This can lead on to a classification task (described in the next section). After this, learners do the same guessing task with each other, in pairs. They then hear a recording of Sandee doing the same task with a colleague and note down differences they hear in the style of interaction. They repeat the same task with another partner and report back on what they have noticed.

(See Appendix 1.6 for a fuller account and to see what Sandee did next.)

4.3.4 Tasks for real beginners

Taken more slowly, this last task ('Junk we carry round with us') would also be suitable for beginner learners. If learners need consolidation of the new vocabulary, a task like this could subsequently be turned into a memory challenge game by covering up the objects once they have been taken out. Then learners in pairs can draw or write a list of the objects they remember. The challenge is then to see which pair can remember the most objects. You can give them clues if they get really stuck early on. And finally, after seeing all the objects again, learners (or teams of learners) can take turns to tell the teacher what to put back in her bag. To make it more fun, this could also be done as a memory challenge (with the objects concealed), each learner naming one thing that has not been mentioned before until all the objects are back. This sequence of small tasks offers plenty of opportunities for learners to recycle the names of common objects as well as exposure to natural interaction as their teacher talks about them and the activities themselves.

'International words' is an example of a teacher-led listing task that can be done by most classes of complete beginners. It does not put pressure on learners to speak, only to listen and understand as much as possible and to try pronouncing some words. It helps beginners to get used to the flow of English and to recognize words they know in that context. It works because quite a few English words have become international; but of course the number of familiar words also depends on the learners' own mother tongue and their life experience.

Topic: International words of English

The teacher starts with a class brainstorm, drawing or writing on the board some words the learners probably already recognize in English, e.g. 'taxi', 'football', 'television', 'supermarket'. The teacher talks a little about each word as it comes up ('Who likes football?' 'Who plays football? You?') using gestures and facial expression to help them understand. The teacher might then ask learners to supply other words of English they already know, and to practise pronouncing them the English way.

International words

internet café bus no football hotel

tennis police TV no problem!

music singer cocacola burger stop

supermarket Hello teacher disco taxi

O.K. radio goal

Figure 4.3 International words (1)

At the end of the lesson, learners count how many words of English they already recognize. That they know so many is usually a surprise to them. This illustrates one basic principle of TBT: it is far more positive to build on what your learners already know, than to start with what they don't know. As one teacher put it, think of your learner's cup as being half full, rather than half empty.

4.3.5 Evaluating a task

What makes a good task? A good task not only generates interest and creates an acceptable degree of challenge, but also generates opportunities for learners to experience and activate as much language as possible. This applies to all tasks, but the examples below are for listing tasks.

READER ACTIVITY 4A

Evaluating tasks in terms of language use

Which two of the following tasks would be likely to generate the most useful language for intermediate learners? And which two the least useful? Which might be usable as an initial but brief teacher-led brainstorm to lead into a topic?

Topic: Cats

a Make a list of six typical things that cats tend to do.
b What different breeds of cats can you think of? Make a list.
c List the different colours that cats can be. How many can you get?

Topic: Planning a party

d What events in your country might people celebrate by having a party? Make a list.
e Make a list of things you have to do when planning a party.
f Who might you invite to your next party? Make a list of people you would ask.

Pick one task from the examples above that would generate useful language and think what you would do at a priming stage. What steps you would take to set it up for your learners to do?

Commentary

One obvious question would be 'Do learners really need to know the words for different breeds of cat?' Such words are very rarely used, and the time spent teaching these would be far better spent on more common words and phrases. Colours of cats might generate a few common colour words and phrases, 'black and white', 'sort of orangey-brown', but others like 'tabby' or 'marmalade' are far less useful. These two, b) and c), then seem to be the least worthwhile tasks. Equally, a list of names of people to invite to a party (f) would have little value in itself, but could be made marginally more useful by adding 'Give reasons for your choice', which might well generate a little more language use, especially if they were asked to agree on a list of five famous people.

Task d) is a simple task requiring learners to name or explain in English any national holidays or events when parties are held or rites of passage like special birthdays or school-leaving parties; language use would be quite limited but could prove useful if learners needed to talk to foreigners about customs in their country and explain them. However, if done quickly as a teacher-led brainstorm in a priming stage, it could help learners decide what kind of party to discuss plans for, and thus prepare the way for a task such as e), which is more likely to generate a variety of longer utterances like, 'Well, you'd have to choose a day and time when most people are free …'.

Task a), too, usually generates a wide range of language use: 'Cats often damage the furniture', 'They miaow when they are hungry', 'They sleep in the sun', 'They like to lie in warm places', 'They wake you up at night', 'They catch mice', 'They kill birds and bring them inside', and so on. Most of the words and phrases here are quite common, and if they don't know words like 'damage' they can always paraphrase or use gestures.

4.3.6 Pre-task priming and post-task activities

Just as for text-based tasks, learners would need some priming before the task, so that they can understand the topic, activate relevant schemata, recall or ask for useful words and phrases and get ideas flowing. Depending on the topic, you could use pictures, or brainstorm words associated with the topic, find out if anyone has personal experience of it, and so on. For example, on the topic of cats, at a priming stage before task a) above, we usually start by asking learners who really likes cats and who doesn't like cats. We have a good friend who hates cats so we tell them why. Some learners will join in at this point. We then tell the class about a cat we used to have and that our children named 'Garfield' like the cartoon cat. We show a picture of him and talk about the things he did—some funny and some infuriating. Learners like hearing about teachers' personal lives, so this usually works well, but you may have other ideas that would get learners listening and interested in the topic.

Once learners have done the task they can compare their lists in a report stage and possibly collate their ideas making one longer list. They might hear a recording of other people doing a similar task, for example talking about what cats do, and see if their ideas are on the list they made. Finally, move into a focus-on-form stage, with the teacher highlighting useful language forms and letting learners practise useful patterns, and record useful words and phrases in their own 'phrase books'.

4.3.7 Summary

To summarize, the outcome of a listing task will of course be some form of list, which can be drawn, written, remembered, compared with other people's, or turned into a guessing game or quiz.

The advantage of starting a sequence of tasks with one or two simple listing tasks is that they can serve as a useful introduction to the topic, and provide a chance for setting the scene and introducing relevant vocabulary. In fact they act as facilitating tasks, helping to lighten the processing load when learners are tackling more complex tasks, as by then, many of the topic words and phrases used for listing will already be familiar.

Another benefit of starting with a listing task is that items on lists can be ordered or sorted or classified in some way or other, for example by making a mind-map, allotting items to categories.

4.4 Tasks involving ordering and sorting

This broad category includes a variety of cognitive processes, including sequencing, ranking, and classifying, which all require a little more thought and cognitive effort than simply listing. Some involve ordering items according to purely factual criteria, like dates or prices; others involve a certain amount of decision making, based on personal choice or opinion.

4.4.1 Sequencing

This may be chronological sequencing, for example, arranging a series of jumbled pictures to make a story, or a jumbled list of events to recreate the order in which they happened. It could entail describing in sequence the steps of a particular process. It could call upon learner's prior knowledge, their imagination, or knowledge gleaned from a written or spoken or visual source.

Tasks that teachers in Canada, the UAE, and UK have used include:

- Order the steps in a baking recipe (where information may be given in a jumbled form, using words, pictures, or line drawings).
- Describe in detail how to make your favourite food.
- Describe exactly what you have to do to make a phone-call overseas from a phone box in your country.

Sequencing can also be done as a memory challenge using a short clip of a film extract on video (not more than 2 minutes) or a film trailer, or a longish TV advert. Play learners the video once or twice with the sound off. Then ask them to try to list from memory exactly what scenes and events were shown, arranging them in sequence. When you are planning this, watch the extract carefully, listing, and counting the different scenes/actions; you can then give learners a fairly precise number to aim for. The interesting thing is, different students remember different bits, so their lists are nearly always different and can be discussed and compared before showing the video again. This would be a good task to set before asking students to do a comparison of two similar film extracts. (See Chapter 5 and Glen Poupore's movie scene comparison task in Appendix 1.5.)

4.4.2 Rank ordering

Learners could list and then rank their school subjects with their favourite ones at the top; they could list seven kinds of pet and then rank them according to how much trouble they are to keep at home. In both cases, to stimulate more language use, learners can be asked to justify their order of ranking.

Lists can be ranked according to many different criteria like cost, popularity, practicality, or fun value—different topics will obviously need different criteria. With the topic of professions/jobs, criteria for ranking these could include ranking according to rates of pay or likelihood of job satisfaction, working conditions, likely levels of stress, suitability for a working parent with children of school age, and so on.

Here are some ideas used by teachers for tasks involving ranking, some preceded by listing tasks.

Potential holiday destinations could be listed and then ranked in order of popularity with the class, based on criteria such as price, weather, accommodation, facilities, or activities on offer. These are in fact the actual criteria that Rosane Correira's class in Brazil arrived at through an earlier teacher-led brainstorming session, after talking about places they had been to on their vacations.

Qualities of a world leader: Mikey Kelly in Japan (inspired by an idea from his former colleagues) gets his learners to brainstorm, first silently on their own, up to eight qualities of a world leader and then in pairs or groups, to come to a consensus, agreeing on five of them. (Both these steps work better with time limits.)

Then, learners as individuals arrange these five in a ranked list, according to criteria they have chosen, and next discuss together, debating and justifying their decisions and referring to current world leaders. This prepares the way for a second task, where real world leaders are introduced on the board, and groups rate each of those leaders out of 5 stars according to their agreed criteria.

Talking about families—how strict are/were your parents? Tim Marchand in Japan explains how he set this task up after an initial explanatory priming phase:

This task sequence has three stages: a listening stage, a language focus stage and a speaking stage; I sometimes adapt the order according to circumstances. The listening stage comprises a recording of four people talking about how they were treated by their parents, and the students have to listen and decide which parents sounded the softest, and which ones sounded the strictest. They discuss that in pairs, giving evidence/ reasons for their ranking.

The speaking stage is simply to talk with a partner and discuss their feelings towards their parents, and report back to the class whose parents were stricter.

At this point, to promote more class discussion, you could attempt to get the class to rank their parents—from softest to strictest!

Tim reports: 'I've used this task several times, and it always goes pretty well. The students have no problem finding things to say about their parents, although there is sometimes a debate over whether "easy-going" is a positive attribute for parents!'

Here the listening stage introduces the topic that the learners will take up later and provides valuable exposure to the kind of language that can be used in this context. This provides excellent priming for learners who are about to do the task themselves. The focus-on-form stage offers a chance to highlight or consolidate features of that language. (See Chapter 6 for ideas for form-focused activities and the recording transcripts for Tim's task.)

We have seen above that selecting criteria for ranking may be done by the students themselves, in a class brainstorm, or they can be decided by the teacher. For more insights into selecting criteria, try the activity below.

READER ACTIVITY 4B

Appraising criteria for ranking

The first activity below is a listing task which serves as a lead-in to the ranking task in the second activity. Which two of the four criteria for ranking in task 2—a), b), c), or d)—below might stimulate the richest interaction for this particular task? Which of them might be best in your context?

Ways to improve your English outside class

On your own, make a list of four ways in which people in your situation could learn more English outside class. Then exchange ideas with a partner and agree on a list of five possible ways.

Then, with your partner, rank order your list according to two of these criteria: a) expense, b) popularity, c) practicality, d) likelihood of success. Give your reasons.

Commentary

Learners come up with all kinds of ways to improve their English, depending on their age, where they live and where they are studying. Ideas include: surfing the net, emailing pen-friends, reading comic strip books in English (including Asterix or Tin-Tin), reading bilingual books, exchanging conversation lessons with a person wanting to learn to speak their mother tongue, finding foreign residents to talk to in English, offering their services as a tourist guide to foreign visitors, listening to English CDs/tapes while driving or travelling to work or school, taking extra English lessons, keeping an English note-book and writing down expressions they hear or read, finding a foreign or English speaking girlfriend/boyfriend, attending or starting an English speaking club or social circle, buying and reading English newspapers or magazines, getting a voluntary job in a charity shop, company or place where English is spoken … .

Given this list of suggestions, ranking according to expense is not likely to stimulate much interaction, as many of these ideas involve very little expense (except extra lessons, buying books, magazines, etc.). Ranking according to popularity would depend on how this was done—if it was a class survey using a 'hands up if you would like to try this' approach, very little interaction would happen, but individuals interviewing class-mates and then reporting back might stimulate more. It is likely that c) and d) would be most likely to stimulate discussion, especially if learners ranked them silently first, and then formed pairs and then fours, and were obliged to come to a consensus within a time limit.

Beginning with silent ranking helps learners to commit themselves to a solution and engage personally with the task, as they can get their ideas together and plan how to express them, before talking to others about it. It is a way of reducing the mental demands and pressure of the task itself.

A surer way to find out which criterion for ranking is best is to experiment and try out all four kinds, with four different groups in the same class. Observe the groups carefully while they are doing the tasks, and then let them report their results to the whole class. Notice which ranking system seemed to work best. Ask each group for their feed-back, too, once they have heard all the results.

4.4.3 Classifying

Learners can either be asked to work out their own categories for classifying, or to allot items in a list to categories already given.

For her 'Junk we carry round with us' task, Sandee Thompson asked her learners to think of ways of classifying the things from her bag. They thought of categories like shape (rectangular or round), things with perfume, things that make a noise, objects to do with money. Different learners came up with different ways of classifying. It is this variety of response that can stimulate rich discussion. It also makes for interesting teaching—you can do the same task with different classes and it is different each time—learners can be very inventive.

When priming learners to choose their own categories, it is helpful to give them one or two ideas first or to do a parallel task with the whole class, like classifying the contents of a classroom cupboard or a desk drawer.

However, if the task instructions give the categories, learners sometimes feel more secure. It makes it a more straightforward task, having only one stage. But this may also reduce the amount of language use it will generate. Which alternative you choose will depend on the degree of challenge your learners are happy with. Here are some ideas for categories you can give. We start with two-way categories.

Giving positive/negative categories works well with many themes:

- After the task about cats, have learners make a list of things cats tend to do, and then ask them to sort their list into 'nice things' and 'not such nice things'.
- *Food*: Learners can classify food items (list provided) twice: first into 'foods they like' and 'foods they don't like', and later into food that is 'reasonably healthy' (that you can eat a lot of) and food that is generally considered 'unhealthy' if you eat a lot of it.
- *Family values: agree or disagree?* For this task, Shaun Manning gave his South Korean learners a set of slightly controversial statements and asked each learner to decide whether they agreed (put a tick) or disagreed (put a cross) with each statement. Then, in small groups, they had to reach a consensus and change the wording of the statements the group disagreed with to make them acceptable. They presented these to the class, compared their adapted statements and discussed the changed wordings.

This last task is a good example of one that starts out with a simple two-way classification and builds up to a serious decision-making task involving a negotiated outcome: the list of adapted statements. (For the full task, with statements and evaluation, see Appendix 1.3.)

The above examples of classification tasks were all based on two categories, but of course there can be more. Animals can be classified in many ways, so can clothes.

'International words' (see the Beginner's task in 4.3.4) can be classified into: things to eat, things to drink, sport, transport, electronic media, school words, etc. The teacher draws columns on the board for these categories and gives an example for each (Figure 4.4). Even beginner learners can say which category the listed words best fit and possibly add one or two more words to each one.

media	sport	people	places	Things you say	Things to eat or drink
International words					
internet café bus no football hotel tennis police TV no problem! music singer coca cola burger stop supermarket hello teacher disco taxi O.K. radio goal					
TV radio	tennis golf	singer	disco	hello	burger

Figure 4.4 International words (2)

4.4.4 Games based on classified sets

Classified lists can be used as a basis for designing 'Odd word out' games, and/or 'What do these have in common?' quizzes. Sets like the following can be used to revise topic vocabulary. Try them for yourself.

What do the items in each set have in common, and which item could be the odd one out and why?

a apples, bananas, biscuits, oranges
b fish, chips (=French fries), hamburgers, cheese
c car, taxi, bus, bicycle

Once learners have got the idea, they can be asked to build up three or four sets like this at home to test the class. They can also be asked to write out the answer keys. For example, in a) they are all sweet but the odd one out is 'biscuits'—the others are fruit; the b) set is all savoury, but the odd one out is 'fish' as the others are all less healthy as they are high in fat content. In c) they are all means of transport but only 'bicycle' is environmentally friendly and healthy. There will always be other ways of classifying, and it is this that provides added interest. For example, for b) you could argue that 'cheese' is the odd one out as the others are all generally cooked or fried, or 'chips' because the others all contain protein. But this is good because exploring alternatives stimulates genuine language use in class.

4.5 Visual support: charts, tables, mind-maps, etc.

Seeing information set out within a framework can help learners process and organize information in a more structured way. This can both make a task less cognitively demanding and give learners a sense of security. It can also stimulate more interaction, as learners like to add their own ideas to fill any spaces. So, if columns are supplied for the 'International words' task above (4.4.3), learners can be asked to add three more words to each column (with the help of a dictionary if need be). In the Sport column, they might add 'golf'. They might feel the need to ask the teacher for words they want to add but don't know—for example, 'basket', where the teacher can respond with 'Yes, good one, but we say 'basketball' in English'. The teacher gains a chance here to expand on learners' verbal offerings, creating opportunities for language exposure tailored to learner's interests and knowledge levels. Such exposure should form comprehensible input for most learners.

4.5.1 Charts and tables

A simple six-cell chart (see Figure 4.5) was used by Yvonne Beaudry, in her 'Earthquake safety' task for her low intermediate learners in Japan. After brainstorming vocabulary for natural disasters ('floods', 'wildfire', 'Richter scale', 'shelter') she reports:

> Small groups discussed questions on earthquake preparedness and safety and filled in the top section of this chart. The cells of the chart were divided into 'before', 'during', and 'after' stages of an earthquake.

Yvonne followed this up with a reading activity with each group reading a different pamphlet on earthquake safety (for example, a Red Cross advice leaflet), adding locally relevant information to the bottom row of cells in their charts. They compared charts with other groups and added their ideas, too. So the chart gave sustained support through several task cycles. (See Appendix 1.1 for a full account of the task.)

Charts and tables also help learners to focus on relevant information when doing listening tasks—the classification is already clear; they simply have to listen for relevant facts to fill the boxes. Charts and tables with headings can also help learners to think of what aspects of the topic to talk or write about, and how to organize information coherently. They have the security of a framework within which to work; this reduces anxiety which, in turn, should allow language to flow more freely.

	Before an earthquake	During an earthquake	After an earthquake
You and your group			
Pamphlets and other groups			

Figure 4.5 Earthquake safety

To raise the degree of challenge for a classifying task, give learners an empty chart or one with only a few headings. Ask them to think up their own headings and then order the headings so they begin with general information and go on to the more specific. They can then write them into the table.

4.5.2 Mind maps

Mind maps have the same advantages as charts but they are more open, flexible, and can be added to more easily. Learners can use their artistic skills to make them look attractive. Like charts, they can be started on the board in preliminary discussion and then built on and filled in by learners.

READER ACTIVITY 4C

Drafting a mind map

1 Add a few ideas to the 'Planning a party' mind map. (See next page.)
2 Select three topics from the 'World map of topics' (Figure 4.1 in section 4.2) which might lend themselves to an initial brainstorm to build up a mind map.
3 Spending no more than one minute on each, rough out a possible mind map suitable for your learners to extend.

Teaching learners how to do mind maps would make a good teacher-led task in itself.

Figure 4.6 Mind map for planning a party (for learners to adapt and complete)

4.5.3 Time lines and storylines

Linear visuals are excellent for tasks based on sequencing. A time line could simply be made from a long piece of thick string or a washing line running along one wall of the classroom. To this can be attached dates and pictures with captions denoting historical events (for example, 'A history of our school/college') or stages in a manufacturing process (for example, 'Cheese making: from cow to retail outlet'), or events in a story narrative. In children's classes, storylines are often drawn on a poster or a wide piece of card. The process of making a storyline or a time line involves deciding what to include and how to draw or verbalize it so that it is clear to others; as such it is an engaging process and at the end there is a concrete outcome— something to show others—which can be interpreted and enjoyed. Different groups can produce their own and then display them, and present them orally to other groups who can then ask questions about them.

One use of a storyline using pictures/drawings is exemplified by David Coulson for his false beginners in Japan. It is based on a dictogloss activity but instead of getting learners to reconstruct verbally and write down the story he tells them, he gets them to work in pairs and draw whatever they can. On a second telling, they refine their drawings and, at a later stage, are encouraged to add any words they can catch. This results in learners listening out for key words and trying to get the gist of main events which they can draw. Finally, they compare their results with neighbouring pairs and try to justify their story pictures to each other by telling the story in English as best they can. On subsequent re-telling, they refine even more.

Whereas dictogloss activities focus learners' attention closely on the language forms used to express the meanings in the story, these picture dictogloss activities encourage learners to listen for the story events they understand and not worry about what they don't quite catch. David reports:

> I originally tried this exercise in the normal format of having them recreate the story in their own words. At their linguistic and motivation level this did not work very well. However, I have found the picture version useful for pointing out just how much they really can understand, once they are allowed to express a reaction in a way they are good at. Sometimes they embellish my story with extra, cheeky details, but it is always good-natured. Once we have had a laugh, I ask them to try writing what they can in English. This may not exactly constitute their own communication, but it does allow them to want to express the meanings of their own pictures. I see the value here particularly in de-stressing the language class atmosphere, which 'tasks' can do very well.

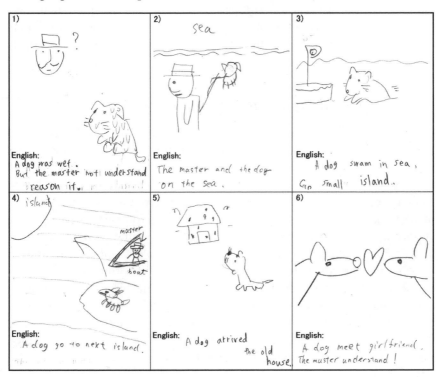

Figure 4.7 A picture dictogloss done by one of David's students

Figure 4.7 shows the illustrations the learners did—an illustration of a story about a romantic dog who swam between islands everyday to meet his girlfriend on the old island he used to live on before his family moved. His owner could never work out why he came home wet every night. So one day he follows his dog to the beach, has to get in a boat to follow the dog swimming the strait, and finally works out the mystery. The text on the picture reveals how wide the gap is between learners' receptive abilities and their productive ones. It points up the value of starting off with the pictures exercise.

READER ACTIVITY 4D

Design a task with some visual/organizational support

1 Think up one or two tasks based on your topic that involve learners in sequencing, ranking, or classifying.
2 Apply one or two of the ideas for visual frameworks above to help you draft clear instructions for your task.

The criteria and categories used for ranking and classifying tasks form a very useful basis for tasks which involve making comparisons, as they give learners specific aspects to compare. The use of visual frameworks/ representations such as charts or mind maps can help them to organize their thoughts and present their comparisons in a systematic way. Comparison tasks will be covered in the next chapter.

4.6 *Integrating reading and writing*

It is often thought that tasks are mainly for improving oral and aural skills, and certainly many of the tasks sent in by teachers for this book have involved a good deal of spoken interaction. This may be because many of their students have been taught in rather traditional ways with a heavy emphasis on grammar, reading and writing, or have textbooks with only a small proportion of genuine speaking activities. Up to now they have lacked opportunities to speak, so teachers have been designing tasks to get them talking. But if you have learners who are already reasonably fluent, and/or who need to practise writing, or to focus more on formal accuracy, it is equally possible to ask them to brainstorm in writing, either individually or in pairs, and then to present their ideas in writing. They can write by hand in class and pass it round or pin it on a wall for others to read; they can email their writing to each other, or use their word processing packages to produce a polished piece of work that can be used for public display or go up on the class website.

Although the tasks in this chapter do not generally start with a text, there will be many occasions where written or spoken texts on a topic can usefully be introduced part of the way through a sequence of tasks. Towards the end of her set of Earthquake Safety tasks, when learners had already drawn up a chart and presented their own ideas, Yvonne Beaudry brought in published pamphlets from several sources. Learners read and compared the information in the pamphlets and used some of it for refining what they had already written in their own charts. Tim Marchand played his class a recording of four people talking about their parents and discussing how strict they were, to give his learners some idea of how to do the task themselves. So he started off his sequence of tasks with a listening task followed by transcript study. Once you have chosen your topic, if there is no suitable text in your textbook, you can do a search on the web to find something that your students will find interesting and incorporate that into your sequence of tasks.

4.7 *Review*

In this chapter, we have explored the process of selecting topics and looked at ways of designing two broad kinds of task and around ten subcategories of task. (See Section 4.1 for a note on classifying task types.) Also, thanks to the teachers who sent in their favourite tasks, we have presented ideas for tasks on around 25 topics, illustrating some of them in detail.

We have also begun to explore various aspects of tasks like linguistic complexity, and have practised different teaching skills, including evaluating a task in terms of potential language use, giving visual/representational support (charts, mind maps, etc.), and planning and grading sequences of tasks. Your task sequences can be further extended when you read the following chapter, where we cover another five broad types of task.

4.8 *Follow-up activities*

General topics like 'pollution' or 'natural disasters' can be narrowed down and made more specific.

READER ACTIVITY 4E

Narrowing down task topics(1)

Work out ways you might narrow down these topics for an intermediate class:

1 pollution
2 natural disasters
3 family
4 clothes
5 sport
6 transport.

Commentary

1 With 'pollution', you might either like to focus on one specific form of pollution, or narrow it down to one or two sources of pollution in the local area or region where your students live. You might then design a task which explores the effects of different types of pollution on local people, and another task might be to propose a long-term solution to one of those problems.

2 With 'natural disasters', you might begin by brainstorming with your class different kinds of natural disaster, and exploring which kind individuals most fear. So you might narrow down to a task on 'The scariest natural disaster'. Or you could choose one kind (e.g. earthquakes) to investigate further, or suggest that your learners (in twos) choose one kind themselves.

3 With 'family' as topic there are many angles possible: family trees; a family you will always remember; middle children; how to be ideal parents; family values. These topics can be further narrowed down as you design tasks for them: e.g. how strict are/were your parents? Is it better to be the older child, younger child or a middle child?

4 'Clothes': old clothes you remember; buying clothes; your best clothes bargain; favourite clothes/most hated clothes/childhood clothes.

5 'Sport': healthiest sports; cheapest ways to keep fit; most dangerous sports; sports in your neighbourhood.

6 'Transport': ways of travelling between two major cities; getting to school or work; a disastrous journey; future transport systems; air travel, ferries.

READER ACTIVITY 4F

Narrowing down task topics(2)

Choose three topics from the topic map in Section 4.2 that you could use with your students. Narrow each of them down. Plan a Priming phase for each of them and then think of a listing task and a sorting task that learners could do in twos.

You might like to use some kind of visual framework to help them assemble their ideas. You might like to integrate some writing … . Exchange ideas with a colleague.

---

5 FROM TOPIC TO TASKS: MATCHING, COMPARING, PROBLEM-SOLVING, PROJECTS, AND STORYTELLING

5.1 Introduction

In Chapter 4, we outlined ways of selecting topics and illustrated two broad types of task derived from the cognitive processes of *listing* and *sorting*. We saw how tasks that involve sorting can often be based on the results of a preceding listing task. In other words, things on lists can often be ranked or classified. We looked at ways of building up a task sequence based on a chosen topic. In this chapter, we explore ways of generating five more types of task, many of which will lead out of the preceding ones. This will enable us to extend our task sequence, possibly culminating in a project or an outcome that can be shared or made public.

We will begin with tasks that involve matching and comparing. These are common classroom activities and not difficult to demonstrate to learners. Textbooks tend to use a lot of them, and so do examinations.

5.2 Matching

A whole range of tasks can be generated here—suitable for all levels. Many of them can be teacher-led and are thus ideal for real beginners who need lots of exposure before having to speak themselves. In fact, many can be done as 'Total Physical Response' (TPR) activities, as formalized by James Asher in the 1960s, and described recently by Richard Frost. (See Further reading at the end of this chapter.)

5.2.1 Listening and matching

Even true beginners can listen to and watch their teacher talking about a range of objects (for example, food items like fruit) or pictures and relate words and phrases to meanings. Teachers often pick up or point to the relevant object(s) while talking about it (for example, 'bananas—nice yellow bananas. Mmm—I love bananas—I eat one or two bananas every day— Who likes bananas? Who doesn't like bananas? How many have we got here? Four bananas? Can you see how many?') as this aids comprehension. After a bit, learners can start to identify which picture or object relates to what they hear without the teacher showing them ('Who can point to the bananas? How many bananas are there? OK—can you draw a banana—just one banana.'). So here, they are matching sounds or words with objects and responding physically. Often called 'Listen and do' activities, these are very common in children's language lessons, and can be used for adults too, even before learning the alphabet, reading, or writing.

A popular matching task for slightly higher levels is based on the idea of an 'Identity parade'. Learners are shown four pictures of people, and listen to a description of one them, in order to identify the person described. Sometimes they hear all descriptions and simply match each to a picture. Alternatively they can hear three descriptions and identify which person has not been described. Matching tasks like these are often used in formal assessments, and the pictures can denote anything from simple objects, patterns with shapes, to buildings, house plans, maps, or street scenes.

A graded sequence

A sequence of tasks on one topic can be built up gradually, so they form a graded sequence of tasks, from easy to more challenging. Here is one such set of matching tasks (all listening activities), but they have been mixed up, so they are no longer in a graded sequence.

READER ACTIVITY 5A
Grading a set of tasks

Topic: Understanding street directions

In which sequence might you do these four listening activities with an elementary class? Be prepared to justify the order you have chosen and say how you might set each one up. Note: you might not want to do them all in one lesson! What would be a good follow-up task for your learners?

a Learners hear a recording of someone giving street directions starting from a 'You are here' point, but not knowing what their final destination will be. They draw the route on their street map. Do they all end up in the same place? What landmark is it nearest to? They can do this several times with different destinations.

b Learners listen and match words or phrases denoting local landmarks (for example, post office, petrol station) to corresponding pictures.

c The teacher tells them about particular local landmarks and how to find them on the street map they have.

d The teacher demonstrates with a section of street map on the board, talking the class through the route she needs to take to go from A to B, with phrases like 'turn left', 'right', 'go straight on', 'second on right', etc.

Commentary

There are several ways of sequencing these according to how familiar your learners are with the area of the map and the names of local landmarks. For low level learners, you could start with b) and maybe turn it into a memory game by giving out pictures to the class (talking about them as you give them out, so the words for the landmarks are heard several times). Then call out the landmarks one by one to see if the class can remember who has each one. (Learners place them face down on their table and hold them up when they are identified.) Then go on to task c)—predominately a listening and identifying task—where students put an X and a number on their map for each landmark; continue with d), maybe asking the class to make the gestures the speaker would use for each direction. And finally do a), which would be a less familiar, more remote voice, and is a typical testing format. To help learners get to grips with it, you could play it several times over, with pauses, but without telling learners if they were right or not. Then they have to keep listening to double check. This also prepares them for a typical test situation. Once done, they can compare their final destinations with people near them.

You may well justify a different sequence, depending on how familiar your learners are with these concepts. You may for example feel that task c), which gives lots of exposure to useful teacher talk, would be better before task b).

As a follow up, to introduce a focus-on-form stage, you could replay the recording, getting learners to repeat and practise phrases indicating location, (for example, 'the third turning on the left'), then phrases indicating movement and/or direction (for example, 'turn left', 'go straight on'), then perhaps phrases indicating distance or time. There may also be instances of repetition and clarification that would be worth pointing out.

5.2.2 Reading and matching

If learners can read, then the above tasks can be adapted to incorporate some reading and/or writing components. For example:

- labelling objects, including things or people in pictures, shapes, colours, etc.
- matching caption cards or short texts to pictures or photos
- matching descriptions to pictures
- matching written summaries to longer written texts
- matching words to jumbled definitions
- reading street directions and matching them to a route, or drawing a route on a street map.

For this last example, you could give learners a map with four different routes drawn on, all leaving from the same starting point. Learners listen to or read three sets of directions and match each one to a route, in order to identify which route was not described. Note that if you give an equal number of routes and sets of directions, learners won't need to listen to or read the last set, as the remaining ones must match up. A more challenging task would be to give them a street map with no routes marked, on which they trace the route they hear. Tasks like these could form part of a longer task sequence, ending up with learners giving directions for routes they choose and the class following them to see where they get to. Here is an example:

'Giving directions' task sequence
Sandee Thompson designed a task sequence on this theme, with a matching task coming second, for a mixed class of beginners in Halifax, Canada. At the Priming stage, she gave out to pairs of learners small maps of Halifax, talked a little about where the school was on the map and then asked them to tell their partner how to get to their home from the school. They did this as best they could in English, using the map to help them. So the learners found out where their partners lived, even though they used very limited language. For the main task she gave out a sheet of written directions to her own house and learners had to read them and match them to places on the map, and trace the route she described. See Appendix 1.7 for the full version of Sandee's task sequence, and read how she continued the lesson from this point and what happened outside class as a result.

The rationale for asking learners to give their own directions first is that by the time they had to read Sandee's more complex directions, they were thoroughly tuned into the kinds of meanings that would be expressed. They were probably also aware of their own linguistic gaps and thus more likely to notice words and phrases that they could have used.

Several teachers have found that if you personalize tasks in some way it results in higher interest levels and engagement amongst learners. Sandee, above, gave directions to her own house and her students found out where others were living. In the next example, Tim Marchand used photos he had taken of his own summer holiday and links several tasks together for the first lesson after the summer break with his low level teenagers:

'Summer holiday' task sequence
Tim displayed his summer holiday photos and asked his learners to match them to captions he had written for them. He then read out loud an account of his summer, and students had to decide the order in which the photos were taken. So here, the captions used in the matching task prepared students for some of the language they would hear in the ordering task. His learners then went on to interview other people in their class to find out what they had done in their holidays and to draw appropriate pictures on a blank holiday postcard for them. The final task

was to write the postcard, describing their holiday. For this, learners worked in pairs helping each other.

Tim reported that the novelty of seeing a teacher's personal photographs and hearing about his own holiday caught their interest and increased their engagement in the tasks that followed. They enjoyed drawing postcards for each other, too. Tim is sure that 'personalization is the key' to keeping a less motivated or low level class interested.

READER ACTIVITY 5B
From task design to task instructions
Choose one of the topics illustrated above or take a topic of your choice.

1   Design two different tasks involving matching that you could use with one of your classes. Think how you would introduce the topic and task at priming stage—you may want to do a teacher-led brainstorm to activate or present useful vocabulary. Write brief instructions for each task and be clear about what the outcome will be at the end.
2   Plan a 'Mystery tour'. Find a street map of your local area that learners may be familiar with. Choose a starting point—and mark this with a circle. Then decide where you could walk to in 20 minutes and which route you would take. Note down any landmarks you would pass. In your head, mentally rehearse the directions you would give learners to get there and see how long this takes you. If you can, record yourself giving directions for this route. Do not mark your route on the map. Give the map to someone else and play your recording. Can they follow your route? Note down any questions they ask. Record it a second time so you now have two versions.

You might like to ask a colleague to do the same, without telling you their destination. Record them doing this and see if you can follow their directions to identify where he/she ends up.

Choose one of your recordings to play in class when you next do a direction-giving lesson. The advantage of having a recording is that you can play it many times and rest while students are listening! If you transcribe it, (or parts of it) you will have an excellent text for some form-focused work.

Tip: to make it more interesting, before you start playing your 'Mystery tour' directions get your learners to guess one place you could get to in a 20-minute walk and put a cross on the map. See which learner gets the closest to your destination.

One big advantage of using tasks involving matching, is that learners gain a very rich exposure to language within the security of a tight and well-defined framework.

5.3 Comparing and contrasting: finding similarities or differences

5.3.1 Comparison tasks

Learners can talk to each other in small groups of three or four to compare:
- their morning routines—who gets up and out the quickest?
- the length of their working day and/or their journeys to and from work
- what times they go to bed—who is generally the latest?
- their family trees and the balance of men and women in their close families
- their best and worst clothes bargains
- their favourite holiday places
- their language learning strategies.

For example, Sandra Wiecek, on the topic of 'Travelling experiences', got her intermediate learners to bring in pictures of their 'Favourite places'. She asked them: 'What place(s) did you enjoy most and why?' Then told them: 'Walk around looking at your friends' pictures and showing yours so that you can share and compare your travelling experiences. Find out if you and your friends have been to the same places. Were there any similarities in your trips?'

As a follow up to this, a variety of target tasks are possible: learners could write a comparison of two of the favourite places they had heard about, or a short summary of the most interesting travelling experiences. Or they could each write a list of what they considered the top five (or fewer) places, with a brief description of each place and why it was a favourite. This could then be passed round for the others to read and compare. The places could then be compared in more detail, with learners listing similarities and differences.

Sandee Thompson got her mixed nationality class of adult learners to compare the strategies they used for language learning and compile a list for themselves. They then heard a recording of fluent speakers having the same discussion, and compared their own strategies with these. Shaun Manning's 'Family values' task (Appendix 1.3) involves both comparing and matching. He got groups of learners to read, change and agree on a list of ten statements (for example, 'Children should only leave home after they have got married') and then compare their list with other groups' lists to find one that matched their own group's opinions.

The above examples are all personal topics, but learners can find out about other things too and compare them. Topics of language and culture can be chosen for comparison, for example, greetings systems in different countries, specific social customs like weddings, or educational systems. Going further afield, learners using the web or other sources could compare refugee camps in different countries, or two different types of volcanoes, or the tourist facilities in two (or more) national parks; the possibilities are endless.

Comparison tasks can also be based on two or more texts or transcripts on a similar theme, for example texts from two or more different newspapers.

- Yvonne Beaudry distributed authentic pamphlets on 'Earthquake safety' from the Red Cross and other organizations. Her learners then compared the official information on what to do either 'before', 'during', or 'after' an earthquake to what they had already written themselves in their own charts.

This formed part of a whole set of tasks; see Appendix 1.1.

- For his '*Moulin Rouge* movie trailer comparison' task, Glen Poupore, in South Korea, used a DVD which contained two different trailers, one designed for a North American audience, and one for a Japanese audience. He got his intermediate level students to watch them twice and note down as many differences as they could. Later, they were asked to explain the reasons for the differences in the trailers—which led to a fruitful discussion about cultural differences. Finally, to promote a focus on language form, he gave them transcripts of the trailers to study.

For a full account, see Appendix 1.5.

Tasks to practise more specifically the process of contrasting can be based on different media versions of the same news story, or film review or obituary, taking stories from two or three different newspapers, or different TV or radio stations. Mail-order catalogues (for clothes or household items or music) have whole pages where very similar items are illustrated and described. Learners can be asked to choose three similar items and decide which is best value. Some teachers use recordings of two TV adverts for a similar product—car adverts are a possibility (and also good for memory challenge sequencing tasks, as we saw earlier).

5.3.2 Games: find the similarities or differences

Comparison often forms the basis for games and other challenges, for example 'Spot the differences', or talking about personal experiences to find things in common.

Focusing on similarities, the following tasks are generally productive:

Things in common: Tell your partner what you usually do at weekends at this time of the year. Then find out what your partner does. Try to find at least three things in common or see how many things that you can find in three minutes you have in common.

'Will your paths cross?': Talk to your partner about what they are doing over the next few days. Find out if your paths are likely to cross at any point over this period. For example, you might be going to the same supermarket for your shopping.

Find someone who has the same birthday: Use the list of seven birthdays that you made earlier (see 4.3.2). Choose four birthdays and commit them (and the people) to memory; fold your list up and put it away. Go round the class asking others what birthdays they found out about and see if you can find someone else with the same birthday. Note down whose it was before continuing. (For some statistical reason there is a strong likelihood of this occurring if more than 30 birthdays are involved.)

Spot the difference: This classic game, based on two nearly identical pictures, can in fact be done two ways: co-operatively, with two people in collaboration, looking at both pictures and helping each other to spot a certain number of differences and writing them down in a list. Or, it can be done in A/B pairs where each learner looks only at their own picture, and they find the differences by each describing their picture in turn, and stopping when their partner thinks they have found a difference to check it out and write it down. Or, instead of describing, A can ask B questions about the details in their picture, and then change over.

There are in fact three possibilities mentioned in the last paragraph. Stop for a moment and reflect on the patterns of interaction and language use that each possibility might give rise to. Which one might your class find easiest to do and which the hardest to do? (More on this in Chapter 8, Section 8.5.)

READER ACTIVITY 5C

Plan a task sequence ending in a comparing task

1 Take your topic and think up two different comparing tasks for classes you teach; write a short set of instructions for each.
2 Write the steps you would take to set up one of these comparing tasks. Think whether you want to allow learners opportunities to write rather than speak, or a balance of both.
3 Preparation stage: what priming activities might you do at the start of the task sequence? Maybe one or two facilitating tasks—listing, ordering, or matching? You could, for example, start off with a teacher-led brainstorm or listing task. Or ask learners to brainstorm and list criteria or aspects that could be taken into consideration when doing the comparison.
4 Learners might benefit from some visual support: some kind of a chart or table to help them organize their information. If so, draw this and fill out some of the cells.

5 You may want them to examine and explore any useful linguistic features of the texts you could use; this could be done either before (as we did above, when we introduced vocabulary for landmarks before the 'Giving directions' task) or after the task for a form-focused stage. Write some suggestions.

6 Show your draft sequence to a colleague and talk it through with him/her. If possible, try out the tasks together. This will allow you to foresee any difficulties and could give you some idea of how it might go in class.

7 Write or record clear instructions for each task, giving examples based on your topic.

Matching and comparing (as well as ordering and classifying) are also useful processes for activities focusing on language form. And all the above task-types can make good facilitating tasks for problem-solving tasks, which we are now going to look at.

5.4 *Problem-solving tasks and puzzles*

Problem-solving tasks invite learners to offer advice and recommendations on problems ranging from the very general, like global warming, to the very specific, like what to do if your neighbour's cat is causing trouble in your garden. These tasks can stimulate wide-ranging discussion and also offer scope for a variety of writing activities, including note-taking, drafting, and finalizing proposals for solutions.

There are many topics that naturally lend themselves to problem-solving tasks. Take a look at the mind map on p. 94. These ideas have been proposed by teachers in different countries, teaching different ages and in a wide range of social contexts. See which ideas would best suit your own classes. Add your own.

5.4.1 Preparing learners for problem-solving tasks

Problem-solving tasks can stimulate rich discussion if learners have already thought out some ideas to share. They will benefit from time to think beforehand; they can then get to grips with the problem and work out possible solutions and how to express them. In some cases there may be a suitable website or pamphlet that gives some useful background information. This means it is often best to introduce the topic and do a relevant priming phase in a previous lesson, explaining the nature of the problem and telling learners that the task will be to discuss and agree a solution to this problem. Obviously learners are more likely to become engaged if the problem is a local one that affects them, or one that is within their own experience, and one that they feel confident talking about.

Global/international issues
- People Smuggling
- Illegal immigration – fictitious marriages
- Unsustainable resources (e.g. oil, coal)

Classroom or institution-based problems
- A large amount of L1 is used in English lessons
- Very few students do their homework
- Unequal learner participation in lessons
- The snack-bar/canteen food is cheap but unhealthy

Teenage issues
- Smoking and peer pressure
- Quarrels
- Lack of money
- Lack of communication between parents and teenagers
- No place to hang out and meet up with friends on neutral territory

Problems for tasks

Environmental issues
- Lack of parking in town centres
- Traffic congestion
- Water shortages
- River and sea pollution
- Overcoming opposition to wind farms

Social/family contexts
- When your grown-up children won't leave home…
- Loneliness at an overseas university
- Being out of work
- Being blind or deaf
- Dealing with death

Work contexts
- Preparing for job interviews
- Boring meetings – how to survive them
- Selling your products – dealing with market competitors
- Inequality in the work place
- Juggling work and family

Figure 5.1 Problems as a basis for tasks

5.4.2 Problem-solving task sequences and scenarios

These often comprise other task types, and it is useful to break down the discussion into a set of mini-tasks, which might include some of the following, but not necessarily in this order:

- listing and ranking the effects of the problem in order of severity
- pooling and comparing personal experiences of the problem
- listing and comparing ideas for possible solutions
- listing and evaluating the criteria with which to appraise solutions

- drafting notes for an oral presentation of recommendations or advice
- writing up a final proposal for others to read.

Some topics, for example, what to do with your cat or pet while you are away, might not warrant more than a few minutes pair discussion doing two or three of the above mini-tasks: there are not many options available for holiday care for cats and each one would require only a sentence or two to outline and evaluate. In the real world, this would be a simple advice-giving interaction, possibly interlaced with an anecdote or a recounting of a personal experience. It is not the kind of problem that would lend itself to a serious written follow up.

A problem-solving task sequence on a more serious topic (like some of those listed above in Figure 5.1) might proceed like this:

Preparation and priming: with a teacher-led class exploration of the effects of the problem and the possible causes, and/or sharing personal views or experiences of the effects of the problem.

Task and report phase: Small groups or pairs could then be asked to think of two or three different solutions, compare them and choose one proposal to put forward to the whole class, justifying their plan of action and saying why they think it is best. Preparing this proposal becomes the 'target task' as defined in Chapter 2, 2.2.

Writing phase 1: Drafting. After the whole class plenary, learners can be asked to write up their proposal in draft form, taking into account the class feedback. They could do this individually at home.

Writing phase 2: Finalizing and 'publishing' the target task. The next lesson they can peer edit their writing, or collate ideas and draw up a single final version—identified by a number—to display on the classroom wall for others to read. Learners can choose three or four to read, note the number and write a brief evaluation of each, which could be shared with the writers in private or put up on the wall for all to see. If the problem is an authentic topical issue, for example, criticizing the opposition to a local wind farm proposal where there is a public enquiry underway, the best recommendations could be sent off to the appropriate official body, and/or sent to a local newspaper as a Letter to the Editor.

Focus on form: If, in the course of their problem-solving task, learners have used written sources of material, these can be re-used for a more explicit focus-on-form stage. If you have a recording of other people trying to solve the problem, this could be exploited for useful language; see the suggestions after the task below.

A note on *grading* is needed here. The degree of linguistic challenge of problem-solving tasks will depend on the familiarity with the topic, complexity and breadth of the problem, the type of initial guidance and/or preparation, how explicit the instructions are, and so on. A very practical down-to-earth task like the cat problems above would probably be far less demanding linguistically than the second sequence described. But it is generally possible to make a complex problem easier by breaking it down into a number of smaller (facilitating) tasks.

Beginning with a text

Some problem-solving tasks can begin with a short text setting out the problem, like a problem page letter, which promotes class or group or pair discussion. David Cox, for example, adapted this task from Nunan (1995: 106), for his learners in Japan:

TASK 2

What advice would you give to the person who wrote this letter? Discuss your ideas and then agree on the two best suggestions.

```
Dear Angie,
My husband and I are worried about our daughter. She
refuses to do anything we tell her to do and is very rude
to us. Also, she has become very friendly with a girl we
don't like. We don't trust her anymore because she is
always lying to us. Are we pushing her away from us? We
don't know what to do, and we're worried that she is
going to get into trouble.
Worried Parents
```

Tasks like this could begin with individuals jotting down two bits of advice they would give and then discussing their ideas, presenting some to the class. They could end with learners drafting a letter of advice, and reading and evaluating each others' according to criteria they select themselves.

A focus-on-form stage could follow. If you can get two fluent speakers/writers to record and/or write their advice, you could use their texts for this. Both in the letter above and in the recording that David got his friends to make (see Appendix 3.1 for a transcript), there are many phrases expressing negativity; classifying these according to structural criteria (those with a negative verb, those with an adjective, other) could provide a rich learning opportunity. In the recording there are several useful phrases with the word 'can', for example 'that's about the best you can do', 'for as long as they can'. Looking at phrases beginning with the word 'I' or 'you' would highlight some common features of spontaneous spoken interaction for example, 'I don't think ...'. 'I would say ...', 'I mean, you know ...' and a study of 'Yes', 'Yeah', and 'No' might even prove fruitful.

More complex problem-solving scenarios, such as those used in business communication skills lessons (see Ellis and Johnson 1994), or for training embassy staff, would usually be introduced with a written description of the background, the roles of the people involved and a statement of the problem. For two examples, see Yevgeny Slivkin's 'Fictitious marriage' role play interview scenario in Appendix 2.5, and Claudia Beh's 'People smuggling' scenario in Chapter 10 (10.3).

Prediction tasks for content-based teaching

We looked at some prediction tasks based on texts in Chapter 3. The purpose of these was to prepare learners for reading a written text or understanding the gist of a listening text. Other prediction tasks can be set up as a stimulus for oral discussion or a writing task. These make excellent preparation for content-based learning. Here are two examples, one for ELT methodology and one for science.

This task sequence was designed by Heidi Vande Voort Nam for pre-service teacher trainees in South Korea who also needed to improve their classroom language.

> *Methododogy area: 'vocabulary teaching'*
> As a warm up we played a guessing game, based on words and their definitions. Then the teacher-trainees brainstormed methods of teaching vocabulary in English. I then gave the trainees a page from a high school English textbook and asked them to predict
>
> (1) which words high school students would ask questions about and
> (2) what method the teacher would use for presenting the vocabulary. Then we listened to a recording that I had made of myself teaching that same lesson to high school students, and the trainees checked their predictions.

Prediction tasks are similar to puzzles in that they engage your curiosity and there is usually a definite solution. Here is one based on a science experiment for you to do.

READER ACTIVITY 5D

A prediction task

Read the outline of a simple science experiment which three of Lorie Wood's adult learners set up as part of a longer project on atmosphere and weather. Can you predict what will happen at the end? Why do you think the black paper is suggested? Make a list of three predictions that children of twelve might come up with.

'Mystery experiment'
Materials
Plastic water bottle (clear plastic, not coloured), an ice cube, some very hot water, some black paper.

Experiment
1 Fill the bottle with hot water.
2 Wait five minutes so the bottle gets hot as well.
3 Empty about half the water out of the bottle.
4 Put an ice cube on the neck of the bottle.
5 Watch closely!

How might you set this experiment up in class to generate maximum oral participation from each learner? What writing task could you set arising from this?

For an outline of the complete project and the answer to the mystery, see Appendix 2.3.

5.4.3 Problem-solving games and puzzles

Other types of problems include puzzles and logic problems, for example: 'Rachel was born in winter but her birthday is in the summer. How come?' These too start with a short text, but will probably generate a different style of pair interaction. Note however that if the cognitive load is too great, i.e. if the problem is highly cognitively demanding, learners will have less spare mental capacity for composing what to say while trying to find the solution in real time. Their language is often hesitant and staccato—all the more reason for giving learners at least some time to prepare a possible solution, and to prepare to report their solution back to others afterwards, in a more formal way. You may also need to show learners how to use a grid for working logic problems out.

Who did what? Where? A logic problem for low level beginners

Peter, Mary, and John all went away last weekend. One of them went to Birmingham, one to Manchester, and one to London. One of them went to the theatre, one went to see a relative, and one went to buy a computer.

Who did what? Here are two clues to help you: one of them went to London to visit her mother; John bought a computer but not in Manchester.

- Work with a partner. Write one true sentence about each person—Peter, Mary, and John.
- Can you explain to another pair how you did the puzzle? Did they do it the same way?
- Now listen to the recording. Did you have the same answers? Did they do it the same way as you?

(This task first appeared in J. Willis and D. Willis 1988.)

There are many sources for such puzzles. We googled and found a website http://pages.prodigy.net/spencejk/YPjan2003.html by someone called Judy which has sections for young people's logic problems, with single stars for easy ones. The important thing is that the game or puzzle you select will give learners useful exposure to language and generate opportunities for learners to express themselves and later to compare solutions.

READER ACTIVITY 5E

Appraising the task in terms of language exposure and use

1. What might your learners actually say when solving the problem about Peter, Mary, and John above? (If you can, ask two people to do it while you listen and take notes or record them.) See transcript in Appendix 3.2 to see what two fluent speakers said.

2. Look at the three follow-up activities in the problem task above. Which would give most exposure to language in use? Which is most likely to get them talking? In writing the true sentences, how much can learners 'mine' from the text? How might your learners express themselves when explaining how they did it?

3. For an explicit focus on form, look at the text of the logic problem and its rubric above. Underline four or five useful phrases that your learners might pick up. What might learners notice if asked to find eight examples of phrases with 'to' and divide them into two categories?

4. How far would it matter if your learners did most of the first step of the puzzle task above in L1?

5.5 Projects and creative tasks

We saw above how problem-solving tasks can be broken down into a sequence of shorter tasks exploring the problem and evaluating possible solutions, leading up to a solution to the target problem. A similar design process can be used to set up projects.

Simply put, a task-based project comprises a sequence of tasks based around one specific topic, each task with its own outcome or purpose, which culminate in a specified end-product that can be shown to others, displayed, or made public in some way, for others to appreciate. Possible end-products are shown here:

£ $ £ $ £ *a funding proposal for a local improvement* £ $ £ $ £ $

portfolio journal LEAFLET booklet a class magazine or newspaper

Poster a guided tour

tourist brochure

a short radio programme

AN ENTERTAINMENT

a short video recording a performance a web-page

Figure 5.2 Some possible end-products

READER ACTIVITY 5F

End-products for your projects

Choose three topics from the topic lists in Chapter 4 (4.2), or from your own syllabus. Look at the end-products above and simply select two or three that might be suitable for your learners to work on for each of your topics. You will build on these in a later activity.

Projects are normally done on a collaborative basis, with learners in pairs or small groups of three or four, but can be done by individuals. They are normally spread over a longer time-span than task sequences, with time in between project-oriented lessons for learners to research as individuals and prepare for each step.

Projects can be mainly classroom-based but are often enriched by including visits by 'experts' or 'informants' from outside. For example, for her 'First aid' project on emergency procedures in a working environment, Lorie Wood asked a registered nurse from her local medical centre to visit her class. First she divided her class into four groups and each chose a specific first aid situation—emergencies that sometimes occur in their lines of work (electric shock, hypothermia, burns, heart attack). Each group had to become 'experts' in administering first aid procedures and demonstrate them and teach other groups. When the nurse came in to class, students asked her about first aid procedures for these, and checked to see if the procedures they had prepared for their presentations were correct.

Lorie also gets her adult students to each create their own newspaper. They have to read some English language newspapers and collect sample articles and items from each genre (editorial, adverts, global issues, etc.), and then write their own pieces (she specifies what) in an appropriate style. Lorie arranges for a local reporter to visit her class and give a presentation on conducting interviews, after which her students practise on each other and then interview a native-speaker for a 'feature story'. Once they have written their pieces, she also asks a newspaper editor to come in as guest speaker, to help them with the design of their newspapers. More details in Appendix 2.4.

Alternatively, learners doing projects can get their data by going outside class. In rural Sri Lanka, school children of 11 and 12 went out in small groups and found out about nearby local places and buildings that visitors or tourists might find interesting. In class, guided by their teachers, they designed, wrote and illustrated in colour a series of leaflets in English on each location. These were laminated and lent to visitors to their village.

A more ambitious project for tertiary level students on the subject of Cuba was set up by Alicia van Altena who teaches 'Spanish in the Media'—an upper intermediate course that uses the journalistic genre to teach Spanish as a second language in the United States. Although this was designed to teach Spanish, a parallel procedure could be used to teach English.

Groups of three students prepare a twenty minute radio programme called 'Tertulia' ('informal social gathering') which is recorded in the professional radio studio of the Center for Language Study (CLS) at Yale University. She describes it thus:

> Topic: Cuba—two opposing views
> The project involves learning how to make a radio program, followed by conversation, evaluation, and discussion with a recent Cuban emigrant about Oliver Stone's documentary *El Comandante*, in which Lourdes Gómez interviews Stone on Castro's policy in Cuba and his film.
>
> - The students read excerpts from journalism texts in Spanish on how to prepare a radio program. Discussions on the main characteristics: clarity, precision and brevity. Students listen to Spanish radio programs and copy those models in practice exercises.
> - Use of the voice: pronunciation and intonation. Students' attention can also be drawn to specific forms of the language in the models.
> - Students read a transcript of Gómez's interview with Oliver Stone.
> - Students watch the documentary *El Comandante*.
> - We use the questions in the interview done by Federico Mayor Zaragoza with Fidel Castro in 2000 for discussion.

- The students work in groups and choose the best five questions of Zaragoza and answer them with the material from the documentary.
- They prepare the script for the radio program with a brief introduction to the guest and the topic and the questions focusing on what, in their view, are conflicting statements. Example: 'If Castro is a dictator and Cuba is so poor how can you account for the high level of literacy and medical benefits?'
- We set a time in the studio and record a 20-minute program that is transferred to DVD and posted on the audio website of the CLS for the general public.

The total time for the project was two weeks, meeting twice a week for an hour and a half, for the equivalent of six contact hours. The students read the interviews, watch the movie, listen to model radio programs and sketch a draft of their radio program as assignments outside class. We devote the class time to explanations, summaries of important aspects, general and small group discussions of the written interviews or movie, some language focus work and the correction of the sketches for the radio program.

Groupings. This year there were nine students in the class divided into three groups. I wanted to get three Cuban dissidents to be interviewed, one per group, but unfortunately due to scheduling problems we only had one person who ended up participating in the three radio sessions.

Student evaluations of the activity were very positive. Some quotations from their feedback follow: 'we translated what we were doing in class to the real world'; 'fun to use and interactive'; 'I felt like I was in a real radio broadcast; high tech equipment was intriguing and novel'; 'it sharpened listening skills and beneficial responding to the guest's comments off the top of one's head'; 'it offered a different perspective from what we had read and seen in Stone's movie'.

READER ACTIVITY 5G

Identifying learning opportunities

The ultimate aim of tasks and projects is to give learners the opportunity to learn more of the language and deploy it effectively. In this case the target language was Spanish, in an English-speaking environment, where Spanish is not widely heard or used.

1 Read the description of the above project and list the sources of exposure to Spanish that learners will have had (both listening and reading) during the project.

2 To whom will they have been speaking Spanish? For about how long?

3 At what points in the above sequence of tasks might the teacher focus on language form?

4 What topics might your learners like to make a radio programme on? Even if you do not have access to a professional recording studio, you can use a tape recorder with a microphone in a quiet non-echoey room. (There are plenty of websites with advice about making good quality recordings and radio.)

5 For an example of a radio programme project for young teenagers, see Aurelia Garcia's 'Radio Talk Show: Healthy teens' in Appendix 2.2.

For the project above, Alicia found three Cubans who were native Spanish speakers for her class to interview. If you teach English in a big city it should not be too difficult to find fairly fluent English speakers willing to come to class to talk to learners about their special field or an aspect of their lives. Or there may be places where tourists or foreigners may readily be found and politely asked to take part in a survey or be interviewed on a specific topic. Or a similar interaction could happen using a web-based community like Webheads, set up by Vance Stevens (2004).

Franziska Lys, who teaches a German writing course in the USA, gets each of her students to seek out a speaker of German (not necessarily a native speaker) living in the area. Her students arrange to interview them once a week over a period of a term to hear about significant episodes in their lives. They write up each week's 'episode' and post it on their own web-page for the others to read. To do this they learn how to create their own web-page, how to upload photos, and search the web for pictures and illustrative details on the places mentioned in the life stories, check copyright and add those to their website. They refine and redraft as they progress and by the end of term they have a fascinating website for others to visit. (See Lys 2004.)

If you cannot find fluent speakers of English locally, then you can do what Aurelia Garcia does in Argentina. Many of her projects entail learners (secondary school age) going out into the local town and doing surveys with local people mainly in Spanish. They then return to class and work out how to express the results in English, write up a formal report and then give an informal oral presentation to the class in English. See Appendix 2.1: 'A new cafeteria'.

Shane Sweeney in United Arab Emirates sends his college students out to local businesses to learn about a trade and write about different aspects of it; for example, the women might go to a local beauty parlour, men to a car sales showroom or industrial plant. They make several visits to explore different aspects of the business or manufacturing process. Although they will do much of this in Arabic, they have to report and present their projects in English. They also have to hold 'end-of-project public exhibitions', and it is through a combination of their information gathering processes and their end-of-project reports, presentations and exhibitions that students are awarded their final grade. (This is fully reported on in Sweeney 2004.)

One reason why students were so positive about all the above projects was that, in addition to finding out about new people or different work environments or angles of a topic, they had learnt new life skills like making a radio programme, setting up a website, working on a reception desk, doing a market survey, interviewing, editing a newspaper, producing a tourist leaflet, and evaluating safety or waste disposal in a factory.

Another alternative is to set web-based projects using specified sites on the internet. You can either prepare your own projects and find suitable websites like Lorie Wood did for the topic of ecotourism and other topics on her syllabus—see Appendix 5—or you can use ready-made projects such as 'webquests'. Check this site for examples: http://www.theconsultants-e.com/webquests/

There are many topics to choose from on this site; for intermediate learners—try Lisa Haugh's webquest 'Adventure sports'. This is clearly written, addressed directly to the learner, carefully staged with excellent web-links, well-defined goals, and evaluation procedures. Learners work partly on their own, partly in pairs or groups, and always end up with some piece of work that can be shown to others and evaluated. Planning projects from scratch takes up a lot of teacher time—finding resource materials, checking websites and libraries, setting up visits, and so on— so finding a resource like webquests is invaluable.

READER ACTIVITY 5H

Planning a project and/or scenario

Read the sample projects and scenarios in Appendix 2 (2.1–2.5) and check the webquest sites for projects that might be suitable to adapt for your classes.

Take two topics and decide on possible end products. (These might be the ones you identified earlier in this section.)

Break each possible project down into a series of shorter tasks destined for one of your classes.

Plan in more detail some priming activities.

Look closely at any texts used—for language features that might be useful to highlight or focus on later.

Appraise your project by listing the sources of exposure to English they will get, and the different uses they will put their English to.

5.6 *Sharing personal experiences: storytelling, anecdotes, reminiscences*

In our everyday social lives, for example with visitors, with friends over a drink, in break-times, we spend a large proportion of time recounting personal experiences and telling stories. When giving advice, for example, we often fall back on recounting what we or a friend did when faced with a similar problem. When telling stories or anecdotes our aim is often to 'cap' the preceding story—ours must be better or more dramatic. We often tell the same story again to different people, so we get plenty of chances to refine it and make it more entertaining or dramatic. If our learners are going to take part in social interactions with speakers of English, it is important they feel comfortable talking about their own experiences, or embarking on a story, so they need plenty of practice in class. Good storytelling contributes to everyone's enjoyment and generally enhances our social experience. The same is true in the classroom.

Some of the tasks described in this book have contained elements of storytelling, for example in Chapter 3 (3.2, learners had to predict from the headline 'Hello! I've just jumped off the Empire State Building' what the story might be and tell it. Reordering events to make a story, as in Monty's monster (3.7.3), or recalling the sequence of events in a video clip would contribute to storytelling skills. Many of the topics suggested in this book so far could give rise to a round of storytelling: for example, an earthquake you remember, a journey that went wrong, your best summer holiday experience.

Maybe because of our tendency to want to 'cap' stories we have just heard, many of the ideas for stories sent in by teachers contain superlatives:

> Your most memorable childhood experience
> Your most frightening experience
> The scariest thing you have ever done
> Your most embarrassing moment
> The funniest person you know

Maggie Baigent, who teaches university students in Italy, regularly uses storytelling tasks at all levels. Recently, she used this with pre-intermediate learners:

> Write an anecdote from your personal experience when something exciting/frightening/special happened.

She followed these stages:

- individual thinking/preparation at home;
- 5 minutes' class time for individual vocabulary queries, private rehearsal;

- tell story to partner
- individual review of performance and a chance for further quick questions
- prepare to retell
- change partners and retell story
- analysis of the organization and language of two similar anecdotes in coursebook (previously used for grammar practice)
- group/class story writing of a short video clip
- write own story for homework
- next lesson, read other students' stories (at least 2 or 3 depending on time).

She reports: 'Both the learners and I felt the effect of repetition on fluency; we enjoyed hearing and reading different stories'.

Several teachers recommended task repetition as a means of encouraging fluency and confidence. Jason Moser regularly does a lesson with his Japanese learners where conversations are repeated three or four times with different partners. He covers a different topic each week. Here he reports on one he had just completed.

'Talking about animals and pets'

1 Priming: (10–20 minutes)

To save time, I write ideas for learners to talk about on the board:

What's your favourite kind of animal?
Have you ever had a pet or do you have one now?
How would you describe its character?
Do you have an interesting experience or story about a pet?

Students do unguided planning—writing their own ideas down, checking words in their dictionaries. They must put all these on one side when actually doing the task.

2 Task

Talk about pets, changing partners three times on my word. No notes or books allowed. Each conversation to last 8–10 minutes.

Next, students write a report based on their last conversation. They work in twos with their last conversation partner and draft one report. They talk about the language itself, what is the correct grammar, the right word, etc. As I go round to help, I encourage them to put in as much detail as they can—this makes the reports more interesting to listen to afterwards.

In the end I read their reports to the class. I correct and recast, and just as importantly I try to 'push their output' even more by exploring deeper into their reports. One girl says her dog doesn't like to go for walks. I ask why and how does she know? I also ask what he likes to do instead.

3 Post-task

With the remaining time, I assigned for class work the vocabulary section in their homework book on describing animals and character traits. Next week we are going to do the unit in the textbook on describing people's characters.

Evaluation
The conversations were noisy—lots of laughing, and lots of English. I have noticed that from task repetition there emerges more 'language play' and 'risk-taking' as students get comfortable. The repetition really helps the students to open up.

Overall the reports were very interesting. Many funny stories about goldfish! One report was about how a girl used different methods to keep a cat out of her garden. There is no doubt that students are taking their language to the limits.

Both teachers allowed learners time to prepare in advance, and expected learners to get on with their own planning. Maggie gave her learners time to reflect before repeating the storytelling task, whereas Jason's learners had to repeat the task immediately. Both got their learners to write up their stories/experiences afterwards, for others to read or listen to, and thus introduced opportunities for some focus on language form. During this, Maggie focused more on story structure and organization, while Jason drew learners' attention to use of vocabulary and grammar . Both sets of learners (and teachers) seemed to enjoy each others' stories and reports.

READER ACTIVITY 51
Planning a storytelling session
Choose one of the task sequences you have been building up during this chapter. Decide on a subject for a storytelling session that would complete the task sequence. Plan what you would do at each stage, and how you might introduce task repetition. Decide how you would get feedback at the end.

5.7 A summary of task types using the 'task generator'

We will end by using a visual representation of the taxonomy of task types we have illustrated in the last two chapters. The aim of this 'task generator' is to help you think up a set of different kinds of tasks on topics of your choice. It is not intended to be a watertight classification—these task types are not necessarily mutually exclusive. As we saw earlier with problem-solving tasks, those near the bottom of the diagram, for example, could well involve some or even all of the cognitive processes from around the top. When telling an anecdote, a speaker needs both to select and sequence the events in a logical or chronological order and decide how to make the ending as effective as possible (a mix of listing, ordering and creating).

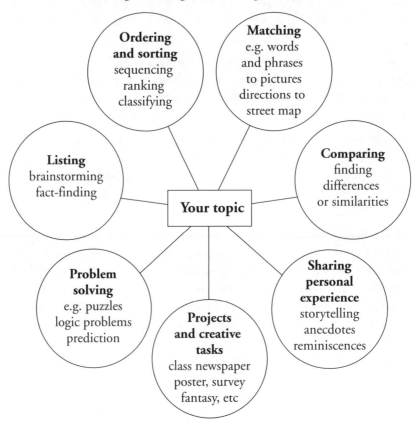

Figure 5.3 The task generator: a taxonomy of task types

There are two points to make at this stage:

- you would almost certainly not want to use all seven types of task for each topic with the same group of learners. Choose the best three or four that link together fairly well;
- not all topics lend themselves equally well to all seven types of task. For example, we found that for 'Cats' it was quite hard to think of matching or problem-solving tasks just about cats that would be suitable for our particular classes. If you find the same difficulty, then omit that type in your set of tasks for this topic. If you chose a topic like 'parking' or 'earthquakes', it would be quite easy to think of problem-solving tasks, but maybe less easy to think of a good ordering or sorting task.

READER ACTIVITY 5J

Generate a set of tasks

1 Choose a topic you haven't used so far—maybe one from the topic list you made in Chapter 2 (2.2). If you can't decide, take the topic of 'Cats'.
2 Start at the top left of Figure 5.3 and take each task type in turn. Brainstorm aspects of your topic to find ones you could list, ones you could sort or classify or organize in a specific order, and aspects that you could match, compare or contrast.
3 Then going round the bottom of Figure 5.3, think what problems your topic might be associated with and what kinds of solutions might be workable. For experience-sharing, think what kind of anecdotes, memories, or opinions might your learners share on this theme? Think of one or two you could tell your class at a priming stage.
4 Finally think of a project or an end-product that might bring together some of the different aspects and might be rewarding for learners to create together to give a sense of achievement.

Commentary

This process of using Figure 5.3 to generate tasks is best seen as a preliminary brainstorming stage. Most tasks will need further refining and precise instructions will need to be written for them. For example, for the comparing task suggested below: 'Cats or dogs—which make the best pets?' you might end up with something like:

Which do you think makes the best pet, a cat or a dog
- for an only child of 10–12 years old, or
- for an active retired person living on their own and who likes travelling overseas?

Decide on one, discuss with a partner, and give at least three reasons for your choice.

With this in mind, read the ideas below that were suggested by a group of teachers from Malaysia, working at different levels in schools and colleges:

Listing
Make a list of things that cats tend to do/like doing.
List reasons why people like/don't like cats.
Think of three pieces of advice for cat owners.

Ordering and sorting
Classify your list of things that cats tend to do into nice things and not such nice things.

Collect pieces of advice from others in your group; discuss and decide which are the most useful. Rank them in order from most to least useful.

Matching
Photos of cats with descriptions of them given by their owners.

Comparing
Cats or dogs—which make the best pets?

Problem-solving
Ways to stop your neighbour's cats from coming into your garden.

If you had a cat at home, and were planning to go away for three weeks, what could you do? Think of three possible solutions and evaluate them.

Creative project/survey
Make a small wall poster about cats that reveals your attitude towards them; prepare to talk about one aspect of your poster to the rest of the class. Interview three people about a cat or other pet they have kept or remember well. Find out whether they would recommend having a cat in a family with small children or in a family where everyone is out all day long. Write this up as a short piece to display on a wall poster.

Create a wall newspaper about cats, asking people in your group to contribute something. As well as pieces based on the above ideas, you could add photos, pictures and captions, sayings, beliefs, or poems about cats.

Sharing personal experiences, story/anecdote-telling
Think of a cat you know or remember, or a story about something amazing a cat has done, and prepare to tell your partner about it. Discuss and decide whose cat story is the most interesting. Write it up for the class to read.

5.8 Review

We have seen in these last two chapters how it is possible to start with a topic, narrow it down and design different types of task, each one leading into the next. From the learners' point of view, the advantages of following a graded sequence of tasks are clear. They start with a comparatively simple listing task, and each subsequent task presents a slightly greater cognitive and linguistic challenge. Once tuned into the topic itself, and familiar with some of the topic vocabulary, learners can more easily take part in consecutive tasks, each working towards a different outcome. Learners will be re-using words and phrases and building up new ways of expressing themselves. Thus useful topic vocabulary is recycled and extended naturally whilst learners explore different angles of the topic.

In the following chapter we shall be looking at stages in the task cycle which naturally stimulate learners to think about the language they are using. We will also look at activities at the end of the task sequence which will help learners to focus on and consolidate some of the forms they have come across.

Further reading
On Total Physical Response (TPR)
Frost, R. http://www.teachingenglish.org.uk/think/methodology/tpr.shtml.

On webquests
A good introduction can be found at

Shelton, S. *Teaching English Using the Web.* http://www.onestopenglish.com.

For a more thorough look at an 'across the curriculum' approach, try the link to San Diego University where it all began: http://webquest.sdsu.edu/

On task design for younger learners
Estaire, S. and **J. Zanon.** 1994. *Planning Classwork—a Task-based Approach.* London: Macmillan ELT.

Pinter, A. 2006. *Teaching Young Language Learners.* Oxford: Oxford University Press: Chapters 5 and 6.

On task design for adults
Leaver, B. L. and **J. R. Willis.** 2004. *Task-based Instruction in Foreign Language Education: practices and programs.* Washington D.C.: Georgetown University Press: Chapters 10 and 11.

On storytelling and projects
Yeh, A. *Telling True Stories: Task-based classroom work in Taiwan.* http://dcyeh.com/sy0304/2ndsem/groupb_projects/stories/.
This uses a mix of traditional teaching, multimedia, and online chat.

Fried-Booth, D. 2002. *Project Work* (Second edition). Oxford: Oxford University Press.

Philips, S., S. Birwood, and **H. Dunford.** 2000. *Projects with Young Learners.* Oxford: Oxford University Press.

Ellis, M. and **C. Johnson.** 1994. *Teaching Business English.* Oxford: Oxford University Press.

Note
A photocopiable worksheet that can be used for a Task Design workshop can be found in Appendix 4. It gives suggestions for aspects of a topic that can explored for each type of task, and an outline for a task-based lesson.

6 LANGUAGE FOCUS AND FORM FOCUS

6.1 *Some basic principles*

In Chapter 1 we argued that tasks should be central to language learning. This means that in order to promote language development we should provide a rich diet of activities which focus on meaning. We should not allow form-focused activities to detract from a focus on meaning. If we have spent time presenting and practising specific forms immediately before introducing a task, then it is likely that learners will be concerned to display the target forms rather than to concentrate on getting their messages across. The task is likely to become a 'further practice' of form activity. This suggests that learners should complete a task cycle before the teacher isolates specific forms for study. Learners are then more likely to use a far wider repertoire of language to express themselves during the task; they will deploy whatever language they have already learnt from earlier lessons, and experiment with language they are not sure of in order to get their meanings across.

At different stages in a task cycle there will be different kinds of opportunities for learners to focus on language. A focus on language occurs naturally when learners pause in their attempts to process language for meaning and switch to thinking about the language itself. They may stop to search for the right word to express the meaning they want, or to look up in the dictionary a word they are not sure of. Or they may stop to wonder if a sentence they are planning to produce is grammatical, or if it can be improved in some way. This switch of attention can take place at any stage in the task cycle, but we can allow for it specifically in the priming stage at the beginning of a task cycle, and also at times during the cycle, when we allow learners time to prepare what they want to say or write.

The task cycle, then, is predominantly concerned with meaning, but there is likely be a focus on language, especially on lexis—words and phrases—at the beginning when the teacher is priming, or setting up the task sequence. There will be occasions during the task sequence when learners have time to prepare not only the content of their message, but also the kind of language they want to use to deliver that message. We use the term 'focus on language' when learners are working with meaning and are thinking about language on their own initiative, independently of the teacher.

At the end of the task cycle there is a focus on form. This is different from a focus on language. Focus on form occurs when a teacher isolates particular forms for study and begins to work on those forms outside the context of a communicative activity. Let's see how this works in practice.

6.2 A sample task : 'How strict were your parents?'

In Chapter 4 (4.4), we looked at Tim Marchand's task in which his adult learners discussed how strict their parents were, and then decided whose parents were the strictest. Tim normally begins the task sequence with a typical priming stage, introducing the topic, making a few comments of his own and then eliciting comments from the learners. During the priming the basic words and phrases are likely to crop up: 'strict', 'let me', 'didn't let me', 'made me', 'had to', 'forced to', 'easy-going', 'freedom'. This priming could be adapted to lead into the listening task quite precisely by introducing some of the topics there. The teacher might, for example, ask how many people had to do jobs at home like washing the car and helping with the house work. How many had to do their homework before supper? How many were scared of their parents? This could even be incorporated into a questionnaire:

When you were a child:

a Do you think your parents were strict or easy-going?
b Did they allow you to stay out late at night?
c Did they let you go on holiday on your own?
d When you went out did you always have to tell them where you were going?
e Did you always have to do your homework before supper?
f Did your parents make you help about the house?
g What jobs did they make you do?
h Did you have to wash the car?

Tim also used a recording as part of this task sequence. He asked four of his friends to tell him about their parents, and recorded what they had to say:

A Well I grew up in the UK in the eighties, and my parents were quite strict with me actually. I wanted to go with the school to Turkey, there was a school trip to Turkey and it sounded a bit of an adventure, and there was an explanatory evening for the parents. My Mum and Dad went along, they heard about all the freedom we'd have there for a month. And then we got home they said no! 'Far too much freedom for

you, young lad', and so they didn't let me go. I was quite upset, so yeah
I think they were quite strict.

B Well I think my parents were quite liberal with me. They never
imposed any schedules or their opinions on me, and they never made
me do any horrible chores, you know? And they were quite open for me
to ask questions. I could talk to them as a friend really, so yeah a very
positive experience.

C My Dad is a quiet man really, so he didn't really make me do much at
home. He sometimes asked me to wash his car or cut the grass, but I
was never forced to do it, and I could usually get some pocket money
for it as well. I think my Mum was also pretty easy-going; she let me
stay out late with my friends. As long as she knew where I was, she
wouldn't mind so much what I did.

D My father was definitely stricter than my Mum. If I had been in trouble
at school, it was always left up to him to tell me off. But I wouldn't say
that my Mum was easy-going exactly. She would sit me down
sometimes and make me do my homework in front of her, or force me
to eat my greens, things like that. I guess I was just more scared of my
father.

There is, therefore, a good deal of text wrapped around the task. Some of
this, the teacher's introductory priming language, is ephemeral, it has not
been written down or recorded. Other language, the questionnaire and the
recording are permanent. They are available for detailed study. Let us put
these elements together to see how we might build up a unit complete with
language-focused and form-focused activities.

6.3 Priming

The purpose of the priming stage is to prepare learners for the topic and to
make available the vocabulary. By 'vocabulary' we mean words and phrases
they are likely to need for the task. We have proposed that this should be done
either by a teacher-led introduction, or a questionnaire, or a combination of
the two. The teacher might reinforce the introduction by leading a class
brainstorm on words and phrases relating to the topic and/or writing up a few
central items on the board. At this stage, however, there would be no emphasis
or insistence on formal accuracy on the part of the learners. The teacher could
then follow the introduction by asking learners to answer the questionnaire as
individuals and to share their answers with a group of three or four.

As we saw in Chapters 4 and 5 one possibility would be for the teacher to
provide a brief introduction to the topic of the next task at the end of one

lesson and give learners a questionnaire to do for homework. This would afford learners the opportunity of preparing for the next stage, for example thinking what to say about their own parents and perhaps mining the questionnaire for useful language. The next lesson could then begin by taking up the teacher-led introduction again, before going on to the next stage of the sequence.

So priming can be flexible. It will probably include a teacher-led introduction of some kind. This may be reinforced by the use of a written text. The timing can be varied, either allowing the learners plenty of time to think about the problem for homework, or asking them to do it fairly quickly in class. The priming can also be supplemented by group work.

There will be at least two parameters governing the teacher's decision as to how to shape the priming. The first question is to do with the complexity of the task and the associated language. The second question concerns the learners' ability. Low level learners will be more likely to need the written input from the questionnaire, and the opportunity for homework preparation. This task could equally well engage a class at a much higher level. In this case a teacher-led introduction might be enough on its own.

6.4 Language focus

It is important to keep in mind that language focus involves thinking about language in the context of a meaning-focused activity. Learners are thinking about language in general terms as the need arises, not about specific forms identified by the teacher. The priming stage has already offered opportunities for language focus. During the teacher introduction learners may ask the teacher for the meaning of particular items. If given the chance, they may mine the questionnaire for useful language. If the questionnaire is followed by a group discussion learners may take the opportunity to work together to clarify language problems. So we can provide opportunities for learners to think carefully about language as they are getting ready for a meaning-focused task.

It is also possible to build in further opportunities for language focused work. Central to the framework outlined by D. Willis and J. Willis (1987) and J. Willis (1996) is a task cycle called *task → planning → report*. Learners begin this cycle by doing a task, in this case a discussion of their upbringing and their parents' degree of strictness. At a later stage they are asked to tell the rest of the class about their discussion, but before they do this they are given time for a planning stage. At this stage there will almost certainly be time spent on language focus, on preparation for the more 'public' report. The planning might be taken in two stages. Once the task has been completed the teacher could begin by asking learners to work as individuals to summarize the discussion. After this they could be asked to pool their ideas to prepare for the report stage. All of this planning is likely to involve preparation, focusing at least partly on language.

This can be supplemented by written work. Learners might be asked to make notes to summarize their discussion. They could even be asked to write a report as a group, describing who had the strictest parents. These reports could then be read out, or put on an OHT for the class to see. Speaking is a real-time activity, in which there is normally no time for careful consideration of language. Writing, on the other hand, allows time to think about language. So building written work into the planning and preparation increases the likelihood of a focus on language. But the writing does not take place in a vacuum. It is going to be used to inform the rest of the class. So the focus is primarily on meaning. It is a focus on language in the context of a communicative activity, not a focus on isolated forms. We must, however, be careful that learners do not begin to use writing as a crutch when speaking, by relying on written notes rather than spontaneous speech.

We can, therefore, identify a number of opportunities for language focus. We can increase the likelihood of a concern for language by allowing more time, for example by setting preparation work for homework. This likelihood will be increased even more if we ask learners to put their ideas down in writing. The required level of language focus and the time given to it will depend on a number of factors. It will tend to be higher with low level classes. It will be probably be higher with an examination class than with a general class, and it will be higher if the teacher feels that the load of new language is particularly heavy.

6.5 *Focus on form*

6.5.1 Identifying items for a focus on form

The choice of what forms to focus on normally depends to a large extent on the nature of the task and the associated texts.

READER ACTIVITY 6A

Identifying topic-related items

Look at the two texts above in section 6.2: the questionnaire and the four recordings. The task is to do with parental attitudes and with duties, responsibilities, and privileges. Given this, what forms do you think learners could usefully be asked to focus on in these texts?

Commentary

Working with the recordings, Tim Marchand chose to focus on the contrast between 'make' and 'let', and also on lexical items like 'strict' and 'easy-going'. These language features are all closely involved with the task and topic.

The words 'make' and 'let', and the patterns that go with them, are very important because they are so frequent and so useful. In the questionnaire there is also one occurrence of the form 'have to', the most frequent way of expressing obligation.

There is one occurrence of the word 'allow' in the questionnaire. But the passive form, 'be allowed to', which is a frequent way of expressing permission does not occur in the texts. It is, however, a very useful form but there is another passive phrase: 'was (never) forced to do it'.

Words like 'strict', 'liberal', and 'easy-going' are less frequent and therefore less generally useful, but they are so closely connected to the topic that they are likely to be memorable from the context, and are therefore worth highlighting.

There is a possible linked topic—household chores. In the texts we find expressions like 'help about the house', 'wash the car', 'cut the grass'. It might be useful to extend this list by asking learners to list things they had to do as children. The list would contain useful everyday vocabulary and expressions like 'do the … -ing' (shopping, ironing, washing-up, etc.); 'do the dishes/garden/housework/beds' etc; 'help with the …'.

The teacher may choose to identify these items and lift them from the context so that they are isolated for a form-focused activity. Tim Marchand identified phrases in the listening like this:

> made me, let me, allowed me to, didn't make me, I was forced to, would force me to

and asked his learners to divide the phrases into those that were associated with strictness and those that were associated with an easy-going attitude.

Alternatively the teacher might find some way of helping learners to identify these language features for themselves. One possibility would be to start from meaning. The teacher might begin by asking learners to read out from the questionnaire about what people had to do, and what they were allowed to do. There are six of these phrases in the questionnaire: 'Did they allow you to stay out late?' 'Did you always have to tell them where you were going?' 'Did they let you go on holiday on your own?' 'Did you always have to do your homework?' 'Did your parents make you help about the house?' 'Did you have to wash the car?' They could then be asked to work in pairs to pick out similar phrases from the listening text: 'So they didn't let me go'; 'My parents never made me do any horrible chores'; 'He didn't really make me do much at home'; 'I was never forced to do it'; 'She let me stay out late'; 'She would … make me do my homework or force me to eat my greens'.

Another possibility would be to start from a given word. Learners could be asked to pick out phrases from the questionnaire with the word 'you'. This would lead them to: 'did they allow you to'; 'did you always have to'; 'did they let you'; 'did your parents make you'; 'did you have to'. They could then look at the listening text and pick out three word phrases with 'me'. This would highlight: 'never *made me do* any household chores'; 'he didn't really *make me do* much at home'; 'she *let me stay* out late'; 'she would *sit me down*'; '*make me do* my homework'; '*force me to* eat my greens'. The teacher could then focus on the verb phrase with 'have', 'let', 'allow', 'make' and 'force'.

It might also be useful for learners to pick out all the phrases with 'quite': 'quite strict with me'; 'I was quite upset'; 'quite liberal'; 'quite open with me'. They could then be asked to find another word in Text C which means the same as 'quite'. This would direct them to the phrase: 'pretty easy-going', which illustrates a very common use of the word 'pretty'.

Yet another possibility is to start from part of a word. Endings like '-ing', '-ble', for example, can lead to interesting discoveries. In Tim's listening text there are a number of phrases containing words ending in '-ly':

> … my parents were quite strict with me actually.
> I could talk to them as a friend really,
> My Dad is a quiet man really,
> … he didn't really make me do much at home.
> … and I could usually get some pocket money for it …
> … I wouldn't say that my Mum was easy-going exactly.
> My father was definitely stricter than my Mum.

This highlights the use of words like 'really' and 'actually' and also the phrase 'not exactly', all of which tone down a statement, making it more tentative and moderate, and which contrast with the use of 'definitely'.

All of the phrases identified above are taken from texts that the learners have processed in the course of the task sequence. This is important because it means the forms that they focus on are rooted in a meaningful context. This will not only ensure that the meaning of these phrases is more easily recognized, it also makes them more memorable.

It is also useful to ask learners to choose for themselves phrases they think will be useful and write these down in their notebooks. The teacher can then go round the class asking a few learners what phrases they have picked out. This can be varied by asking one group of learners to pick phrases from one paragraph and another group from a second paragraph, and so on. Learners then listen carefully to the choices others have made.

READER ACTIVITY 6B

Identifying useful forms to focus on

Look at the text about the young man in Chapter 3 (3.3 Stage 5). What items from that text might you choose for activities focusing on form?

Commentary

The text provides a good opportunity to focus on reflexive pronouns. There are five reflexive phrases:

> to kill himself, threw himself, found himself, poured myself, Jim Burney himself

These cover the use of the reflexive for emphasis ('Jim Burney himself'); its use as a direct object ('kill himself', 'threw himself', 'found himself'); and also as an indirect object ('poured himself'). The expression 'found himself' to express location is particularly frequent in both spoken and written English, so it is worth highlighting. Other frequent phrases are 'I said to myself ...', 'He thought to himself ...', 'help yourself', 'do it yourself', 'by myself'. The reflexive as indirect object is very common. You can practise the forms of the reflexives ('myself', 'yourself', 'himself', 'herself', 'ourselves', 'yourselves', 'themselves') by asking learners to complete sentences like these with reflexives:

> I cut ... a piece of cake.
> She got ... a drink.
> They made ... a few sandwiches.
> etc.

Verbs commonly found with a reflexive indirect object are 'hurt', 'enjoy', 'teach', and 'cut'. These are worth exemplifying. You can refer your learners to a grammar book exercise on reflexives, but you should also tell them to keep looking out for them in the language they meet, because the grammar of reflexive pronouns is very complex, particularly the restrictions on their use.

Like many narratives the text contains several phrases of time:

> over Christmas, for a moment, then, half an hour later, at the time

and of place:

> in New York, off the Empire State Building, to the top floor, where he held on to the safety fence, threw himself off, towards the cars, moving along Fifth Avenue, over 1,000 feet below, on a narrow ledge on the 85th floor, outside the offices of a television station, where the strong wind had blown him, knocked on a window of the offices, crawled in to safety; on duty there, coming in through the window of the 85th floor

and of quantity:

> hundreds of cars, a lot of invitations.

Phrases of time, place and quantity are so frequent in the language that they justify a lot of classroom time. Encourage learners to keep a double page for each of these in their notebooks in which to write new phrases.

Other interesting features include:

- the use of 'took' with a means of transport: 'took the lift'. You could ask learners how many words they could put in the place of 'lift' in this phrase in other transport contexts i.e. 'take the/a ...'. Ask them to see who can come up with the longest list of words. This will stretch their language to cover as many forms of transport as they can.
- the collocation 'strong wind'. You could get learners to use a dictionary to find what other words collocate with 'strong' (for example, 'current', 'swimmer', 'team', 'possibility'); we also use it for drinks like tea and coffee).
- the contrast between 'decided to' and 'decided that'.
- 'the idea of ...-ing'.

It may not be worth spending time on all these phrases in this particular lesson, but it is well worth making a note of them. Later on, when you come to deal with pronoun indirect objects, for example, you can refer learners back to this text and ask how many examples they can find here.

Most texts contain so much useful language that it would be confusing and tedious to cover it all. It is a matter of selecting what can best be covered with a particular text and taking note of useful illustrative material which might be used later to reinforce another text.

6.5.2 Correction as focus on form

Teachers often rephrase learner contributions to the discourse. When they do this, they are behaving as participants in the discourse, so we would regard this as a focus on language. Sometimes, however, teachers use correction as part of a form-focused activity. This kind of correction fulfils three important functions:

- It helps prevent fossilization. Learners are alerted to the fact that they still have some way to go in mastering a given form.
- If used sparingly it helps motivate learners. Almost all language learners expect and want correction. They see it as a necessary part of the teacher's role.
- It provides useful negative feedback. Sometimes negative feedback is the quickest and most efficient way of putting learners on the right track. For example, learners often produce sentences like

He suggested me to go.

by analogy with

He persuaded me to go.
He asked me to go.
etc.

Even when they are aware of the form

He suggested to me that I should go.

they may still believe that 'He suggested me to go' is an acceptable alternative form. They can never come across anything in the input to show them otherwise. The only way they can get this information is through correction.

So correction is useful. But it is not nearly as effective as we would like to think. We have already seen how learners persist in errors with forms like 'do'-questions in spite of constant correction. So correction should be used sparingly. It is better to provide a positive focus on appropriate forms than to spend too much time on correction.

6.5.3 Finding texts

We need to think carefully about where to get texts for language study. You may be able to use the texts which occur in your coursebook, even if the coursebook is not designed for task-based teaching. In Chapter 10 we will be looking at how to adapt coursebooks to give them a more task-based flavour. In the example we have just looked at, Tim started from the idea of finding a challenging and interesting topic for discussion. He then decided to create a listening text by asking some friends to talk about exactly the topic that his learners were going to discuss. This produced a spoken text with a lot of rich variation. We added to this the possibility of a questionnaire. This produced a written text which highlights very directly the relevant language items, but which is much less rich and varied.

Spoken texts

So one way of creating a text for a focus on language or on forms is to make a recording which parallels the task in some way. Here, Tim interviewed four separate people so the results are four spontaneous spoken monologues. The great advantage of making recordings like these is that you and your learners gain the benefit of a text which is rich in many of the features of natural spoken language. Other tasks are more overtly interactive; for example, David Cox made a recording to support his problem page task. David asked two friends to actually do the task he was going to set for his class. (See Appendix 3.1.)

There are, of course, practical limitations. Tim Marchand did not have the facilities to make a recording of sufficiently high quality for classroom use, so he transcribed the recordings, read the texts out himself in class and then gave the learners the transcript. Spontaneous recordings like David Cox's are not always easy to use in the classroom. We will look at some of the problems together with the considerable advantages of using these texts in Chapter 7 (7. 4).

Other sources of spoken texts include

- recordings supplied with coursebooks or resource materials (but beware stilted or overacted scripted dialogues—unnatural examples of speech);
- short recordings from radio stations—for example, topical news bulletins, weather forecasts, adverts. Phone-in programmes are particularly useful if you can find them because they have all the features of spontaneous interaction;
- recordings made by learners themselves. Many language schools in English-speaking countries send their learners out to interview members of the public. If you are not based in an English-speaking environment you may be able to persuade English-speaking colleagues or friends to be interviewed. You could also consult the learners themselves. Do they know any proficient English speakers who would consent to be interviewed?

Those taking part in the recordings certainly do not need to be native speakers; they simply need to provide a good model for learners. Possibly the best model for a monolingual group of learners would be native speakers of their own language who have a high level of proficiency in English.

Written texts
A second possibility would be to provide a written text. This might be found in the library or on the internet. In Chapter 4 we looked at a task from Yvonne Beaudry about earthquake precautions. Yvonne found a number of safety leaflets to provide supporting texts. These would certainly provide material for language study and also for a focus on form. Alternatively a written text might be specially created. Instead of asking his friends to talk about their childhood, Tim could have asked them to write down their experiences. It is not always possible to find helpful friends. Teachers could record or write down their own experiences, or could ask their colleagues to help. It is often possible to build in texts at an earlier stage in the task sequence. For example we thought of supplementing Tim's recording with a written questionnaire. It is possible for teachers to produce questionnaires of this kind for themselves. The sort of supplementary text will depend on the topic or task.

READER ACTIVITY 6C

Finding or creating texts (spoken and written)

Think about some of the tasks outlined in Chapter 4:

- Make a list of things cats typically do.
- Describe in detail how to make your favourite food.
- Rank school subjects in order of popularity.
- What criteria would you consider in choosing a holiday destination?

What supporting texts (spoken or written) might you find or create to provide for language focus and focus on form?

Commentary

Any of these four topics could be supported by a listening text. You could record a friend or colleague doing their version of the task. If you have the resources, you could get a group of two or three people together to discuss the question and make a recording. This would provide a listening text with many of the features typical of everyday conversation.

For the food task it should be possible to find a number of recipes in English. If you do not have access to recipe books there are plenty of recipes on the internet. (Try, for example, www.bbc.co.uk/food.) For holiday destinations you could find holiday brochures or, again, search the internet. For example, just google the Malaysian island of Penang, and see how many tourist sites you come up with.

You could provide supplementary material for the favourite food task by giving learners a mixed up recipe and asking them to reorder it. You could write a number of statements about holiday resorts known to the learners and ask them to read the statements and guess which resort they referred to. For the school subjects topic, you could write sentences about your own schooldays omitting the subject and asking learners to guess what subject each statement referred to:

> My favourite subject was … because I was quite good at it.
> I hated … in the third year because the teacher gave us so much homework.

You will certainly have come up with more ideas of your own, and if you pool ideas and materials with colleagues you will come up with a rich variety of texts.

6.5.4 Some form-focused activities

When we ask learners to look at a text and identify items for themselves, there is an element of discovery involved, particularly if they are asked to begin from meaning. We gave an example of this above, where learners were asked to identify things that people 'had to do' and things that they were 'allowed to do'. They had to read rapidly through a familiar text and pick out phrases according to their meaning. We can think of this as a consciousness-raising activity. Learners have to apply their own initiative and work things out for themselves. This process is likely to increase their awareness of the language.

But after they have done this exercise and also identified the other phrases with 'have', 'let', 'allow', 'make', and 'force', they could be asked to say which two verbs behave differently from the others, so that they recognize that 'make' and 'let' are followed by the plain infinitive, without 'to'. Asking them to work things out for themselves can have two beneficial effects. It may make the insights more memorable, and it encourages learners to look carefully and critically at the language they are exposed to.

It is also useful to explain to learners how these phrases work and demonstrate their use. You could refer them to their grammar book, or work through some grammar-book exercises with them. You could make up exercises of your own, a gap-filling exercise for example:

My parents … me do the dishes.
I … to finish my homework before supper.
They never … me stay out after ten at night.
etc.

It is also possible to create exercises involving *grammaticization*. By this we mean taking a string of words, removing many of the grammatical markers and asking learners to restore them. You might, for example, take this part of the listening:

My father was definitely stricter than my Mum. If I had been in trouble at school, it was always left up to him to tell me off. But I wouldn't say that my Mum was easy-going exactly. She would sit me down sometimes and make me do my homework in front of her, or force me to eat my greens, things like that. I guess I was just more scared of my father.

and ask learners to study it carefully. You could then give them this version:

father definitely stricter Mum. If in trouble school, left up to him tell me off. not say Mum easy-going. sit me down make/do homework, force eat greens, things like that. guess more scared father.

and ask them to work in groups to restore the text to its original 73 words. Alternatively you could ask them to look carefully at the questionnaire, and then give them this version, which they have to complete without looking back at the original:

a think parents strict/easy-going? (9)
b allow stay out late night? (10)

c let go holiday your own? (10)
d went out always tell them where going? (15)
e always do your homework supper? (10)
f make help about house? (9)
g wash car? (7)

In each case the number in brackets gives the number of words in the sentence. This prompts learners to think carefully about what they are doing and ensures that they will try to recall the original sentence word for word. On one level this is a very mechanical exercise, to see if learners can recall the sentences. But of course recall is much easier if they can recall the general structure of each sentence, so there is also a consciousness-raising element here. After they have done this kind of exercise once or twice they realize this and begin to pay careful attention to the small words which often mark syntactic relations and functions.

Another recall exercise is known as *progressive deletion.* The teacher writes a sentence up on the board, for example:

He sometimes asked me to wash his car or cut the grass, but I was never forced to do it.

Then two or three words are rubbed out:

He _____ asked me _____ wash his _____ or cut the grass, but I was never _____ to do _____.

and learners are asked to recall the full sentence and read it out from memory. Then two or three more words are deleted:

He _____ _____ me _____ wash his _____ or _____ the grass, but I _____ never _____ to do _____.

and again learners are asked to read the sentence from memory. This goes on until the whole sentence has been deleted. You can make the activity easier putting dashes for each letter to show the length of each word, or by asking learners to do it in groups, or by having the sentence read out two or three times at each stage. This looks like a mechanical exercise, a very mechanical exercise. But it makes learners think hard about the structure of phrases and sentences. The most important thing is that they see it as a real challenge and almost always enjoy it.

These recall exercises are valuable because they cover a range of language items. Different learners will be learning or consolidating different things. In the exercise in which they are asked to complete the questionnaire questions, for example, some will be thinking hard about the question forms. Some will be working on the forms expressing obligation and permission. Yet others might be trying to remember the position of adverbs of frequency.

Finally the teacher might consolidate by asking learners to write down a few sentences for homework: 'two things you had to do or were forced to do'; 'two things you were allowed to do'; 'two things they didn't let you do'. This could be the focus of a memory game in the next lesson, in which learners are asked to give their statements, and then other learners are asked to remember what they have been told and by whom.

In addition to focusing on the main themes in a text, it is important to identify useful phrases which the learners are likely to come across again. Tim Marchand's rich listening text includes:

> grew up, in the eighties, quite strict with me actually, a school trip, it sounded a bit of an adventure, went along, far too much, I was quite upset

David Cox's recording includes the following phrases:

> Well I don't know, She seems to be having a lot of trouble, I would say …, it's hard not to worry, speaking from experience, I think you're right, Just being as supportive as you can, that's about the best you can do, make it clear that …, I think those would work

It is also very useful to give learners the opportunity to find useful phrases for themselves. You might, for example, ask each group to pick out three phrases which they think will be really useful in the future and write these down in their notebooks. This will mean that they work carefully as a group to decide on which phrases to choose. They could then read out their phrases for the rest of the class—or, better still, put away their notebooks and give their phrases from memory. Another possibility is to give each group a different section of the text to work on and ask them to pool ideas at the end. When this happens, learners are likely to listen carefully to what other groups have to offer.

Once they have identified and shared useful phrases, you could go back over some of them and see what other words typically occur in the main 'slot'. For example:

> in the eighties/seventies/sixties
> a school trip/a work trip/a business trip
> It sounded a bit of an adventure/a disappointment
> having a lot of trouble/problems
> being as supportive/helpful/friendly as you can

So the idea is to identify useful forms, build on them, and extend them to cover other experiences and contexts that your learners may meet.

6.5.5 Putting texts together

In the questionnaire and listening for the 'Strict parents' task, there was good coverage of expressions of obligation and permission. But very often we want to look at an aspect of language that is not covered neatly in a single text.

Let us say, for example, that we are interested in adverbs which modify adjectives: both modifiers like 'quite' and 'fairly', and also intensifiers like 'extremely' and 'absolutely'.

In Tim Marchand's recording for the 'Strict parents' task we noted a number of uses of the adverb 'quite' to tone down an adjective:

> quite strict with me, I was quite upset, quite liberal, quite open with me.

and one occurrence of 'pretty' used in the same way:

> My Mum was pretty easy-going.

There is also an occurrence of 'not exactly' with the same sort of meaning:

> I wouldn't say that my Mum was easy-going exactly.

There is enough here for the beginnings of a form-focused exercise on modifying adverbs, but we would need more examples. In the text on velociraptors in Chapter 3 (3.9) there are four occurrences of 'very', one of 'really', and one of 'incredibly'—all used as modifying adverbs:

> this will be *very* familiar to a lot of you; they could move *very* fast; to turn *very* quickly; it was always *very* sharp; they could turn *really* quickly; it had *incredibly* powerful jaws

Here is a text in which someone is telling the story of a frightening experience:

> Yeah, I was OK until I had a *rather* nasty experience about er, height. I was okay. I could go anywhere. But er, I was er, on a lighthouse actually. We were being taken round it. We went up all the stairs and to the light, er, room. And then the chap says 'Oh, come on. Right we'll go out here'. And I went through the door and I was on this *very very* narrow little parapet with a rail about … perhaps eighteen inches high, and then a sheer drop of about a hundred feet or something. I was *absolutely* petrified. I've never been as scared like that before or since.

So in each of these texts there are examples of adverbs which intensify adjectives, ('very', 'very very', 'really', 'incredibly', 'absolutely'), or moderate them ('quite', 'pretty', 'rather').

Let us imagine learners are to be exposed to all of these texts, first the frightening experience story, later the velociraptors and finally the strict parents. There are a number of possible teaching strategies. We could draw attention to 'rather nasty experience', 'very very narrow little parapet', and 'absolutely petrified' after the first text, then after the velociraptors ask learners to pick out two uses of 'very' and find another word similar in meaning. Then in the strict parent text we could ask them to find four expressions with 'quite' and one with 'pretty', and ask learners if they can recall another word with the same meaning, prompting them, if necessary with the frame: 'I had a … nasty experience'.

Another possibility would be to wait until learners have treated all three texts and then design an exercise to highlight all the occurrences we have referred to. For example:

Look at these sentences from some of the texts you have read and heard. Can you remember which of these words are used to fill in the blanks:

   absolutely, exactly, incredibly, pretty, quite, rather, very, very very

1 My parents were … strict with me actually.
2 My Mum was … easy-going.
3 I wouldn't say my Mum was easy-going ….
4 The velociraptor could move …fast.
5 It had … powerful jaws.
6 I had a … nasty experience about, er, height.
7 I was on this … narrow little parapet.
8 I was … petrified.

It is, of course, unlikely that any one learner will be able to recall the texts clearly enough to complete all of the sentences, but it is very useful to ask learners to work in groups to try to recall, then to lead discussion comparing their answers before showing them the original sentences. It is important to point out that some of the learners' guesses may be 'wrong', in the sense that they are not the original words, but the important thing is that they are still acceptable forms of English. You can move on after this, or in a later lesson, to look at modifiers and intensifiers with your learners in their grammar books.

6.6 Organizing language-focused and form-focused activities

In looking at priming we showed how learners could be asked to work on priming tasks in advance—to answer a questionnaire, or prepare a topic for discussion. We need to organize our task sequences over a period of time, not simply in a single lesson. We have seen, for example, how the 'Strict parents' task might bring in vocabulary about household chores. If you recognize this in advance you might set an earlier task which deals with this topic—for example a class survey about who in the learners' households do various jobs about the house and garden. Then when learners come on to do the 'Strict parents' task you can have a quick review of the household chores task. Preparation is likely to be particularly effective when learners are asked to incorporate the language of an old task within a new one.

The same applies when learners are asked to repeat a task or to engage in a parallel task. After we have done the 'Strict parents' task we might go on some time later to look at what learners have to do at school. They could, for example, be asked which school rules they think were sensible and which were not. This would generate the same language of obligation and permission, though in a different context. In priming for this task the teacher could begin by asking learners to recall what they had to do at home, and what they were allowed to do. They could then move on to talk about school rules; this would involve much of the same language. So in preparing the 'School rules' task, learners are likely to draw on their experience of discussing what their parents made them do and allowed them to do. Some of the texts associated with strict families could be reviewed for homework before learners go on to school rules. In doing this it is important to avoid learners coming to a task believing that they will be assessed on their ability to produce specific phrases. So it is probably better to direct their attention first to the texts rather than to specific language items. After they have completed the text on the new topic, they can review their language of permission and obligation in texts associated with both tasks.

After working with a new context, teachers can extend learners' repertoire by referring them to their grammar books and asking them to manipulate de-contextualized sentences using gap-filling, rewriting and multiple choice exercises. This leads naturally on to examination practice in which learners tackle questions in the format appropriate to any examination they might need to take.

We saw in Chapters 4 and 5 how choosing a topic is a useful starting point for designing and organizing tasks. It is also useful to look at ways in which the concepts and language in one task may be incorporated in another. So the vocabulary of household chores becomes a part of a task on strict parents, which in turn later provides part of the priming for a task on school rules. It is vitally important to begin with this meaningful exposure which makes language memorable. Finally learners can be asked to manipulate the same grammatical forms using de-contextualized sentences and, where necessary, examination practice materials.

As you build up a repertoire of tasks and get more and more experience with these tasks in the classroom, you will begin to see more and more opportunities for language reinforcement building on from one task to another.

6.6.1 The pedagogic corpus

We have shown how more than one text can be put together to provide input for language work. Clearly learners do not simply work with a single text in order to develop their language. In fact they will draw on all the language they can recall to help them build up a picture of the language. We have shown how the course writer and teacher can help them by looking at similar language items associated with different texts, for example by looking at the language of permission and obligation when talking about strict parenting and also when talking about school rules.

We can take it further than this by drawing their attention to similar language features in a range of texts they have studied. We might, for example, look at phrases and sentences exemplifying the use of a preposition like 'in' or 'of' from a whole series of texts. This will give learners a large number of examples from which to draw conclusions. In this way we can use a set of texts to provide learners with examples of the use of specific features of the language in contexts which are familiar to them.

When grammarians use a set of texts to make discoveries about the language and to illustrate those discoveries, we use the word *corpus* to refer to the bank of texts they are using. In the same way when we use a set of texts to help learners find out about the language we can talk about a *pedagogic corpus*. By this we simply mean the texts learners have studied which provide them with material which will help them to build up their insights into the language and the way it works. We shall have more to say about the pedagogic corpus in Chapter 9 (9.4).

6.7 Preparing for examinations

TBT aims primarily at helping learners get ready to use the language in real-life situations. But it is also important to prepare learners for examinations, whether they be school or public exams. Nowadays many public examinations incorporate communicative activities. (See Chapter 9 (9.3.2), and FAQ 10.13 in Chapter 10.) Many tests and examinations, however, involve a focus on form. In a test of grammar or vocabulary candidates often have to do multiple-choice questions, gap-filling or sentence completion. It is obviously important for them to have practice in handling test items of this kind. After they have completed three or four task-based sequences you can ask them to go over the work they have done and then give them a short test along the lines of the examination they are preparing for.

Learners may be asked to answer traditional comprehension questions or multiple-choice comprehension questions. After a task sequence you can give them one of the texts they have worked through and ask them to answer comprehension questions which mirror the exam. As an alternative, you can ask learners to set their own examination questions, using the student as question master as we did in Chapter 3 (3.5). After they have studied a number of texts you can ask different groups to prepare tests on different texts. Take in the tests and go over them to polish them up before you give them to the rest of the class.

Provided you give them plenty of examination practice you will probably find that task-based learners are actually better prepared for examinations than their form-focused counterparts. The real language work that they have done in task-based activities makes language so much more memorable than a solid diet of form-focused activities.

6.8 *Review*

We have looked at two ways of getting learners to think about language. Figure 6.1 summarizes these two ways. In the first, which we have called language focus, they think about language as they prepare to take part in a communicative activity, a task. They may be given time to do this in class, or they may be asked to do it for homework. In focusing on language they may refer to a dictionary or a grammar book, or they may pool ideas with other learners. But the important features of this language focus are that it is in preparation for a meaningful activity, and decisions are taken by the learners themselves. It is the learners, not the teachers, who decide what to focus on and why.

There are also form-focused activities. Learners think about language under teacher supervision, usually at the end of a task sequence. The teacher identifies useful items from a text or a collection of texts and finds ways of making these language features noticeable and memorable. Learners may be asked to find words and phrases associated with particular meanings, or they may find specific words or endings. Once language material has been gathered, the teacher can then elaborate on it in a number of ways—by grammatical explanation and demonstration or by setting gap-filling or sentence-completion exercises. It is also useful to encourage learners to pay careful attention to the wording of a text by encouraging activities which involve grammaticization, recalling the precise wording of a text from lexical clues. Finally it may be useful, particularly with examination classes, to set tests at the end of a task sequence or of a series of task sequences, based on the language that learners have focused on in those sequences.

Thinking about language

Language focus and form focus compared diagram:

Language focus

Learners think about language in the context of a task-based activity. They help and correct one another or consult an authority (grammar book, dictionary, their teacher) to help them express their meanings more effectively. They are likely to do this:

- at the priming stage when they ask for the meanings of specific items;
- when they *mine* written language in preparation for a coming task;
- when they work together to prepare for a task;
- when they work together to plan a report for the whole class;
- when they are making a record of a task either by putting it in writing or making an audio-recording.

Form focus

In form-focused work learners work on recognizing or manipulating the forms of the language in a number of ways:

- **Consciousness raising:** learners work with text to find:
  — ways of expressing specific meanings (e.g. ways of giving permission; time phrases)
  — phrases with specific words (e.g. learners might be asked to identify phrases with 'me' as a way of highlighting permission and obligation; or phrases with particular prepositions as a way of highlighting time phrases)
  — words or phrases they think will be useful in the future

- **Recall:** Learners work with familiar texts doing grammaticization, progressive deletion and gap-filling exercises to oblige them to focus on grammatical words and phrases

- **Extension:** Teachers extend beyond the texts learners have studied by giving grammatical explanation and gap-filling, multiple choice and other exercises with topics or situations not covered in the texts.

- **Correction:** If used sparingly correction is useful to motivate learners, to avoid fossilization and to give learners negative information which they cannot find in the input.

- **Exam practice:** Learners prepare for form-focused exam questions by setting and answering questions in the appropriate format.

Figure 6.1 Language focus and form focus compared

Further reading

Thornbury, S. 2001. *Uncovering Grammar.* Oxford: Macmillan Heinemann ELT
Full of useful ideas for working with texts and for other consciousness raising activities.

Willis, D. 2003. *Rules, Patterns and Words: Grammar and Lexis in English Language Teaching.* Cambridge: Cambridge University Press.
Chapters 4 to 9 have many examples of activities that focus on different aspects of form.

Willis, J. 1998. 'Concordances in the classroom without a computer: assembling and exploiting concordances of common words' in **B. Tomlinson** (ed.). *Materials Development in Language Teaching.* Cambridge: Cambridge University Press. Chapter 2 pp. 44–66.
This chapter illustrates how a pedagogic corpus of textbook texts can be exploited by learners themselves.

7 THE TASK-BASED CLASSROOM AND THE REAL WORLD

7.1 Classroom language and the outside world

Every discourse arena has its own typical discourse structure. In their classic study of discourse in 1975, Sinclair and Coulthard showed how classroom discourse tends to be teacher dominated. The following is a typical exchange:

TEACHER What's the past tense of 'bring'?
STUDENT 'Brought'.
TEACHER 'Brought'. Good.

So, a typical exchange consists of a teacher question, a student response and a teacher's evaluation of that response. In most classrooms the teacher evaluates the content of the response—is it the right answer? In the language classroom teachers tend to evaluate the form of the response—is it acceptable language?

TEACHER 'I get up at eight o'clock.' Can you make the question?
STUDENT When you get up?
TEACHER do you ...When do you...?
STUDENT When do you get up?
TEACHER Good. 'When do you get up?'

The problem with this kind of teacher-dominated discourse in the language classroom is that it gives learners relatively few opportunities to use the language. Learners would be restricted to making limited responses. They would have no opportunity to speak at length and no opportunities to control the discourse. So language teachers have developed a number of techniques to compensate for this. They ask learners to engage in role play, or to compose dialogues, and so on. In particular, tasks of the kind we have been looking at in this book give learners the chance to produce real and extended discourses of their own. They engage in argument about the consequences of drug addiction. They exchange anecdotes about their childhood and how strict or easy-going their parents were. A well-balanced task-based programme will ensure that learners experience an appropriate range of discourse types.

So one of the advantages of the task-based classroom is that it enables us to escape the restrictions of the classroom, and involve learners in different types of extended discourse. It provides an arena for informal spontaneous interaction. It also provides reasons to read, in order to check one's beliefs or predictions, and it requires learners to engage in extended monologue, detailing their arguments or elaborating on their stories. In carrying out these tasks learners will find themselves doing many of the things that we do in spontaneous language use outside the classroom: agreeing and disagreeing, interrupting, asking for repetition and clarification, changing the subject or the emphasis, highlighting the important part of the message, guessing at meanings and making inferences and so on.

But the classroom is still restricted as a discourse arena. In the outside world learners experience an infinite variety of social relationships and working roles. They may find themselves having to adjust their language to the demands of entertaining a distinguished visitor in English, or talking to a friend's three-year-old child. In real life some learners may be involved in service encounters as hotel or restaurant staff, while others visit hotels and restaurants only as customers. It is impossible to reproduce all these social and working relationships in the language classroom, but this does not absolve us from the responsibility of preparing learners to deal with the wide range of language encounters they may experience in the real world. In this chapter we will look at ways in which the classroom reflects the world outside and also at ways in which it fails to do so, and we will look at ways of remedying these failures.

7.2 Real-world tasks

In the Commentary on Reading activity 1c in Chapter 1 (1.5), we looked at the question of how far classroom tasks mirror the real world. We established three levels. First there was the level of *meaning* in which learners produce meanings which will be useful in the real world. Second was the level of *discourse* in which learners realize discourse acts which reflect the real world—the things we have highlighted above, such as agreeing and disagreeing, guessing at meanings and making inferences. Finally, at the level of *activity*, they engage in a communicative activity which reflects very directly the way language is used outside the classroom—they tell stories, get involved in arguments, explain how to do things, and so on. In this section we will look at tasks which relate to the real world on all these levels.

7.2.1 English for specific purposes

In some teaching situations such as English for academic purposes (EAP) and English for occupational purposes (EOP), we can mirror very closely the way our learners will be going on to use the language in the real world.

We can provoke discussions and set readings which reflect precisely the discussions and readings which will be involved in their future work or study. In Chapter 3 (3.4), we looked at a jigsaw task designed by Joann Chernen for her trainee bakers. Learners read a text on making chou paste, with different groups taking notes on different parts of the text. Then the groups came together to pool their knowledge. The reading and note-taking reflect precisely the study process. The discussion also reflects a study process. Learners exchange knowledge and, in the process, check and question that knowledge. Joanna has imposed one artificial condition—the learners take notes on only one part of the process. She has done this for a good reason— in order to create a need for the discussion. In spite of the artificial restriction, all the stages involved in the task sequence are a true reflection of a study process.

Prediction tasks can play a large part in reading for academic purposes. Many scientific research journals, for example, begin with an introduction which sets out the aims and stages of the research. Often scientists read this introduction rapidly to decide whether or not it is worth their while to read the whole article. We can reproduce this process in the language classroom. Let us imagine we have selected an article relevant to the learners' area of specialization. We might then provide a set of instructions like this:

1 Work in groups of three.
2 Read the following summary of a research article.
3 List three important questions which may be answered in this paper.
4 Do you know the answers to these questions?

This will promote a group discussion which can then lead to a general class discussion led by the teacher. In the group stage, learners will be using the language of their specialized subject as readers, as speakers, and as question-ers. There will be opportunities to ask people to clarify their opinions, to challenge those opinions, to set up alternative views. The group discussion will be a rehearsal for the teacher-led class discussion. Finally the learners will have a reason to go on to read the article in question to resolve some of the questions left unanswered.

An important feature of the tasks outlined above is that they involve real language use. There is an immediate problem to solve. In each case the language use reflects very directly the kind of language learners would need in their real-world situation. This is largely because in each case language is used primarily to exchange information. In some situations, however, the social dimension of language use is at least as important as the exchange of information. For workers in the tourist industry, for example, the need to treat clients in the hotel or the travel agent's in an appropriate manner is almost as important as the need to provide them with accurate information. An attractive solution to this problem is to set up a role play activity. Learners might, for example, be given a timetable problem to solve. One group of learners preparing to play the part of a client might be given the following instructions:

> You wish to book return flights to London for a conference running from April 3rd to 5th. You have been given a travel grant of $450.00 to cover the cost of the flight, so you do not want to pay more than this. You would prefer to fly from X airport in order to save money, but you are willing to fly from Y if necessary because it is closer to your home.

Another group, the travel agents, might be given these instructions:

> A client wants to book return flights from to London for a conference running from April 3rd to 5th. What alternatives can you offer? Would you advise your client to fly from X or from Y?

One member of each group could then be asked to role play the situation, the travel agent equipped with timetables and prices either in print or, more realistically, accessible on a computer terminal.

The advantage of a role play is that it mirrors real life. Trainee travel agents can see themselves dealing with clients, answering their questions and helping to solve their problems. The disadvantage of a role play is that it imposes an unnecessarily heavy load on learners. It asks them not only to solve a problem, but also to act out a role while doing this. The role requires them to act within certain social and professional conventions. What forms of address should they use? With what degree of formality or deference should they address a client? Should they engage in social chit-chat or concentrate on the essentials of the business? It is extremely difficult for learners not only to solve a problem, but also to play a role as they are doing so.

A solution to this problem is to separate out the role-playing element from the task, or problem-solving element. First simply set a problem. Group A are asked to:

> Ask B for information on flights to London from April 3rd, returning on April 5th. Find out:
>
> a   the cheapest flight from X airport
> b   the cheapest flight from Y airport
> c   the most convenient flights from X and Y in terms of timing
> d   the best flight from X and Y in terms of convenience and price.

Group B are asked to:

> Find flight information for flights from X and Y to London on April 3rd, returning on April 5th. What questions do you think a client might ask about these flights? What answers would you give?

Learners then work in A/B pairs on an information exchange task in which As solicit information from Bs.

When learners have worked on the information exchange they can listen to an experienced travel agent dealing with a customer. They can be asked to make notes on the social dimensions of the exchange:

How does the agent address the client?
Are there any apologies? How are they expressed?
Does the agent make recommendations? How is this done?

Once they have listened to a real life exchange learners can be asked to script a similar exchange. After they have done this they can reasonably be asked to role play the exchange. In the problem-solving activity the learners simply choose the language that solves the problem most efficiently. There is no pretence involved. The language they use is prompted entirely by the outcome they are seeking to achieve. In role playing the activity there is an element of pretence. Learners are obliged to behave in an artificial way which they believe would be appropriate in a given social encounter. They try to treat a fellow student as though he or she were a valued customer, and they try to act out a relationship which is quite different from that which exists between them as classmates. These demands make it difficult enough for experienced language users to act out a convincing role play, never mind a learner who, by definition, still has problems with language processing.

A useful classroom strategy is to take learners through a sequence in which they first solve a problem, then learn to play a role, and finally learn to solve problems while playing a role. This separates out the difficulties, allowing them first to concentrate on the problem, and then on the social context. As they progress through their course they will need less and less preparation for the social context, the role playing element, until eventually they can enter into a full-blown role play without the need for controlled preparation. We shall have more to say about this in section 7.5 below.

7.2.2 Everyday English

Many of the tasks we have looked at are to do with everyday language—making conversation, reading newspapers, finding our way around the world by asking other people or looking at written sources on paper or electronically. Many of these tasks have clear links to the real world at all three levels. In everyday conversation we discuss things like how strict our parents were or what subjects we would like to have on the school curriculum, and we argue about things like dangerous drugs. A lot of conversation involves storytelling. Sometimes these are personal anecdotes; sometimes they are second-hand stories in which we report something we have read in the newspapers or seen on TV. So a storytelling task may be based on learners' own experience or it may be the outcome of a prediction exercise like those described in Chapter 3 (3.3). Either of these would reflect real life storytelling. After doing a storytelling task which links to the real world in this way, we should make the links clear to learners. For example, it is worth pointing out to learners that a lot of everyday conversation consists of storytelling.

All of us have a repertoire of stories and opinions in our first language. We produce these stories on appropriate occasions, and stand ready to offer our opinions when the occasion arises. Often what sounds like a spontaneous narrative or an opinion expressed for the first time is actually a repetition of a routine we have used many times before. It is widely accepted now that a lot of language is made up of phrases which are more or less fixed. It is equally true that a lot of much longer stretches of language are relatively fixed. The good storyteller has told some of his stories many, many times before. We are all used to explaining a bit about the place where we live, to complaining about traffic congestion, to comparing prices in the shops. In the same way we talk about films and TV programmes we have seen and books we have read, summarizing and evaluating.

We have these routines in our first language and it is important to build up routines in a foreign language. So summarizing and discussing these things in class contributes directly to language use outside, building up a repertoire of conversational gambits.

When learners listen to a recording of a discussion, you can identify ways in which speakers highlight stages in their argument: 'the main thing is …', 'this means that …'; or ways in which they contradict each other: 'yeah, but …', 'well, I'm not sure about that'. You can highlight learners' attempts to achieve the same discourse functions, commenting on their success or helping them, to shape their language more effectively. It is also valuable to make comparisons with the first language. How do you interrupt someone politely? How do you change the subject? This shows learners that these are things we do in the real world, not simply in classroom activities.

After a discussion it is worth asking learners if they have ever had a discussion on this topic in their first language. It is also well worth while engaging learners in the choice of topic wherever possible. What interests them? What subjects do they think they might have occasion to discuss in English? Once you have a list of topics you can design tasks around them, designing questionnaires, for example, and looking for suitable texts to feed into the discussion.

7.2.3 Electronic communication: writing and reading

Some years ago most learners would probably expect to do relatively little in the way of writing in a foreign language in the world outside the classroom unless they were likely to study or work in the medium of English. With the widespread use of email and chat rooms that has all changed. There is now a good chance that learners will need English for email correspondence either with native English speakers or with others who use English as a common language or that they will enter a virtual chat room where English is required. At the same time the internet has vastly increased the opportunities to read English. There is such a demand from people who want to use the internet in a language other than their own, usually English, that the search engine, Google, actually provides a set of language tools, including a translation program.

Email communication can be an object of study in itself. You can begin by discussing with learners how email communication differs from 'snail mail' correspondence. What advantages does email have? Obviously it is much quicker. You can attach documents and pictures. It is easily stored and retrieved. Are emails different in form from other letters? Learners can talk about this with reference to their first language. You can then bring into the class samples of correspondence and ask learners to guess whether they are email or snail mail. How can they tell, if indeed they can? You can bring in a sequence of emails omitting one email from the chain and asking learners if they can reconstruct that message, trying to get as close to the original as possible. If the sequence and the omission are carefully chosen, this can be an engaging task. Use a sequence of emails as a text following through some of the ideas set out in Chapter 3. The important thing is to make them aware of the form of communication that is involved in email. It is fast moving, often abbreviated and usually relatively informal.

Learners should certainly be encouraged to use the internet in English. They can be given useful web addresses to help them prepare topics for discussion. You can set them questions to be answered by using the internet: 'What is the most expensive hotel in London and how much does it cost to stay there for one night?' 'How long does it take to fly from Singapore to Hong Kong?' 'What is the cheapest package holiday you can find for a fortnight in Cuba?' You can set twenty questions allotting five to each learner. They can go home and find the answers then come back and compare answers next lesson. It is not difficult to think of internet tasks along these lines. You can use the internet to supplement the reading in your coursebook. Readings often throw up questions. Instead of looking for answers to these questions yourself you can ask learners to find the answers for themselves on the internet.

Unfortunately not everyone has access to the internet and to email, but it is so important in today's world that you really need to bring it into the classroom if most of your learners do have access. So you will need to allow for those learners who cannot join in these internet tasks. You can set internet work well in advance so they have the chance to access a computer either at school or in a library or internet café. You can provide print-outs for some learners and, if necessary you can set alternative homework for those who do not have access to a computer.

7.3 Artificial tasks

In Chapter 2 (2.3.2) we looked at a task which was quite clearly artificial, in that it did not mirror anything learners are likely to want to do in English in the real world—anything that is likely to figure in their needs for English in the real world. But this task still related to the real world on the first two levels, the levels of meaning and discourse. This was a game in which learners tried to remember the positioning of objects on a tray. Games like this do not reflect target activities, but do involve real-world meanings. In the real world we do not normally try to recall and talk about the positions of objects on a tray. But we very often refer to objects by describing where they are in relation to others: 'It's in the drawer next to the knives and forks'. The tray game obliges learners to handle these real-world meanings.

As well as real-world meanings these tasks involve real-world discourse acts. In games like this it is important, for example, to monitor information carefully and to ask a partner to clarify what has been said to make sure we have a precise understanding of what has been said. This is exactly what happens in the real world when, for example, we give or receive instructions or directions. Other games practice more complex discourse skills. In 'Twenty questions', for example, it is important to phrase questions precisely in order to get the information we want. When we ask a series of questions in the real world we do so in order to home in on specific information which we cannot uncover with a single question. Precise questioning like this is a part of many real-life activities—finding what sort of goods or services a shop business can offer, or what sort of goods or service a customer requires. Twenty questions is an artificial way of creating the need for careful questions in the classroom.

So artificial tasks may not offer a precise reflection of the real world, but they do oblige learners to engage in real-world meanings and real-world discourse acts. Let us go on to look at the language generated by a task to show how it reflects many of the features of spontaneous discourse.

7.4 Spontaneous spoken discourse

If we are to link the classroom and the real world, it is obviously important to bring into the classroom samples of language which reflect the world outside. This is not too difficult with written language and also some spoken language—broadcasts, lectures and so on. But it is very difficult to introduce recorded samples of spontaneous interactive spoken discourse into the language classroom. This discourse is usually characterized by a shared environment, shared purposes, and shared knowledge. This can lead to all kinds of omissions and abbreviations. When one adds to this the false starts and illogicalities that are very much a part of spoken discourse it is hardly surprising that spontaneous spoken discourse can be very difficult for an outsider to follow. Consequently the dialogues used in teaching materials tend to be scripted. As a result they are usually over-explicit and fail to incorporate many of the features which are typical of spoken discourse.

One way of bringing spontaneous spoken language into the classroom is by making recordings of experienced speakers of the language carrying out tasks of the same kind as the learners themselves will be asked to carry out. Let us look at an example.

Two native speakers are looking at photographs of places and trying to guess what country each picture was taken in. The learners have the same photographs and have already had a chance to try the task themselves. Here is an excerpt from the recording. As you read through it take note of the way the participants express their opinions:

PK   What do you think of the one in the top left hand corner here Mary?
MS   Well I'm absolutely positive that that's New York. That's in er, North America. What do you—Okay?
PK   I think—I agree, yes, with the Statue of Liberty and all those skyscrapers. Mhm. Yeah.
MS   Yes.
PK   Erm . . . What about the one in the middle here at the top?
MS   Well when I see a . . . er . . . a windmill I always think of Holland, so I would say Holland, for that.
PK   Mhm. Yes I think I agree with you. It's flat as well isn't it?
MS   Yes.
PK   Yes. So it must be Holland.
MS   Right.
PK   And the third one along the top?
MS   Not too sure about that. Er. . .
PK   Somewhere oriental perhaps?
MS   Oriental definitely. It could be, er, Thailand? With that type of . . .
PK   . . . that sort of roof?
MS   . . . roof?
PK   Mm. Yeah.
MS   Erm
PK   I think Thailand. I don't know enough about it to sort of say it's China.
MS   It could be China—or Thailand. Shall we plump for . . . ?
PK   I think Thai . . . I think Thailand. I would plump for Thailand there.

MS Okay and erm, how about this one with the big vase?

PK Yeah. Next row. Big vase. Makes me think of Greece.

MS And me. Mm. And er . . . Looks like a Grecian urn. And it's hot.

PK It's hot, and tourists always look like that in Greece don't they? Dressed for the summer.

MS Yes. Okay, Greece.

(J. Willis and D. Willis 1988)

Figure 7.1 'It could be Thailand'

READER ACTIVITY 7A

Identifying language items

1 How many statements of opinion can you find in this dialogue?

2 What do speakers say when they are sure? What about when they are not sure?

3 How many questions can you find?

Commentary

There are the following expressions of opinion:

a Well I'm absolutely positive that that's New York.

b I think—I agree, yes, with the Statue of Liberty and all those skyscrapers.

c I would say Holland, for that.

d Yes I think I agree with you.

e So it must be Holland

f Somewhere oriental perhaps?

g It could be, er, Thailand?

h I think Thailand.
i It could be China—or Thailand.
j I would plump for Thailand there.
k Looks like a Grecian urn.
l Okay, Greece.

a), e) and possibly l) express certainty, so speakers say 'I'm positive' and use the modal 'must' to show they are sure. They show they are not sure:

- by using the modal 'could': g) and j);
- by using the modal 'would': a) and i);
- by saying 'I think': b), d) and h);
- by using rising intonation to signal a question: f) and g).

An activity like this draws learners' attention to the means used to reach agreement.

READER ACTIVITY 7B
Looking at spontaneous speech
What features of spontaneous speech are illustrated in the dialogue above?

Commentary

You can find the following features in the dialogue:

1 false starts and omission:

I think—I agree, yes, with the Statue of Liberty and all those skyscrapers.
I think Thai … I think Thailand.

2 a range of interactive phrases and discourse markers:

Yeah, Okay, Right

3 verbless 'sentences':

What about the one in the middle here at the top?
And the third one along the top?

4 abbreviated sentences:

Oriental definitely.
I think Thailand.
Makes me think of Greece.

5 the use of fillers

and erm

6 vague language

   I don't know enough about it to sort of say it's China.

This is the only one clear cut example here, but vague language is generally very frequent in spontaneous speech. Words and phrases such as the following are used constantly

   about, sort of, kind of, more or less, or something

This illustrates one of the advantages of using spontaneous recordings of tasks. The recordings carry many of the features of spontaneous speech. There are, of course, other features which are not exemplified here, such as:

---

7 the use of sentences that tend to be joined with simple conjunctions, particularly 'and', 'but', 'then' and 'so'. This is particularly true of spoken narrative.

8 the use of colloquial words and forms:

   bloke, fellow, guy (for man), kids (for children)

9 the use of 'tails'

   He's a funny fellow, that George.

10 the use of 'fronting'

   That George, he's a funny fellow.

11 the use of phrases that are constructed by simply adding one element to another ('my aunt, her friend, his neighbour, she said …' Instead of 'The neighbour of a friend of my aunt's said …'). There is an interesting example in the recording of three place adverbials linked in a chain: 'the one in the middle here at the top'.

If spontaneous recordings are used regularly in the classroom, all these features will be exemplified at some stage.

Once we have material of this kind we can begin to work with it to highlight important features for learners to study. By picking out all expressions of opinion we highlight much of the language involved in reaching agreement. By picking out all the questions we promote insights into the way the discourse is structured.

It is important for learners to be exposed to the features of spontaneous speech. Most of us can recall our first exposure to a foreign language outside the classroom, and the feeling of bewilderment which often accompanies this experience. We are suddenly confronted with people who speak rapidly, who use vague language which was never covered in our classroom experience, who make false starts and ask abbreviated questions. This is the real world and we need to prepare learners for it. Discourse markers like 'well', 'right', 'okay', and 'so' carry a huge communicative weight and need to be studied in context.

Once we have identified these features we can begin to look at them systematically and to devise activities to highlight them for learners. It is very useful for learners to listen critically to recordings of spontaneous spoken discourse in their own language in order to raise their awareness of features like vague language and repetition. They can also be asked to work from an edited version of a recording of natural discourse in English from which elements like vague language and discourse markers have been removed. They can then listen to the recording and identify the elements that have been omitted. D. Willis (2003) lists a number of other activities which enable learners to focus on natural spoken discourse. But the most important thing is to provide plenty of exposure to spontaneous speech by bringing recordings into the classroom.

7.5 The social dimension

Language is used in a rich variety of social situations, and the language we use is shaped by social contexts and relationships. In the classroom, however, social contexts and relationships are strictly limited. As we pointed out in section 7.2.1 above, the agent/client relationship does not exist in the classroom. Once learners get to know one another relations are relaxed; indeed teachers often work hard to establish a relaxed informal atmosphere in the classroom. So, when speaking to one another in their first language, learners will tend to use informal language, and they will probably try to carry this over into their use of English.

At first, of course, they cannot distinguish between informality and studied politeness in English. They have to learn the difference between 'Hi Jen, how's it going?' And 'Good morning Mrs Carter, how are you today?' or between 'Can I use the dictionary when you've finished with it?' and 'Excuse me, I wonder if I could use the dictionary after you please'.

Whatever approach is taken in the classroom, we will always need to make learners aware of the social dimension of language use. There are a number of useful ways of doing this in the task-based classroom. Some of these involve a general awareness of cultural conventions, some of them involve knowledge of appropriate language forms. Consider the following:

- Recognize the difference between problem-solving and role play in the way suggested in section 7.2.1. Learners begin with a problem-solving task, for example, and go on to listen to a recording in which a parallel problem is solved in a real-world situation. The example we looked at involved moving from a timetable problem to a dialogue between a travel agent and a client. Learners then looked at the language forms used before going on to role play the agent/client dialogue.

- Part of the task → role play sequence involves language analysis and consciousness-raising. Once learners have handled the language involved in negotiating the problem, they can go on to look at the social dimension of the interaction. This stage would concentrate on forms of address, on the use of modal verbs, on markers of deference such as apologies.
- Encourage learners to think about the social dimension in their own language. Forms of address are important. How, for example, would they address a close friend as opposed to a complete stranger? How would they address someone much older than themselves as opposed to someone much younger? How is politeness encoded in their own language? How and when do they make apologies?
- Make generalizations about social variation. For example, in English longer is generally politer. So there is a cline from 'Please …' to 'Could you … please …' to 'Would you mind …-ing … please'.
- Make sociolinguistic variation the subject of class discussion. This can be done by analyzing language behaviour as it is revealed in texts. It is interesting, for example, to look at a sequence of emails to show how strangers tend to move very rapidly from formal politeness to informality, from 'Dear Dr Willis' to 'Hi Dave'. It is worth looking at letters handling similar subject matter between close friends and between strangers. What differences are there? Look at the differences between the popular press and more prestigious newspapers. How do they report the same events?
- Ask learners to rewrite letters and dialogues varying the social parameters.

We need, therefore, to supplement a task-based approach to take account of social variation. This is partly a matter of consciousness-raising, sensitizing learners to the way the social dimension is encoded, and partly a matter of introducing appropriate language forms.

7.6 Teacher roles

In the task-based classroom teachers still fulfil their traditional role of providing language knowledge and input, but they have also to promote real language use and provide a clear link between the classroom and the real world. The teacher's traditional role is that of knower, someone who imparts and shapes knowledge. This is the role that shapes the kind of classroom discourse we looked at right at the beginning of this chapter. But the most important role for the teacher in the task-based classroom is not so much the purveyor of knowledge as the manager of discourse. Most of the teacher's time will be taken up in leading and organizing discussions, and in class management to enable learners to work on tasks.

Let us look briefly at the roles fulfilled by the teacher in the task-based classroom:

1 Leader and organizer of discussion

Most task sequences begin with a teacher-led discussion. You may then choose to move into group/pair work. But in most cases it is possible to conduct the whole task sequence in teacher-led form. Remember the basic characteristic of a task-based approach is that meaning is primary and comes before a focus on form. It is possible in a discussion-based lesson to move from a teacher-led introduction to learners working individually on a questionnaire. The teacher then leads a discussion of the questionnaire. This is followed by a stage in which learners jot down a few notes summarizing their opinions. The teacher then offers learners the opportunity to share their views with the class. So the teacher controls the class at each stage. The same approach can be applied to storytelling activities or to games. In a game of 'Twenty questions', for example, the class can work as individuals. They can begin by writing down possible questions and reading these out. They can then begin to play the game calling out questions as individuals when nominated by the teacher, with the teacher summarizing where they have got to at certain stages.

There is a an excellent precedent for this kind of procedure. N. S. Prabhu, one of the pioneers of task-based approaches, advocated this kind of teacher-led discussion in his classes in Bangalore in South India. He used no group or pair work (see Prabhu 1987). The great advantage of group work, of course, is that it gives learners plenty of opportunities to talk. But you may feel that there are times when the greater control of a teacher-led approach more than outweighs providing opportunities for learner talk. You may want to adopt a teacher-led approach in the early stages of task-based teaching, gradually using more and more group work as learners become familiar with the idea of doing tasks. You may use a teacher-led approach the first time learners do a particular task or a particular type of task. You may want to rely heavily on a teacher-led approach if learners are, for whatever reason, reluctant to use English in group work. You have to decide this for yourself in the light of the dynamics of your particular class at a particular time.

You should be aware, however, that a teacher-led class is not an easy option. It requires careful preparation, especially with elementary classes. You need to think things through with great care, anticipating the difficulties learners are likely to have and working out strategies for handling those difficulties.

2 Manager of group/pair work

We have pointed out that group/pair work gives learners more opportunity to use the language, particularly the spoken language. The teacher needs to be able to organize this kind of work to get the best out of students. It is important to make sure that learners are absolutely clear about what is expected of them before they move into groups. It is also important to monitor groups carefully to make sure that they are on track. If things do seem to be going wrong you should not be afraid to suspend group work and sort out problems before continuing.

It is sometimes useful to change the composition of the groups and repeat a task. You might, for example, ask learners to discuss a topic, then change groups and ask them to continue the discussion with a new set of partners. This provides useful opportunities for learners to rephrase ideas they have already worked through. The same applies to storytelling. Learners can change groups and tell their story again to a new audience, or they can tell a story they have just heard from someone else in a previous group.

3 Facilitator

You need to find a balance between setting a task which provides the right kind of challenge, and making sure that learners can manage the task. If you are introducing a new task and you are not sure about the level of difficulty, then the best thing is probably to err on the side of making things too easy rather than risk things being too difficult. We will look at ways of adjusting tasks in the next chapter.

4 Motivator

It is very important to give learners all the encouragement you can. There are two basic ways of doing this. First you should be as positive as you reasonably can be in the feedback you give learners. Go out of your way to highlight their achievements. When reporting on group work, pick out some of the useful phrases learners have used and comment positively on them. When a learner speaks to the class as a whole always try to find something positive to say about the performance. You may comment on the breadth of vocabulary and pick out one or two useful words or phrases. You may comment on growing mastery of a new grammatical form. Being positive does not mean that you have to be completely uncritical or that you have to ignore the problems that learners have and the mistakes that they make, but it does mean that you should put a positive gloss on things whenever you can.

The second important way to enhance motivation is to highlight progress. It is worth reviewing progress at regular intervals. What useful new words and phrases have been acquired? What new topics are now available for discussion? What new stories have they added to their repertoire? Have they become noticeably more fluent? Encourage learners to identify their achievements and to take a pride in them.

5 Language 'knower' and adviser

This involves helping learners with meanings. You should join in learner discourse as an equal participant, but one who has greater language knowledge and experience. You can highlight learner contributions by repeating them and sometimes rephrasing. When operating in this role you should resist the temptation to correct learners when they don't really need it but you should be ready to help by answering questions in a language study phase when learners are struggling to find the best way of expressing themselves. It is useful to try to think of yourself as conversing with a group of friends rather than being the teacher.

6 Language teacher
There are, however, stages at which you do adopt the traditional teacher role, explaining, demonstrating, and eliciting appropriate language forms. In a task-based approach this focus on form normally comes at the end of a task sequence. It is an important role, and also a difficult one which demands careful thought and preparation.

7.7 *Review*

It is important to design task sequences which meet the needs of particular groups of students. In doing this it is important to take account of the social environment in which language is used and to make learners aware of this social dimension. It is also important to make learners aware of the way language is constructed—particularly spontaneous spoken discourse. Often a useful way of achieving this is by making them aware of how they use their own language. This will help them to recognize that language varies according to the social environment and the purposes and circumstances of language use.

In order to make tasks work and to provide a suitably rich learning environment you will need to take on a range of teacher roles. It is important to be aware of the richness and variety of teacher roles in the classroom and to take account of this in your planning.

7.8 *Follow-up activities*

1 Think of a lesson you taught recently or, if possible, record one of your lessons. How many different roles did you carry out? How much time did you spend in the role of *language teacher* as it is defined above?

2 Before teaching a particular unit, identify the kind of target discourse, spoken or written, that you are aiming at. Is it informal conversation, an academic lecture, a newspaper editorial, a travel brochure? If the target discourse is written, try to find one or two samples of that discourse in the real world. How far does it match the texts your learners had to deal with in your lesson? Are there any important features missing? For example, do written texts in your coursebook show obvious signs of simplification? If

so, do they still prepare learners to handle this form of discourse outside the classroom?

3 If the target discourse is spoken, try to record one or two samples and ask the same questions. Look carefully to see if the features of spontaneous discourse listed in this chapter are to be found in the recordings of spoken discourse you use in your classroom.

Further reading

Carter, R. and **M. McCarthy.** 1996. 'Spoken grammar: what is it and how can we teach it?' *ELT Journal* 50/4: 369–71.
This is a description of spoken English, showing how it differs from 'standard' written forms and offering suggestions for teaching.

Willis, D. 2003. *Rules, Patterns and Words: Grammar and Lexis in English Language Teaching.* Cambridge: Cambridge University Press.
Chapter 9 gives a description of spontaneous spoken discourse and describes activities to help learners focus on it.

8 ADAPTING AND REFINING TASKS: SEVEN PARAMETERS

8.1 Introduction

Once we have an initial idea for a task, or once we have identified a possible task in a coursebook, we will often need to adapt or refine it so that it meets the needs of our learners more precisely. This chapter offers seven parameters that give us specific aspects to consider when adapting or refining the design of a particular task.

You will be familiar with your own learners' needs in general terms: for example, whether they need more practice in speaking or writing, and if speaking, whether they need more opportunities for spontaneous interaction or for more formal talk. Do they need to extend their vocabulary rapidly? If so, they will benefit from tasks that incorporate a wide range of reading and/or listening. Are they are concerned about passing an exam with a focus on grammar and written accuracy? If so, they will need tasks that provide natural opportunities for more formal writing in exam-like conditions. All this information is useful when we are selecting and refining tasks with specific classes in mind. The present chapter deals with more detailed planning—the fine-tuning of individual tasks—but we do need to keep overall objectives in mind so as to offer a suitable range of tasks over the longer term.

These seven broad parameters can be considered before a lesson when setting up, grading, and writing instructions for tasks. For each one we shall look at different variables that can be selected and 'tweaked' in order to make a task more effective. And occasionally, even if we have planned the task well beforehand, there may be times during a lesson when you need to tweak a task to make it more effective.

We want to illustrate this process initially by comparing two versions of the same task on the topic of work and career moves.

Here is the first version of the task for you to reflect on.

READER ACTIVITY 8A

Improving a task

'Career moves'

What are your opinions about working in a family business, or working freelance from home? Tell your partner.

Imagine that a colleague asks you to advise her on this task—she tried it with a reasonably good intermediate class but most pairs did it in less than a minute, saying very little.

Why do you think it did not work very well? Suggest two or three improvements.

Commentary

There are several reasons why the task as set up here might not work. Firstly, some learners may have no experience of family businesses or working freelance from home, and have no opinions at all. If you think this might be the case, ask them to think of someone they know to whom this might apply. It would also be more precise (and doable) if we changed the word 'opinion' to 'advantages and disadvantages', and included some informative input and engaging pre-task activities to motivate learners to weigh up the two situations. Finally, the instructions are ambiguous because of the 'or'—are learners supposed to talk about both topics or just one? So, another improvement would be to make this clear or learners might think that one opinion for each situation will be enough.

There are other improvements that could be made, but for now let us look at a second version of the same task, taken from a coursebook, and compare the two versions.

The task below is from the middle of a unit on 'Career moves' from *Natural English Intermediate* (Gairns and Redman 2002). It is in a listening skills section titled 'For and against' and follows a three-step listening task about a son working in his father's business, where possible advantages and disadvantages are listed. After this comes a section entitled 'Listening challenge', which has a colour photograph of a smiling mother sitting by her computer at home, holding a young child on her lap while answering the phone. There are toys scattered around.

Comparing this version of the task with the one above, we see that the main speaking task (6) has two pre-task steps (4 and 5) both encouraging learners to engage with a specific situation. The photo supplies visual clues which makes (4) more appealing and human. There is more information available from what Catherine says in the recording, backed up by the tape-script. Compared with the first task above, step 6 instructions are more precise, and

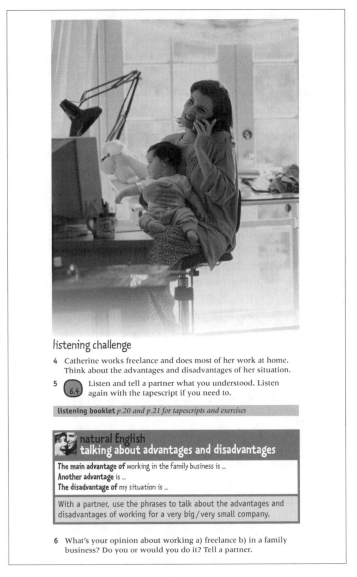

Figure 8.1 Catherine working at home

personalized in that the learners are asked to say whether either option would suit them.

This is, then, a great improvement on the first version: the recording also gives more exposure to language in use and it is likely to generate more interaction. But there are still many ways in which it could be adapted or tweaked to make it more appropriate for specific groups of learners. So let us start with an overview of the seven parameters to see how these could be applied.

READER ACTIVITY 8B

Analyzing and adapting task instructions

1 Look at the mind map (Figure 8.2). Consider each parameter in turn, applying aspects of each parameter to the second version of the task above. Which of these parameters are accounted for in the task instructions, in part or in whole? Which are not mentioned?

2 Applying aspects of these parameters, think how to adapt/add to the textbook task instructions so that the task is likely to generate more language use and a richer learning experience for your own learners.

Make notes based on each parameter, leaving space to add to them or revise them while reading the next section, for example, 'make the interim goals more precise'.

We shall now take each of these parameters and explore them in relationship to the tasks above. Making some of these parameters clearer in the task instructions and/or adapting them is likely to make this task a more effective and satisfying learning opportunity. Our ultimate goal is to end up with a task that engages learners and generates as much meaningful use of language as possible.

8.2 Outcome and interim goals: the need for precision

A *closed* task is one where there is a 'correct' answer, for example in a 'Spot the difference task' where there are five differences to be found. An *open* task is where the outcome is unpredictable—where learners are free to decide what they want, as in the task we have just looked at.

The first version of the task above leaves the final outcome rather vague and open to a minimal interpretation—to give an opinion about working free-lance or in a family business. The second version is less vague in that learners must consider both options and also apply it to their own circumstances, but we do not know how much they will have to say on this topic—they may have no direct experience of either situation. A less motivated learner could achieve even the second task minimally in two utterances to a partner: 'freelance—too risky for me; our family—no businesses' and sit back. A more motivated learner might refer back in the book to the preceding listening task with its list of advantages and disadvantages of family businesses and use some of them. There is also some background information in Catherine's recording that a motivated learner could draw on. However, there is nothing to help learners know how well they have understood the main points of the recording, other than comparing theirs with their partner's understanding.

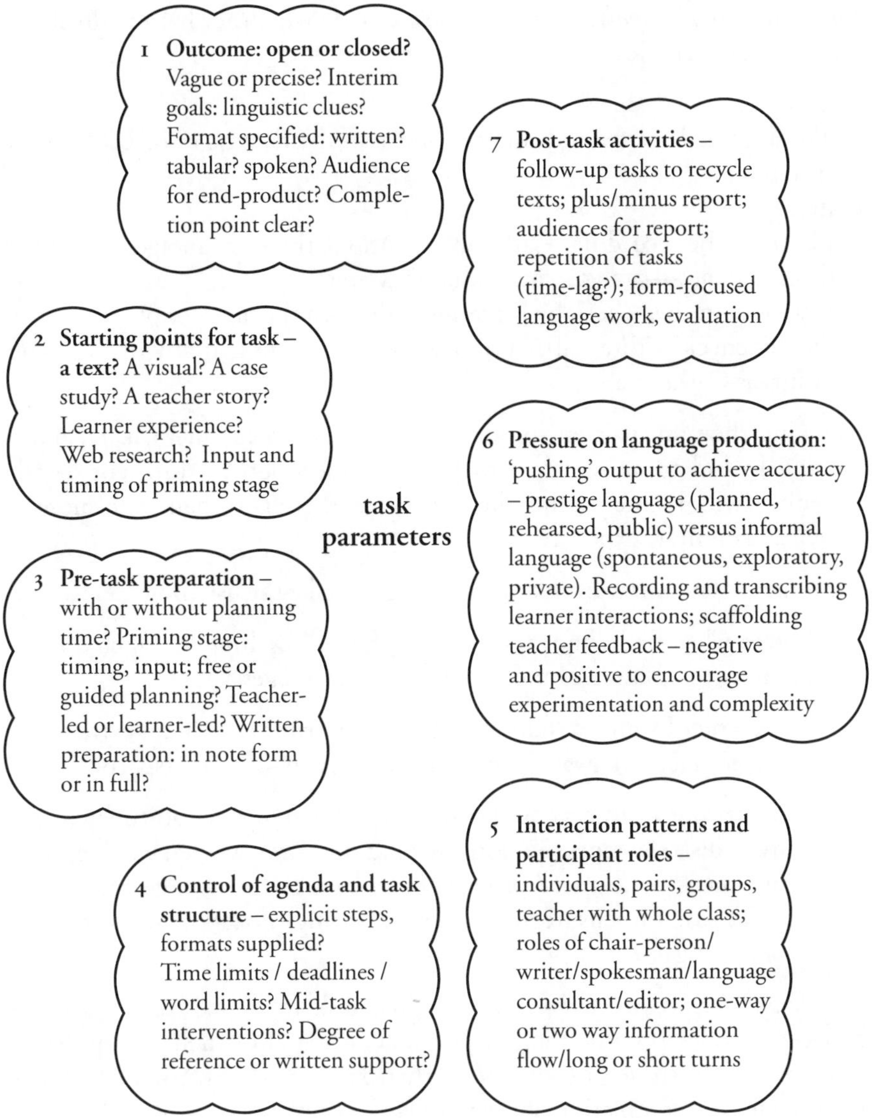

1 **Outcome: open or closed?**
Vague or precise? Interim
goals: linguistic clues?
Format specified: written?
tabular? spoken? Audience
for end-product? Comple-
tion point clear?

7 **Post-task activities** –
follow-up tasks to recycle
texts; plus/minus report;
audiences for report;
repetition of tasks
(time-lag?); form-focused
language work, evaluation

2 **Starting points for task** –
a text? A visual? A case
study? A teacher story?
Learner experience?
Web research? Input and
timing of priming stage

**task
parameters**

6 **Pressure on language production:**
'pushing' output to achieve accuracy
– prestige language (planned,
rehearsed, public) versus informal
language (spontaneous, exploratory,
private). Recording and transcribing
learner interactions; scaffolding
teacher feedback – negative
and positive to encourage
experimentation and complexity

3 **Pre-task preparation** –
with or without planning
time? Priming stage:
timing, input; free or
guided planning? Teacher-
led or learner-led? Written
preparation: in note form
or in full?

5 **Interaction patterns and
participant roles** –
individuals, pairs, groups,
teacher with whole class;
roles of chair-person/
writer/spokesman/language
consultant/editor; one-way
or two way information
flow/long or short turns

4 **Control of agenda and task
structure** – explicit steps,
formats supplied?
Time limits / deadlines /
word limits? Mid-task
interventions? Degree of
reference or written support?

Figure 8.2 Task parameters mind map

It is this kind of situation—where the task is vague and students don't really
know how much they should understand or say, or whether they have done
enough to complete the task—which often leads to difficulties with class
management in TBT.

There are alternative ways of developing this task which would make it more
precise and help learners to feel more confident doing it:

Set specific interim goals so learners know exactly what they have to do along the way. For example:

- in step 4:
  Think of at least two advantages and two disadvantages of Catherine's situation.
- in step 5:
  Listen to the recording. Catherine mentions three advantages and three disadvantages—can you catch what they are?
  Listen again then check by listening again with the tape-script.
  Finally check with a partner and see whether you had any of the same points as Catherine.

Knowing they must listen for six things in total helps them listen more attentively and to know when they have understood in sufficient detail. Listening twice before reading the script gives them two chances to succeed as well as gain more exposure.

Give clues or key phrases from the recording to make the listening task easier:

Listen to what Catherine says about the following things—which do you think refer to advantages and which to disadvantages?

work when I want to, family and children, time travelling, extra time, social contact, get away from work/escape, a lot of room (space)

Add some writing. Learners could make a list of two or three advantages and two or three disadvantages. Looking at what they have written will help you do a rapid check on learners' progress on the task when you go round and listen in. It's easier to ensure all learners are doing the task and not talking about something else!

Give more precise instructions for the final task in step 6, distinguishing between a general opinion and a personal appraisal of their own possible career paths (or those of someone in their family), thus clarifying what is required for the completion of the task. For example:

6 Tell your partner your general opinions about working a) freelance b) in a family business? (Give two main points for each.) Did you and your partner make any points in common?
Then discuss whether working freelance from home or working in a family business would ever suit you or your partner. Say why or why not. How similar are your reasons?

Specifying the number of points and reasons means that learners will know when they have done enough to be sure they have completed the task. Identifying what points they both made and reasons they have in common gives the task a more social outcome—it's the kind of thing we often do in casual conversation.

Precise instructions, interim goals, a clear completion point with an outcome of some kind are likely to increase learners' confidence in their ability to do the task, stimulate richer use of English, maximize student participation and less likely to allow a minimal response. Adjusting these parameters can also help us with the grading of a task, making it more or less challenging.

8.3 Starting points for tasks: input and timing at priming stage

Here we are looking at the very first thing or things we might do when preparing to introduce learners to a task or a set of tasks on a particular topic. Here are some ideas you might use for this initial priming; you may well have others.

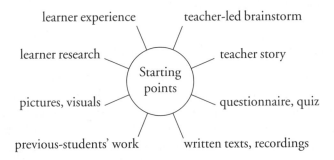

Figure 8.3 Starting points for tasks

The 'Career moves' task above begins with a picture of Catherine working at home and asks learners to think about her situation. So the starting points are a *visual presentation* coupled with *learner experience* closely followed by a *recorded text* which learners then listen to, to prepare themselves for the spoken task. An alternative starting point might be to ask learners, well in advance of the lesson, to find out about someone who works either in a family business or is freelance, and to ask them how they decided to work in that way—so this would start with *learner research* (possibly in L1, but to be reported to the class in English). A good starting point for the task in Chapter 3, 'Hello, I've just jumped off the Empire State Building', might well be a *picture* of the building with a short *teacher-led class brainstorm* about high buildings they know of. The newspaper headline then takes them into the preparation stage, where learners start thinking for themselves. For a general topic such as 'Volcanoes', learners might start by doing some guided *web research* on their own, looking at sites suggested by the teacher; more everyday topics such as 'Cats' or 'Strict parents' could well be introduced by a *teacher's story*, leading into class discussion drawing on *learners' own experience*.

Input at priming stage could take several forms: as we saw above, it could be written, for example, a website or reference source to be read outside the classroom. It could be a straightforward teacher introduction to the topic and explanation of the task; or a teacher/learner demonstration of a parallel task (for example, a 'Spot the difference' using a slightly different pair of pictures), or listening to a recording or seeing a video of a similar task; or it could be seeing sample end-products from students who had done the same task previously.

Timing of priming stage. Very often, this will come in the same lesson as the task. But, as we suggested in Chapter 2, priming could usefully happen in a previous lesson, which then allows learners to do their preparation at home before the task lesson. This was the format that Maggie Baigent's storytelling sequence took. (See Chapter 5 (5.6).)

8.4 Pre-task preparation and planning

Much recent research (for example, Foster 1996; Foster and Skehan 1996) has shown the benefits of some kind of pre-task planning. Learners who are given five to ten minutes just before the task to plan what to say tend to produce task interactions that are not only lengthier but linguistically richer, with a higher degree of fluency and clause complexity. (For details, see Ellis 2003; Djapoura 2005.) This applies especially to more complex tasks, like problem solving or creative tasks like storytelling. Mehnert (1998) found that for tightly structured tasks even one minute of planning time produced greater accuracy, but results seem to vary for different types of task.

With or without pre-task preparation time Although we have outlined the advantages of giving learners planning time, going straight into the task without time to plan or prepare does give learners practice in coping with real-time interaction—a valuable skill they will need for real-life English use. (See Chapter 7 (7.4) on spontaneous discourse.) So maybe we should give learners experience of both alternatives. For example, when we ask learners to repeat a task in a later lesson, this could be done with no preparation time.

Types of preparation—free or guided planning Once learners have been primed for the task, they could be given a specific number of minutes to think about it and write notes, and look up words they want etc. This is free (learner-led) planning. Guided planning is when the teacher (or a handout) suggests language that might come in useful, and/or gives suggestions for ideas to talk about. Interestingly, this seems to result in less accurate language use on task, the speculation being that, with guided planning, learners are trying to express more complex ideas than they can currently manage, and use patterns and grammar that are not yet a part of their natural repertoire (Djapoura 2005). One could argue, then, that learners might benefit from a degree of autonomy at this preparation stage, but if you have learners who are clearly not making much effort, then guided planning might encourage them to try harder and 'push' their output, even if they do make more mistakes in the short term. (See 8.6 below.)

Amount of written preparation, in note form or in full If you give learners time to write out what they want to say in full, (or to prepare this as homework) they may well benefit from the time spent on working out what they want to say and how to say it—thinking of the right words to use, and checking grammar and collocations. Teachers in Japan have found that this gives shyer learners the confidence to speak out in class. (See also Kelly and Gargagliano 2001 and 2004 for approaches to task-based writing.) However, there is always the risk learners will end up reading out loud, or trying to speak 'written English' or even learn it by heart and simply recite it from memory. To help resolve these problems, ask learners to reduce their full account to notes that they can refer to during the task (possibly limiting the number of phrases written).

8.5 *Control of 'agenda' and task structure*

'Agenda' relates to the way the task itself is structured. For example, are there explicit steps or formats for learners to follow? Are time limits, deadlines, or word limits set? Is additional support (reference material, note-taking) specified and/or allowed?

With low level or less motivated learners, it may help if the task agenda is carefully structured and controlled for them, as in the 'Career moves' task above, where we suggested introducing specific interim goals leading up to the target task. On the other hand, with a more complex task or with higher level learners, you may choose to leave some parts of the agenda fairly open to allow space for learners to negotiate their own procedures. In our original task instructions (8.2 above) there was no explicit agenda control at all, no time limits, and no itemized steps. The only 'agenda' specifications were to think about two topics and relay some opinions to a partner. And we concluded that such a broad lack of specification is not generally so conducive to generating rich interaction and opportunities for language learning.

Formats Supplying a specific format, for example, columns, or a diagram or table to complete for an interim goal is often motivating. Having spaces to fill in is engaging and encourages more equal participation. The table below could be used at step 5 (listening) and/or adapted (different headings, more space) to help learners prepare for the final step 6, where they think and talk about their own career situation.

	Advantages	Disadvantages
Working freelance at home		
Working in a family business		

Time limits, deadlines, word limits Setting a time limit for a task (or a step in a task) can help to motivate learners to get on with the task quickly with a focus on the task goal. Teachers tend to find that a shorter time limit works better as learners concentrate more fully. You don't always need to adhere strictly to it; if the task is going really well and everyone is still engaged, let it continue until one or two pairs or groups have finished.

Deadlines can be also be set by giving a specific number of things to achieve, for example: 'When you have thought of/written down three good reasons/ found seven differences, put your hands up'. As teacher, you can decide at this stage how much longer to allow the activity to run.

Setting a time limit for a report back session also helps. 'Plan a 30-second report/a one-minute talk' is much less scary than simply 'Plan a report/talk'. The planning time will almost certainly take a lot longer than the task or report and this is useful learning time. So you may end up with a two-minute task, a 30-second report (this would be around 80 words), with ten minutes or so to plan or rehearse in between the task and report.

Setting a tight word limit for a summary or a written report means that learners have to choose expressions carefully and tussle with grammar to condense the information. (Tip: write a summary yourself first, then count your words to make sure you set a realistic word limit.)

Mid-task interventions Skehan (1998) suggests increasing the challenge of the task by introducing more information half-way through. For example, in a task where learners were asked to decide what they would cook last minute for an unexpected guest, they could be told mid-task that the guest was a vegetarian. Or in a problem-solving task, you could introduce last-minute budgetary constraints or time constraints that would effect the decisions students had made. The decision to do this can be taken during the lesson once you see how the task is going.

Degree of reference support During a speaking task, you may decide not to allow learners to use dictionaries or to refer to notes—after all, in real-life communication outside the classroom such support might not be available. Allowing individual dictionary use tends to hold up the proceedings, too— better to encourage this before and after the task. But during a reading task, you may want to allow dictionary use. You could, however, decide to limit it, for example, 'While doing the task you may look up no more than five words'. This encourages learners to think harder about possible meanings and to explore context clues, and later to pool their knowledge.

The same limits could also be applied to notes or drafts that students make before the task; to discourage students from reading out loud from notes or drafts rather than talking spontaneously while doing the task, you could ask them to reduce these to a certain number of words or phrases and write them on a small piece of paper they can hold in their hand.

Learners setting their own agenda Some teachers reported that they discuss the task with their class right at the start (or even in a previous lesson) and encourage their learners to decide together how they will set about doing the task. This could generate valuable learner–learner discussion on how to set about achieving the goal—a very useful language skill, in fact. This some-times forms a part of 'strategic planning' (Ellis 2003). In other words, students decide jointly on their own strategies and procedures, and set their own agenda, guided by the teacher. Some even make their own rules relating to the use of L1, or at what points dictionaries are allowed.

8.6 *Interaction patterns and participant roles*

In the 'Career moves' task above (8.1), learners work first as individuals, reflecting on the pros and cons of working from home, listening to Catherine, and then finally, with a partner, they check what they understand. Because learners have had a chance to think beforehand and possibly to list their ideas individually, they will definitely have something to listen out for when hearing the recording, and something to say to their partners afterwards.

READER ACTIVITY 8C

Group interactions and learning opportunities

Think how the interaction and learning opportunities in this task might change if, instead of asking students to work in pairs, you had

- groups of three at step 5 (discussing the listening), and
- groups of four at step 6 (the final speaking task).

What possibilities would this open up? What difficulties might it cause? How might you solve them?

Commentary

At step 5 (listening) the level of comprehension might well increase with the combined efforts of three rather than two people. At step 6, four people doing this final speaking task together and drawing on their different life experiences would increase the lexical challenge and enrich their language experience as it would open up a wider range of possibilities. Although each learner gets less time to speak, they will get more practice in turn-taking, interrupting, and dealing with overlapping speech. There is also more likelihood of disagreement which would enrich the discourse. The teacher also has fewer groups to monitor and get round to if there are four rather than three or two in a group. However, some teachers find that doing tasks individually or in pairs is easier to handle and less likely to result in some learners sitting back and relying on the others to do the work.

Participant roles If each member in a group of three or four is given a role with a particular responsibility, this should result in more equal participation and the task stage is less likely to get out of control. For example, one person can act as the *writer/secretary/reporter* for a pair or group, recording in writing what was discussed, or agreed. In a group of three or four, one group member armed with a dictionary could be the *language consultant* whose job it is to look up and take note of any unknown words or phrases. In a group of four, one person could be a *leader/chair person*, responsible for making sure everyone has a chance to talk. (A smart move is to give this role to the person who generally talks more than the others!) Another person could, after the task, act as the *spokesperson* who reports orally to the class or another group. Often it is the teacher who decides which learner has which role, but if you want to generate more interaction in a group, you might sometimes allow them to negotiate which role they each take on. And sometimes you can ask one learner to be an *observer*, investigating one aspect of the interaction, for example, noting down who speaks and how much, or what was said in L1 rather than English.

One-way or two-way information flow? Long or short turns? Learners reporting their ideas to a partner might result, initially, in long turns. i.e. two one-way information flows, as they explain their ideas to the other person. When they work on comparing or combining their ideas, this interaction will almost certainly become a two-way (or in a group, a three- or four-way) flow with shorter turns.

The distinction between one-way and two-way information flows has in the past been oversimplified. 'Two-way' referred to split information tasks (information gap or even opinion gap tasks), where both learners had something to tell the other. 'One-way' was used to describe tasks like 'Describe and draw', where one person held all the information about what was to be

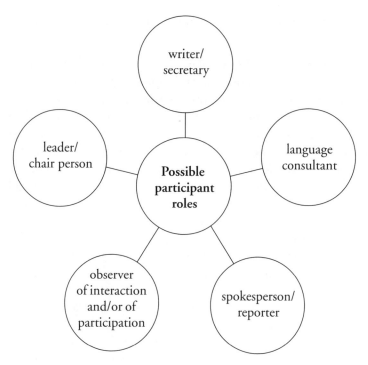

Figure 8.4 Possible roles for group participants

drawn and had to explain to the person drawing in one long turn. But in practice, as drawers progress with their drawings, the interaction tends to become two-way, as the drawer asks for clarification and the speaker checks what has been drawn. So this distinction becomes less useful (Ellis 2003: 88–9).

It is far more important to consider *how much* language use each learner is gaining at different stages in the task cycle, and *how varied* this is (for example, not simply confined to giving instructions or answering questions, or short turns). If, for example, we notice the interaction is dominated by one person, we can compensate for this at a later stage or in a new task cycle by allotting different roles, such as making the most talkative learner become a secretary whose role is to take notes (with no speaking apart from asking for clarification). This will subtly change the interactions within the group and add variety to the lesson.

8.7 Pressure on language production: 'pushing' output to achieve accuracy

TBT is sometimes criticized on the grounds that it promotes fluency at the expense of accuracy. This whole area needs careful consideration. Sometimes pressure on learners to produce accurate language is a good thing, but it is not always appropriate.

In real-life settings, in our L1, we all use a variety of registers when we talk to people. With people we know well and in informal contexts we just get on and chat spontaneously. There is little pressure to speak in a certain way as we have no need to try to impress. Typical features of informal spoken interaction were listed in Chapter 7. However, we naturally feel more pressure on occasions where we have to speak in public—if giving a speech at a wedding, for example. We would also be on our best linguistic behaviour in a job interview, or if interviewed by a radio or TV reporter, or if we are talking to a funding agency, or a student's employer who is paying for their English course. On these occasions we use 'prestige' language; we usually take time to rehearse in our heads things we might say, because we want make an effort to speak appropriately, and this entails being both fluent and precise—and it is not easy to achieve both these goals spontaneously. The difference between *rehearsed, planned, or public* talk and *spontaneous, exploratory, or private* talk is important to recognize. The first, 'prestige' version is more akin to a prepared monologue or language written for a wider audience, where grammatical accuracy and lexical precision matter. However, in spontaneous real-time discourse, unfinished utterances are quite acceptable, mistakes go unnoticed, and if we use a seemingly imprecise word or phrase, the listener can immediately clarify what is meant.

It would seem sensible then to make learners aware of different kinds of language use, and make a clear distinction between *real-time spontaneous talk and writing*, where unfinished sentences and short notes are appropriate and errors may go unnoticed, and *prestige talk* or *planned writing* destined for a larger or public or higher status audience. Preparing a presentation for a less familiar person, or an outsider of higher status, as Aurelia did when her class presented their ideas for a new timetable in English to the school coordinator (Chapter 2 (2.3)), pushes learners to plan thoroughly and use their best English.

If we have learners who lack confidence and are worried about speaking aloud for fear of making mistakes, then we need—to start with at least—to reduce the pressure and encourage them to say whatever they can as spontaneously as possible, encouraging rather than correcting, and not expecting them to speak as one would write.

Coursebooks often cater for such learners. In the task above from *Natural English*, learners talk informally in pairs with a partner who is familiar and of roughly equal status. When talking in twos or small groups like this there is no external pressure on them to produce 'prestige' language—they are less likely to worry about making mistakes or to strive to impress someone in their group by trying to use more accurate or more appropriate language when they are all of equal status. This is, of course, ideal for encouraging shy, less fluent learners to speak.

However, learners who are reasonably confident, fluent but inaccurate when speaking or writing, may need to be encouraged to think harder about the forms they are using, or their errors may simply fossilize. Unless challenged, they will continue to get by on what they know, and avoid language they perceive as 'difficult'. How can we supplement the textbook where needed and challenge them to take more care with their language? Or push them to extend their repertoire of forms and try out more complex language? These are all questions raised by Skehan (1998).

There are several natural ways to increase the pressure on language production, including putting learners in a situation where accuracy will matter or where they are more likely to notice their mistakes, by asking them, for example, to

- give a formal presentation after a task, standing in front of the whole class
- write or record something for public display—see post-task activities below (8.7)
- record themselves doing the task to play back for the class to hear.

Recording learner interaction Get fluent learners to record themselves doing their task (Report stage, 8.8.2). They then take the recording home and listen to it, noting down words and phrases they needed but couldn't recall or didn't know, correcting any errors and making a note of 'good' words and phrases they used. They should write these down. For example, if they have done a narrative task, ask them to listen for correct past tense verb forms, and suggest other adjectives or verbs they could have used. Ask them to show you their language notes at the start of the next lesson, and they could share their 'good' words and phrases with each other.

Learners transcribing and reformulating Get learners to record their task interaction then, at home, they choose a one-minute section of it to transcribe, correct and improve. Get them to write this section out again (you can take this in to look at next lesson) and possibly re-record it. This should help them focus on accuracy and be more aware next time round of the kind of errors they make when talking spontaneously. Some time after this you could get them to repeat the same task or do a similar one with another partner. Transcribing takes time, though, so this is something learners could do occasionally, or take turns to do.

Teacher feedback Feedback from the teacher or other learners which identifies errors (sometimes referred to as 'negative' feed-back) may be useful to help the push for accuracy at a priming stage, or at a planning stage prior to a public reporting stage, or before recording themselves. It is at times like these, when aiming for prestige language, that learners will want to be accurate as well as fluent and are more likely to take note of corrections or recasts. It might also draw their attention to their gaps—words and phrases they should remember but don't. In a written task, encourage co-operative drafting; giving one group member the role of 'editor' can help the push for accuracy. And when they do get things right, reward them with positive feed-back. The 'feel-good' factor is important; success breeds success and this enhances motivation. Learners who feel they have 'failed' generally give up trying.

Positive feed-back can also, in the long term, encourage experimentation with new words or patterns, and use of more complex clauses. Keep a small notebook handy and as learners do the task (or report on it) listen out for and note down any useful words or expressive phrases that you notice in their spoken or written language. Afterwards, hold a feed-back session where you draw class attention to them, building on them if possible. Ask the class for more ways of expressing similar things or for words that go with the same pattern. For example, with 'the problem is, ...' suggest other words like 'thing', 'idea', and add adjectives—'the main problem is ...', 'the worst problem was ...', 'the best thing is ...', 'the awful thing is ...'.

However, as we saw in Chapter 6 (6.5.2), it is sometimes useful to give negative feedback and provide corrective input—especially to more confident learners whose inter-language systems might benefit from being 'destabilized'. But we need to guard against overcorrection as learners who are over-corrected may feel they are failing to achieve the desired standards. If you also praise learners for good words and phrases, they are more likely to take risks and experiment with other new words and more complex utterances in the future, rather than sticking with safe but simple language for fear of making mistakes. As well as pushing for accuracy, then, we need to reward complexity (Skehan 1998; Ellis 2003: 117).

8.8 Post-task activities

8.8.1 Follow-up tasks for recycling texts

In Chapter 3 (3.8), we looked at ways of recycling texts and suggested several activities that could be done after the main reading or listening task: summarizing from memory, rewriting or retelling from a different view point, text reconstruction, puzzles or quizzes set by learners themselves for other groups, and so on. The aim of these follow-up tasks is to encourage learners to read the text or transcript, or to listen again for a second or third time. In this way they process the language of the text slightly differently each time, thereby assuring more chances to notice different linguistic features and maybe to incorporate some of them in their subsequent writing or speaking.

8.8.2 Report stage

Private or public? Small or large audience? Known or unknown? In the 'Career moves' task above, the textbook instructions suggested that learners report their ideas to a partner i.e. in a 'private' setting; this is suitable for less confident learners who have problems with speaking out. You could, however, change or extend these instructions in order to increase the pressure to speak accurately as well as fluently. Each pair could report to another pair and decide on the two main advantages and disadvantages. Then one spokesperson from each group could come to the front and tell the whole class about their group opinions, then it would be more 'public'. If you add in a planning stage prior to this, the group would feel under pressure to help their spokesperson to organize their presentation well, to use a richer vocabulary and to produce accurate language in their report to the class. (See 8.7 above.) This was tested out by Craig Johnston (2005: 191–200) who found that after a planning and report stage, his learners' syntactical accuracy improved, their lexical selection was more native-like and also more varied than at the task stage. This is something you could explore in your own classes.

This 'public' report stage was also exemplified in Chapter 3, where, after a prediction task (3.3), we suggested a fourth stage, where pairs or groups tell the story containing their own predictions to the whole class, who then compare stories. As well as increasing motivation to use more 'prestige' language, it also makes learners want to read the text to find out which of their stories was nearest to the newspaper report.

Generally, the bigger the audience, the more pressure there is to perform well. If, though, you have shy students who lack the confidence to speak out to a larger audience, you might, as an interim measure, move one student to the next group to report to them, or divide the class in halves or quarters and let learners report to one or two smaller groups. Preparing the report with a partner also helps; two learners planning together will correct each other's contributions, discuss grammar points and collocation, thus scaffolding each other's learning and giving that extra feeling of confidence (Storch 2002).

There is also more pressure to use more 'prestige' language if the person you are reporting to is of higher status than you, or unfamiliar to you. Some teachers occasionally set up tasks or projects where outsiders come into class to hear the class report their views on a certain issue relevant to them; or to act as specialist informants, having heard a report from the class on what they are currently studying. For example, Aurelia Garcia's learners presented a report on their ideal boarding school to the headmistress of their school, and Lorie Wood invited a trained first aid specialist to visit her class to check what action the groups were recommending for different emergency scenarios in their workplace.

Glen Poupore's advice is relevant here: when asking students to present their results, you should create a high expectation in terms of the quality of their presentation (be it oral or written) as this will make them focus on accuracy a little more. If it's an oral presentation, you can still collect a written report sheet of their ideas.

The report could, of course, be written instead of spoken, or written up for homework after an oral report in class. The reports could then be read by other groups (inside the class or outside) who read them to compare content, or list interesting ideas, or for some other specific purpose.

We looked briefly in Chapter 7 at teacher roles. When chairing a report-back stage, it is important to react initially to the content of what is said, to summarize the main points, or pick out some of the most interesting details and comment on them. Jason Moser, who found that students' reports were often rather general, began to ask for more details during the report stage, thus pushing their output even more by exploring more deeply. He writes: 'One girl said her dog doesn't like going for walks. I asked why and how does she know? I also asked what he likes to do instead?' Pushing for more detail is also a very useful teacher tactic at the planning stage, between the task and report, as it gives learners more time to think and plan.

If the message is not totally clear, some clarification and occasional recasting of student utterances may be necessary, but it might be more profitable to allow time for some sustained form-focused work after the report-back stage; this follows the principle of meaning first, form-focused work later.

Whether private or public, written or spoken, this report stage allows learners to recycle, refine and extend the language they have already used in pairs or groups when doing the task together. However, there may well be occasions where you feel a report stage is not appropriate, if you are, for example, doing a series of short tasks, or task repetitions (see below), you might simply do one report at the end of the series of tasks, not after each one. Or you might want learners to write or record their own report for homework, to be read or played back in a future class. This allows more time for language reflection—another benefit. Or if the task did not go very well for some reason, it might be best to do a quick teacher-led summary and move on quickly to something different.

8.8.3 Task repetition

The advantages of repeating tasks are many and varied. There is a fair amount of research (Bygate 2001; Ellis 2003; Lynch and Maclean 2001; Essig 2005; Pinter 2006) to show that getting learners to repeat the same task (or the same report) but with different partners results in a richer use of vocabulary and a higher degree of accuracy and grammatical complexity. For example, in the first attempt, one of Essig's learners said: 'I rushed into a mistake train'; in the second, this became: 'I dashed into the wrong train'. Pinter found that, in addition to the above benefits, ten-year-old children doubled their speech rate over three repetitions of a task—they paused less and spoke with more confidence, often picking up new structures from each other.

Jason Moser in Japan makes the point that students are exposed to a wider variety of language when repeating tasks with different people and he reports that, with young adult learners, 'from repetition emerges more language play and risk-taking as students get comfortable. The repetition really helped students open up …'. Learners, even children (see Pinter 2005), often feel slightly dissatisfied with their initial task performance and generally welcome a chance to do it again later and better. We know from our recent experience of learning Spanish that we very often think back over what we've said in Spanish and recall better words and phrases that we could have used.

The time lag between task repetitions can vary from an immediate repetition, or even two, three, or four repetitions with different speaking partners in the same lesson, as reported by Jason Moser (see 'Talking about animals and pets' in Chapter 5 (5.6)), to repetitions after a day or two, or a week or so. Maggie Baigent's students enjoyed repeating their stories in the following lesson, after some in-class analysis of the structure of two familiar stories and a chance to reformulate their own. Task repetition can also be done in preparation for an end-of-term test or an exam. Here, you might tell learners in advance that they will have a chance to repeat some of the tasks they have done that term. And beforehand encourage them to expand their vocabulary, try out new language, and make their contributions as detailed as possible.

In our research for this book, teachers reported setting strict time limits for each repetition. Limits range from between two minutes to eight minutes for an intermediate level conversational task. In a repeat storytelling task, shortening the time limit for each story repetition from 6 minutes to 4 to 2 (an idea from Nation 2001), proved challenging and great fun.

After the final task repetition, most teachers required learners to write a report including the most interesting things they had found out. This gives them time to recall useful words, recycle language and ask about it, and write down points they want to remember.

8.8.4 Post-task language work

In Chapter 6, we made the distinction between language focus and form focus. The first is when learners are focusing on language in the context of the meanings they want to express. This might occur at a pre-task planning stage, or between the task and report stage, when students are shaping what they want to say in their report, helped by the teacher in their role of linguistic adviser. So this is mainly learner led.

As we saw in Chapter 6 (6.5), focus on form is teacher led, and focuses on specific forms (for example, verb phrases expressing obligation, or words ending in '-ly',) that occur in the texts and/or recordings from the task cycle or from earlier lessons that students are already familiar with and have processed for meaning. This kind of focus on form follows the task or task cycle; it is generally pre-planned, and forms part of the language syllabus. Its purpose is to help students systematize what they know, and to expand their conscious knowledge of words and patterns.

For example, in the task we expanded on above, after listening to Catherine's recording, learners could be asked to listen and write down the words and phrases that go either before or after the key phrases they were asked to look out for (see section 8.2), for example, '*don't waste time* travelling', '*take up* a lot of room'. This would help them learn more from the listening text, and they might find such phrases useful for talking about their own circumstances later. (The transcript for this listening text is in Appendix 3.3.)

In addition to these, there are other more impromptu ways of focusing on the language that learners have used.

Teachers collecting examples As suggested in 8.6 above, during the task or report, make a note of useful expressions learners have used, any collocations that need attention, and one or two recurring errors that you can offer alternative wordings for—or cover in a subsequent lesson when you have had time to think. You could also list words or expressions they needed and didn't know. Maria Leedham, for example, listens and takes notes while her learners are doing a 'milling' task, circulating amongst other learners getting answers to questions on their 'question cards'. She explains 'I then deal with language problems (after the task) by eliciting other ways of saying something or eliciting corrections or useful collocations'. As we have said before, it is very important not to focus solely on errors and correction, but to comment on, build on and extend useful expressions and patterns, ending the task cycle on a positive note.

Analysing task recordings If you can get learners to record themselves performing or reporting back on the task, and transcribe a short section for homework, they could compare their interaction with that of more fluent speakers doing the same task. For example, Maria Leedham got her exam class to record themselves doing mock oral test tasks, and when they compared their own task interactions with those done by fluent speakers, they found significant differences in turn-taking procedures and length of utterances. Learners tended to speak in whole sentences very much as they would write, and then stop, to give their partners a chance to say a sentence, while native-speakers used far shorter exploratory utterances—building on each other's contributions. To express agreement, native-speakers used 'yeah', 'mmm', and lexical repetition, rather than whole phrases like 'I strongly agree', which learners used a lot (Leedham 2005: 98). From comparing recordings, learners can notice many other useful linguistic features and widen their repertoire of conversational strategies.

The value of asking learners to record and transcribe was mentioned by several teachers. Heidi Vande Voort Nam reports: 'during the transcription phase, many trainees wanted to write what they wish they had said rather than what they had actually said'. So she allowed them to write a second, more idealized, version.

8.8.5 Evaluation and reflection

At the end of a task cycle, or even in the next lesson, many teachers get their students to think back over the previous task cycle and write down how they felt about it on a slip of paper and hand it in anonymously. It's best to be specific, for example: 'Write two things you enjoyed about the lesson(s) and one thing you didn't like or make a suggestion for an improvement'. Some teachers hold an informal class feedback session after each main task cycle; others occasionally interview students in their mother-tongue in small groups outside the class and note down how they feel. Pinter (2005) did this with ten-year-old Hungarian children with success; some do this and record feed-back to analyse later.

Corony Edwards (Edwards and J. Willis 2005: 264) wanted to find out about one aspect of her teaching: she asked a very quiet, rather unresponsive class to write how they felt when she made an open invitation to the whole class to ask questions or to comment on something. She reports 'the twenty-one anonymous responses I received, written on tiny slips (3 cm × 5 cm), were enough for me to write a three-page report for the students, told me a lot about the way I was managing the group and resulted in much more interactive classes from then on'. Not only did she profit as a teacher, but the students benefited too; they really enjoyed reading the report; they realized others had similar feelings and began to overcome their fear of talking in class.

So getting feed-back does not need to be a cumbersome process—use small slips of paper and allow three or four minutes thinking time, and you'll get some enlightening data which will help you tailor your tasks and techniques to suit your learners even better.

READER ACTIVITY 8D

Applying the parameters: same task but different instructions

Choose one of the tasks you designed while reading Chapters 3, 4, or 5, or a textbook task, or one you have used recently. Bearing in mind the parameters above, write out two sets of task instructions, adapting the task to suit:

1 a class of very shy learners who know quite a lot, write quite well but lack confidence in their spoken English;

2 a class of fairly confident, reasonably fluent but laid back learners who need pushing towards accuracy in their spoken and written English; and

3 decide for one of them how you would get feed-back after the lesson.

8.9 Review

In this chapter we have distinguished seven broad parameters of task design and within each of those, considered different variables that can be selected, adjusted and implemented when setting up and carrying out a task. Keeping these in mind when appraising tasks and planning task-based lessons will help you to:

• select the best parameters for your learners at different points in their course;
• write/give clear task instructions so that learners feel secure and know what to do at all stages;
• evaluate tasks and activities that appear in coursebooks and be aware of the many ways you can adapt them so they suit your students better;
• be more flexible in class—knowing what parameters you can change during a lesson, and how to change them to enhance different kinds of learning opportunities;
• reflect on the lesson afterwards and think what you might change if you did the same task with another class;
• reflect on the lesson and plan what parameters you might change when you set up the next task for the same class, to give variety; and
• explain to others what aspects of TBT lessons you can adjust, and give more specific feedback to colleagues if they tell you they have done a task which didn't work.

8.10 Further exploration: investigating your teaching

These parameters can also help you to plan small-scale action research projects, and become more experimental in your teaching. They can help you narrow down and specify what aspect of your teaching you want to examine more closely, or write about for a course assessment. You can, for example, change just one variable and repeat the task, recording the interactions to see what differences this one change makes. You will always learn something new from exploring your teaching and it can be very satisfying indeed.

8.11 Follow-up activity

Choose a task that you have planned or tried out in class recently.

- Appraise it by thinking about it in terms of some of the parameters above. Which parameter(s) might you change in order to improve the way the task works? Or which might you like to experiment with? Choose one.
- Plan to change this one parameter next time you try the task out. Think how you will observe the results and get feedback during and/or after the lesson. (Record some of the pair work, or a specific section of the lesson? Ask a colleague to observe? Ask learners for their feed-back?)
- Try the task out again, with the new parameter, note down what happens and get feed-back. Tell others about it or write a short report of your experiment for others to read.

Further reading

For a more in-depth treatment of the principles behind some of the parameters in this chapter, read Skehan 1998 Chapter 3 on 'Psycholinguistic processes in language use and language learning'.

For more ideas on what to explore, and how to observe the results, see Edwards and J. Willis (eds.) 2005: 269–76, where Edwards summarizes 18 informal investigations into aspects of TBT carried out by teachers in different countries. Full accounts of these investigations are given in Edwards and J. Willis (eds.) 2005.

If you want some ideas for task-based writing activities, try:
Kelly, C. with **A. Gargagliano**. 2001. *Writing from Within*. Cambridge: Cambridge University Press.
Kelly, C. with **A. Gargagliano**. 2004. *Writing from Within: Introductory*. Cambridge: Cambridge University Press.

More formal research findings and their implications for the design of tasks and TBT in general, can be found in Ellis 2003, especially Chapters 1–4.

9 DESIGNING A TASK-BASED SYLLABUS

9.1 The language-based syllabus

We have seen throughout that a task-based approach to learning and teaching takes meaning as its starting point. In doing this it contrasts with approaches which take language form as their starting point. An approach which starts from language form specifies its syllabus in terms of form. It lists items like 'the present continuous tense', 'the first conditional', and 'the definite article' as learning goals and builds teaching units and sequences around such items. Normally the syllabus has more than one strand. So the basic syllabus specification may list linguistic items like those shown above, but it will also take account of other considerations. There will certainly be a lexical strand to the syllabus. This will probably be topic based. The syllabus designer will list the topics to be covered in the course and will then list the most important words associated with these topics. There will probably be a functional strand to the syllabus. Care will be taken to ensure that learners are able to make suggestions, to offer invitations, to express agreement and disagreement and so on. But the organizing principle of the course will be a list of language forms which will be treated systematically and built up gradually throughout the course.

The problem with this approach to syllabus design is that it rests on doubtful assumptions about the way a language is learnt. It is based on the assumption that language learning is additive, that we acquire one form, then move on to the next which is mastered in turn, and so on. But language learning is much more complicated than this. It is a complex process of formulating and checking hypotheses about the language. When, for example, learners are first introduced to the form 'going to' to talk about the future they may well assume that 'going to' is used for all future actions. Later when they come across the modal 'will' they realize that there are other ways of expressing the future. They have to abandon their former hypothesis and work out, probably with guidance from their teacher, when to use 'will' and when to use 'going to'. They have to adjust their picture of 'going to' to accommodate the use of 'will'.

At a later stage they are introduced to clauses with 'if' and with time conjunctions:

> If you miss your train, you'll be late.
> I'll tell her when I see her.
> I'll come home as soon as I finish work.

At first learners have a tendency to use the modal 'will' in these clauses:

> *If you *will* miss your train you'll be late.

They have to learn that there are restrictions on the use of 'will'. Again they have to adjust their picture of the language in the light of new information. So learning is not simply a matter of adding new knowledge. It often involves reviewing previous knowledge.

A structural approach can make some allowance for this by building a cyclical element into the syllabus. But, surely, this is simply an admission that it is built on insecure foundations. It sets out to achieve item-by-item mastery, and it evaluates learners on this basis. But it then acknowledges that this is unrealistic by recycling items in the hope that they will be mastered at the second or third attempt. It seems that a more realistic approach is to accept from the start that learners do not achieve control of language items in this way and find an alternative approach.

There is, as we have seen earlier, another reason why language learning is a dynamic process. Learners are not simply acquiring language forms; they are learning to put them to use. They are trying to fashion a usable meaning system from the bewildering range of language forms to which they are exposed. By a 'usable meaning system' we mean one which they can operate with in real time. In Chapter 1 (1.5) we looked at the problems learners have in using 'do'-questions with any consistency. They go through a stage when they can form 'do'-questions when they have time to think, in a grammar test, for example. But when they are using language spontaneously the complex 'do'-questions do not spring to their lips. They rely instead on intonation and produce forms like 'Where you live?' and 'What mean X?' So very often they do not simply learn something and then put it immediately to use. They have to go through a waiting period in which the new form gradually becomes more familiar, until finally it becomes automatic. So at any stage the learner's knowledge of the language is very complex. Some items, like 'will' and 'going to' have been learnt, but are in the process of being refined. Other items have been learnt but are not yet applied automatically.

So even though a language syllabus needs to be itemized, we need to recognize that learning is not a simple additive process in which learners gradually add one item after another to their repertoire. But there is a contradiction here, because, in a sense, language teaching must always be additive. We cannot attempt to teach the whole language at once. Once we become involved in teaching we are obliged to break language down into individual items—words, phrases, patterns, rules, and so on. We isolate these items and try to make them accessible to learners. So we adopt procedures which seem to treat learning as an additive process, one which sees learners as adding one item at a time until they have a complete picture of the language. There is, then, a conflict between the dynamic way in which learners learn and the additive way in which teachers are obliged to teach.

How is that conflict to be resolved? As we have already pointed out, part of the answer to this question is to treat the syllabus as cyclical. So that a given item is not simply taught once; it is revisited and reviewed several times. It is, however, possible to propose a more radical solution. In this chapter we shall look at different task-based approaches to syllabus design and finally at the notion of the *pedagogic corpus* which offers a solution to the problem of reconciling the dynamic nature of learning with the fact that teaching is necessarily additive.

9.2 A meaning-based approach

9.2.1 What do learners want to mean?

As we have seen, a task-based approach focuses sharply on language as a meaning system. So as a starting point for a task-based syllabus we should ask the question 'What will learners want to mean?' or 'What will learners want to do with the language?' If we take this starting point, it will first oblige us to acknowledge the importance of vocabulary in language learning. In specifying what learners want to mean we will be very much concerned with specifying the topics they want to handle in English. Secondly we need to ask questions about what learners will want to do with the language and in what circumstances. Will they be concerned mainly with the written or the spoken form? Will they want language for instruction or will they be mainly concerned with the social uses of language? How tolerant will people be of any failings, in other words what degree of accuracy will be expected of them; how hard will people be prepared to work to ensure a successful interaction? For example, there will probably be a high level of tolerance if a learner is acting in the role of a hotel guest, but a relatively low level of tolerance if the learner is in the role of hotel receptionist.

9.2.2 ESP courses

Clearly learners' needs will vary from one group to another. Learners may want English for highly specific purposes. For example, in Chapter 3 (3.4) and Chapter 7 (7.2.1) we looked at tasks designed by Joann Chernen for trainee bakers. The priority in her course was to enable learners to undergo training in English in a closely defined area of study. This dictated not only the kind of vocabulary that she taught, but also the kind of activity she brought into the classroom. In the example we looked at learners were focusing on the vocabulary to do with the making of chou paste, and they were working on activities which involved note-taking and classroom discussion. These were topics and activities which focused directly on the vocabulary her learners would need for their training and the kind of language activities they would need to engage in. So a well-designed specialist course will focus on a limited range of lexical topics and language activities. These topics and activities will be determined by a needs analysis, which involves a close study of the target-language-using situations. This is not a simple process. It involves careful observation, recording and analysis of language in use. But it pays off in the classroom by ensuring that learners' time is well spent because they focus on topics and activities that are important for them.

Jabbour (1997) describes the design of a course for medical students who needed to read medical research articles. In the course of her research she consulted medical experts and medical students to learn more about how they set about reading research articles and what they expected to gain from the process. In most cases the reading involved skimming quickly through the introduction to the article to determine if it was relevant. If the reader decided the article was probably worth reading, the next stage was to skip to the findings section at the end of the article. Only if this confirmed the value of the paper would the reader set about a detailed reading. As a result of this finding Jabbour designed activities which encouraged learners to scan the introductory sections and predict the kind of information that might be found in the section on the findings of the research. Without this careful needs analysis she might simply have assumed that students would read through the article from beginning to end, making notes as they did so. In fact this happens comparatively rarely. So a careful analysis of what language learners will need to process and for what purpose, and how they will use the language, can ensure that valuable classroom time is put to the best possible use.

Content-based courses are sometimes used for more advanced learners of English who are interested in particular topic areas. For example, Lorie Wood designed a task-based course entitled 'English and Global Issues' for her tertiary level students. Her draft Course Plan appears in Appendix 5.

9.2.3 English for general purposes

Learners often want English for everyday purposes, in order to interact with other users of English in a range of settings—as friends, as tourists, as providers and recipients of goods and services, and so on. And many adult classes contain students with a variety of different needs. If we are to define a syllabus for such general learners we need to list what it is that learners want to do with their English, the situations in which they will want to operate and the topics they will want to cover. In some countries, ministries of education stipulate topics and situations and criteria or benchmarks for different levels. The *Canadian Language Benchmarks* is one good example for ESL. Many European countries draw on the *Common European Framework* (*CEF*) (Council of Europe 2001) document as a basis for language syllabus design. This document was produced under the auspices of the European Council of Ministers to specify the content of syllabuses for the teaching of all European languages. It is a brave and seemingly thorough attempt to foresee the needs of general learners. But the *CEF* is far from perfect: it is often very difficult to interpret; and we take issue with it on some basic questions, and find it over-elaborate in a number of ways. It does, however, provide a useful starting point to illustrate the principles of syllabus specification. In section 9.3, below, we will look in detail at the development of a syllabus based on the *CEF*.

9.2.4 English for examination purposes

In many cases learners are working towards an examination. If the examination is well designed it will be a test of learners' ability to use the language. (See FAQ 10.13 in Chapter 10.) If this is the case, then, it will match well with a task-based methodology. Learners will be asked to do under examination conditions the sort of thing they have become accustomed to doing in the classroom. An oral examination, for example, might ask candidates to tell a story and give instructions. They will be marked on their ability to do these things effectively, and their ability to produce accurate samples of the language will be considered in that context. Their reading skill will be tested by testing their ability to retrieve relevant information from English text. So they might, for example, be asked to provide directions to a hotel. In order to do this they may have to match information from an email message with information from a map in order to provide appropriate instructions. In both these cases there is a good match between the kind of things learners do in the task-based classroom and the things they are asked to do in the examination. It will be necessary to ensure that learners get examination practice so that they know what is expected of them and get used to the conditions of the examination, but in general they will be well prepared.

At the other extreme, however, there are examinations which focus very sharply on form rather than on content. Learners are asked to complete gapped sentences, or to answer questions in a multiple-choice format. Activities like this are far removed from language use. But the work that learners do in the task-based classroom will have prepared them for the examination in that their language will have developed in terms of accuracy as well as communication. In preparing learners for an examination of this kind, however, it will be important to follow up task-based and form-focused activities with test items which mirror the form of the examination. At the end of each unit, for example, they may be given a test in multiple choice format which relates closely to the content of the unit, but also goes beyond it. So examination preparation will supplement, but not replace task-based work. For examination classes it is necessary to build an extra strand into the syllabus to ensure that learners have sufficient practice of working with examination formats and in examination conditions.

9.2.5 Starting from the coursebook

There is something reassuring about a glossy, well-illustrated coursebook. Not only is it attractive, but it also carries an appearance of authority. In some situations students demand the security of a coursebook. So teachers are forced to adopt a coursebook and work with it, even if they cannot find a book which really fits the needs of their students. In this case they may choose to work with a coursebook, adapting it along the lines suggested in Chapter 8, or they may choose to adopt one or more coursebooks and build a whole task-based programme round them. This is what Jason Moser decided to do in Japan.

Jason co-ordinated the introduction of TBL into the obligatory two-year language program at Osaka Shoin Women's University. English had become very unpopular, partly because students had no immediate need for it outside the class. They were not motivated by a grammar-based approach because it didn't convince them they could do anything with the language they were learning. Jason's aim was to get all students to enjoy using English socially in the classroom and to use English to learn about life. Jason was working with 28 teachers, ten Japanese and eighteen expatriate, to design a TBL program, with a task sequence for each lesson. The programme was based on three books. The first was *Writing From Within: Introductory* (Kelly and Gargagliano 2004) which Jason describes as 'a task-based writing course which works on the premise that what students won't say orally they will express through writing'. The second was *Touchstone 1* (McCarthy *et al.* 2005). This is not a task-based course in itself, but it does offer opportunities for building in task sequences, some of which are highlighted in the comprehensive teacher's book. Finally there was *Focus on Grammar* (Fuchs *et al.* 1994), which is basically grammatical but has consciousness-raising activities and comprehensive listening and grammar explanations in Japanese. Between them, these books gave a pretty thorough coverage of the language that teachers regarded as important and of the language that students needed for the tasks, for basic socializing and learning and talking about life. Jason reports:

If textbook lessons didn't have tasks or they were too hard/simple, boring or whatever we tweaked or supplemented with tasks chosen on the basis of the need for a variety of task types, pleasure, and difficulty level. We designated a main task for each lesson. So lesson planning meant figuring out how to use the task and then to build a sequence around it. After several months of preparation, seminars, observations identifying 'authentic' i.e. meaning-focused use of language, handouts, keeping journals, constant teacher support during which we solved initial problems like how to sequence a lesson effectively, how to adapt and improve tasks, where and how to push output, we have now got over 700 students learning through a TBL approach, and another (larger) college campus wanting to do the same.

One of the keys that has sold the program to teachers is seeing how much students come to life during the task cycle. Another key to success was providing the teachers with excellent and stimulating material that they would enjoy too. Tasks needed to be fun for both teacher and student.

His advice to other program co-ordinators wanting to implement a TBL program is:

Basically … get all teachers (even dissenting ones) using the same tasks and material and to work from there. This is what I call 'working out of the same box'. This gets people speaking the same language and it challenges them to think. It's important, too, to get teachers thinking in terms of a holistic teaching sequence. Other than that, just courage and commitment to push ahead.

At the end of the year we ask for feedback on the tasks but during the year we go with the tasks we have planned, sharpening them up at the start of every week. If everyone does what they like and chooses their own tasks and supplementary materials, your program won't become TBL. Putting us 'in a box' has pushed teachers to really deal with the issues of TBL. In one way our TBL program has been TBL for our teachers! By setting parameters you force creativity.

9.3 From 'can do' statements to tasks and texts

9.3.1 The concept of 'can do'

The *CEF* lists a number of 'can do' statements at each level. These are described as 'learning outcomes' and list the things learners should be able to do as a result of completing a course at a given level. These 'can do' statements are organized under broad categories relating to the type of communication involved, circumstances of that communication and the level at which learners are operating. Let us look at a sample of 'can do' statements at the elementary level under the heading 'Sustained monologue—describing experience'.

- Can tell a story or describe something in a simple list of points.
- Can describe everyday aspects of his/her environment, for example: people, places, a job, or study experience.
- Can give short, basic descriptions of events and activities.
- Can describe plans and arrangements, habits and routines, past activities and personal experiences.
- Can use simple descriptive language to make brief statements about and compare objects and possessions.
- Can explain what he/she likes or dislikes about something. (*CEF* p. 59)

The next question to ask is what topics should be covered in a syllabus. Here again the *CEF* offers guidelines listing fourteen topics such as 'House and home', 'Health and body care', 'Food and drink', 'Daily life', and 'Weather' (p. 52). These are broken down in turn into sub-categories to give a more precise specification.

Let us take the statements 'Can give short, basic descriptions of events and activities' and 'Can describe ... past activities and personal experiences'. We can combine these with the topic 'Daily life' to help generate a task sequence which might be carried out in the classroom. The sequence could focus on narratives to do with a busy day, along the lines of the task sequence we looked at in Chapter 2 (2.2). The sequence could begin with a recording of someone talking about a busy day. We have used a recording by David Foll, an English teacher working in London, talking about a busy day he had had:

> The busiest day I've had recently was last Monday. I taught in three different schools. So on Monday morning I taught in one school from 9.30 to 12.30. Then I went home and on the way home I had to do a lot of food shopping. Then I had lunch—I just had time to have lunch—then I went out again. I went to another school on the other side of London, where I taught from four to six. Then I had half an hour to get from that school down to another school in the centre of London for six-thirty to eight-thirty. Then I got home and I went out for supper afterwards with friends. So that was quite a busy day.
> (J. Willis and D. Willis 1988)

Learners were asked to listen and work in groups to make a list of what David did on his busy day. They were then asked to make notes of not more than fifteen words and use these notes to tell the class about David's day. Finally they were asked to talk about a busy day of their own and to decide in their groups who had had the busiest day.

This task sequence relates precisely to specific learner outcomes. It involves listening to and understanding an anecdote relating to everyday life. But not all task sequences need to relate directly to learner outcomes. In Chapter 2 (2.3.2) we looked at a task which involved remembering objects on a tray. We pointed out that this was not a real-world task or, in *CEF* terminology, a learner outcome. But we justified this task sequence on the grounds that all the way through learners are concerned with real-world meanings. They are expressing the location of objects relative to one another. It is possible to justify a task sequence, particularly at an elementary level on the grounds that it will contribute to a real world task or learner outcome. Tasks such as these are what Long and Crookes (1992) refer to as 'pedagogic' tasks.

9.3.2 Grading tasks

One of the problems we need to tackle is the question of grading tasks. Skehan (1998: 99) offers a list of variables for assessing the difficulty of tasks. The list is too extensive to include in its entirety here, but it includes features such as:

- *Cognitive familiarity* of topic and its predictability. Some topics, such as the family, will be well known to learners, something they talk about frequently in their first language. Other topics, such as 'Volcanoes' (see Chapter 4 (4.3.2)) might be new to them. They may even need to do some research before being able to handle a topic like this. The 'Busy day' task above would rate highly in terms of familiarity; since learners are talking about their own experience it is clearly something well known to them.

- *Cognitive processing* The amount of computation. How much work do language users have to do in preparing their message, or how much intellectual effort is required in understanding a message? A text about a volcano which simply recounts an anecdotal experience would be much lighter in terms of cognitive processing than a text which explains how an eruption occurs. The 'Busy day' task is not intellectually demanding, so there is little in the way of computation once the events of the day have been recalled.

- *Communicative stress* Time limits and time pressure. A task is much easier if learners have time to think about it before they begin to tackle it. The amount of communicative stress can be controlled. If, for example, learners are asked to prepare the topic for homework, there will be no time pressure, but if they are suddenly asked to produce a narrative spontaneously this will be much more difficult.

- *Code complexity* Linguistic complexity and variety. To some extent code complexity will be determined by the learners themselves. They may be very ambitious in their chosen story, or they may choose something less demanding. We can, however, impose more demands on linguistic complexity. If, for example, learners were asked to talk about their most embarrassing experience this would probably be lexically more demanding. It would also require more in the way of organization and evaluation of events, which again would make more linguistic demands.

Prabhu (1987), one of the first to experiment with task-based teaching, believed that the most reliable guide to task difficulty was the teacher's intuition. Teachers would usually be able to tell simply by looking at a task whether it was appropriate for a particular group of students. A checklist like that offered by Skehan is a useful way of sharpening and focusing teacher intuitions, but it cannot provide any guaranteed solutions. The best way forward is probably to rely on your knowledge of a particular class and your experience of the way they have handled other tasks. You can then design or select a task bearing general criteria in mind. The next stage is to look at the seven parameters listed in Chapter 8 in order to vary the demands placed on learners. If you try a task and it proves too easy or too difficult you can adjust the parameters the next time you use the task.

A strong guide to the complexity of a task is given by the associated texts which you have selected or created as part of the task sequence. Joann Chernen's chou paste task (see Chapter 3 (3.4) and Chapter 7 (7.2.1)) begins with a text. Teachers are used to assessing the relative difficulty of reading passages like this. It is reasonable to assume that if the text is accessible to learners then the associated task will be within their ability. The same applies to the spoken text associated with our 'Busy day' task. It is, then, reasonable to assess the difficulty of tasks by looking at associated texts.

Given this, we can take an inventory of the *CEF* 'can do' statements or learner outcomes together with a list of topics as a starting point for syllabus design. A learner outcome in this sense is a target performance—what we expect learners to be able to do as a result of their classroom experience. Learner outcomes can be used to generate a series of tasks. We can then identify or create one or more texts to accompany each task. Depending on the desired learner outcome, this may be a spoken text as in the example we have given. Given a learner outcome relating to reading such as:

- can find specific, predictable information in simple everyday material such as advertisements, prospectuses, menus and timetables (p. 70)

we would design a task based on a written text.

So far, we have shown that by working carefully with an inventory like that provided by the *CEF* it is possible to design a series of tasks to provide learners with the communicative experience they will need to use the language effectively outside the classroom. There will be careful selection of learner outcomes, texts and tasks to ensure that there is appropriate topic coverage. In designing or selecting tasks and ordering them to create a syllabus we will take account of the perceived difficulty of the task. This perception will be sharpened with reference to a checklist such as that provided by Skehan (1998). Perceived difficulty can be adjusted by applying the parameters listed in Chapter 8. Finally, an indication of task difficulty will be provided by the associated texts.

But there is still a serious omission in our syllabus specification. It does not specify what language will be covered and in what order. Ellis poses the question:

> Which forms should be included and in what order? These questions raise in turn the problem facing linguistic syllabuses in general, namely how the teaching syllabus can be made to match the learner's inbuilt syllabus. A focus-on-forms approach will flounder if the forms taught do not correspond to those the learner is capable of acquiring.
> (Ellis 2003: 231)

This draws attention to the problem identified in Chapter 1 (1.5). We can 'teach' a language feature in the sense of drawing it to the learner's attention and offering some explanation or illustration, but we cannot guarantee that it will be acquired in the sense that learners will make it a part of their spontaneous repertoire. We gave the example of 'do'-questions. Learners go through a stage at which they know these forms in that they are able to understand how 'do'-questions are formed and to produce them when their attention is entirely on form. But at the same time they do not know them in that they consistently fail to produce them on appropriate occasions. The question Ellis asks is how can we ensure that we provide a focus on forms at the appropriate stage in a learner's development. A possible answer to this conundrum is to shift our idea of what constitutes learning. It is not useful to think of learning as the incremental acquisition of a series of language items, because that is not how learning happens. Let us therefore try to think of learning in a more developmental way.

9.4 Language coverage and the pedagogic corpus

9.4.1 The pedagogic corpus

Nowadays, when grammarians or lexicographers go about describing the grammar of a language, they often begin by collecting a very large sample of the language usually running to many millions of words, which they call a *corpus*. That corpus is then assembled on a computer to provide data, on the basis of which they can formulate a description of the language. Once the data is available the scholar can use the computer to summon up in an instant a large number of examples of the language feature which he wishes to study, usually in the form of KWIC concordances. The acronym KWIC stands for 'Key Word In Context'. The 'key word' is the word under study, sometimes referred to as the 'node word'. If we think of the word 'would', for example, as a key word, then a sample from a KWIC concordance might look like this:

1 What *would* you do if you were Mr. Botibol
2 It's not the sort of letter I *would* like to receive.
3 What *would* you cook for an unexpected guest?
4 While we were singing people *would* come up to us and try to speak to us.
5 What advice *would* you give to a young person leaving school?
6 We enjoyed it because people *would* gather round us and they would join in.
7 They announced that the Prime Minister *would* speak on television
8 What precautions *would* you take if you were camping in a game park?
9 Yes I *would* agree.
10 Often there *would* be a village band playing
11 How much *would* that cost in a restaurant?
12 Some of us *would* write our own songs and set them to music
13 Then we said that we *would* play hide and seek
14 Yes, I *would* think so.
15 I suppose the cheapest way *would* be to go by bus.

In a large corpus there would be many thousand occurrences of the word 'would' but a grammarian would probably be content with a sample of around 500. A close look at this sample reveals that 'would' has the following meanings and uses:

1 to express a hypothesis, as in examples 1, 3, 5, 8, 11, and 15 above. When it is used with this hypothetical meaning it sometimes occurs in a conditional sentence as in examples 1 and 8.
2 to refer to a past habit, meaning the same as 'used to' as in examples 4, 6, 8, 10, and 12.
3 as the past tense of 'will' in reported thought or speech as in examples 7 and 13.
4 in a number of fixed phrases such as 'would like' in example 2.
5 to moderate an expression of opinion as in 'I would agree' in example 9 and 'I would think' in example 14.

The corpus linguist will use this information as the basis of the description of 'would'. There is, of course, a good deal more to be learnt about 'would' from concordances. For example, many years ago, before we saw concordance evidence we thought that the second use listed above, 'would' as 'used to', was relatively rare and confined to formal slightly old-fashioned usage. But when we looked at statistical information based on corpora we found that it accounts for around 20 per cent of the occurrences of 'would'. In fact, 'would' meaning 'used to' is more frequent than 'used to' meaning 'used to'! In this way a corpus grammarian builds up more and more information about the language and so builds up a more and more satisfactory description. What other words are used with 'would' to moderate an opinion as well as 'agree' and 'think'? A corpus search would identify 'argue' and 'suggest' as likely items.

There are, of course, important differences between the way a corpus grammarian works and the way a learners works. The grammarian already knows the language in that he is a competent and sophisticated user of the language. He uses a *research corpus* to work towards an explicit description of the language which will perhaps be incorporated in a grammar or dictionary. Learners, on the other hand, are not competent and sophisticated users. They are trying to internalize a working model of the language. They use the language they are exposed to as a pedagogic corpus to help them build up a more and more complex and precise picture of the way the language works even though they may not be able to explain the rules which lie behind their language behaviour. But both the grammarian and the learner are involved in a process which involves using language data to form hypotheses about the way the language works, and then to refine and test those hypotheses.

In section 9.3.2 above we showed how it is possible to move from learner outcomes to generate tasks and then to create or select texts which form a pedagogic corpus. As learners work with these texts they will inevitably formulate hypotheses about how the language works. As, for example, they come across the modal 'would' they begin to formulate hypotheses about its meanings and uses. The same applies to the other language they are exposed to. It all provides input for learning. So as they are processing texts for meaning learners are also using it as input to provide insights into the workings of the target language. This is something that will be encouraged by a methodology which prompts learners to look at language for themselves.

9.4.2 The role of the course designer and teacher

If we see the learner as working in the way described above, then we can see the job of the course designer and teacher as fourfold:

1 to provide a pedagogic corpus made up of texts which contain sufficient and appropriate raw material for learners to generate the insights they need about the target language to enable them to operate effectively as language users. So texts need to contain appropriate vocabulary which covers the domains in which learners are likely to operate. They need also to illustrate the grammatical knowledge learners will need to acquire;

2 to provide learners with guidance, or instruction, to help them make appropriate generalizations about the language they are exposed to;

3 to provide activities which encourage learners to analyse the language they are exposed to in a way which will enhance learning and make it more efficient; and

4 to encourage learners to practise the language they have been exposed to.

The last three of these requirements were the subject of Chapter 6, in which we looked at language-focused and form-focused activities.

A specification of appropriate learner outcomes together with associated texts is likely to provide sufficient coverage of basic grammar. The sample text about a busy day, for example, illustrates the tense patterns necessary for the outcome with relevant time expressions. It links sentences with coordinators like 'so', 'and', and 'then', which are typical of informal spoken discourse. The overall structure of the text is typical of a spoken narrative with an introductory sentence: 'The busiest day I've had recently was last Monday'; and a summarizing sentence: 'So that was quite a busy day'. Overall the text provides reasonable coverage of the grammar which is central to constructing an anecdote about everyday life.

It also offers illustrations of other useful features of language, which we will now look at.

READER ACTIVITY 9A

Identifying a form focus

What other language features can you find in the 'Busy day' text in section 9.3.1 above, which would be useful for learners at the elementary level?

Commentary

You probably found quite a number of useful language features. Here are a few you might have listed:

- time expression 'from … to …': 'from four to six', 'six-thirty to eight-thirty'
- use of 'got' to mean 'reached': 'then I got home'
- uses of 'had':

  for necessity: 'I had to do a lot of food shopping.'
  with time expressions: 'I had half an hour to get from that school …'
  'I just had time to have lunch.'
  with meals: 'I had lunch', '…time to have lunch'

- relative clause with 'where': 'another school,' '… where I taught from four to six.'
- use of 'quite' as a modifier: 'So that was quite a busy day.'

We may draw attention to these features by setting up consciousness-raising activities, for example:

Pick out all the phrases with 'have'. Think of three ways to classify them.

or by using a repetition drill, for example, to highlight the 'where' relative:

What do you call a place where you have lessons?/the room where you eat?/a shop where you buy bread? etc.

Here are some answers. Can you ask the questions?
the bedroom, a shoe shop, a swimming pool, a cinema, etc.

The aim of these activities is not to enable learners to achieve spontaneous mastery of the items chosen. There are, however, a number of reasons why it is useful to highlight items like these:

- Once learners have noticed them in this context they are more likely to notice these and similar features when they come across them in future texts.
- Once we have highlighted them we can draw attention to them again when we meet a similar feature of language in another text. So when, for example, we come to look in detail at 'have' used to express necessity in a later unit we can resurrect the example we have highlighted here. This builds a powerful recycling element into the syllabus.
- There is just a chance that learners are ready to take one of these insights on board and make it a part of their spontaneous repertoire. If we present learners with a single grammatical item we are highly unlikely to hit on something they are ready to acquire. We are much more likely to find an item like this if we offer a range of possibilities.

9.4.3 Integrating lexis, tasks, and grammar into the syllabus

The following diagram draws heavily on Ellis (2003: 237) in important respects. It makes the point that in the early stages of learning the process is very much lexically driven, with strong emphasis on acquiring relevant topic lexis.

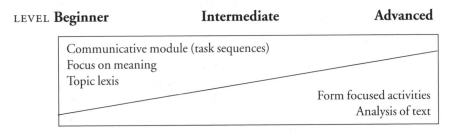

LEVEL **Beginner**   **Intermediate**   **Advanced**

Communicative module (task sequences)
Focus on meaning
Topic lexis

Form focused activities
Analysis of text

Figure 9.1 Changes in the learning process

As learners become more experienced in using the language and have more exposure to language to draw on so they become more able to benefit from that language experience. It becomes more and more realistic and more and more effective to draw on their familiarity with texts. When we begin to do this we begin to see learning in a slightly different light. We no longer see the learning process as adding one item after another to a store of linguistic knowledge. We begin to see it as a growing awareness and sophistication in the ability to process text and to learn from it. We see it as a growing familiarity with a body of texts which have been processed for meaning in the context of a task-based programme. This is a developmental view of learning. We are treating the learners as corpus linguists, accepting that they are involved in a process of discovery. The big difference, of course, is that corpus linguists are engaged in drawing up an explicit description of the language which will go into grammars and dictionaries. Learners are engaged in constructing a usable language system. But there are similarities in that both the corpus linguist and the learner work with text to develop awareness and to discover language.

9.5 Covering important lexis

9.5.1 The most common words

It is unlikely that you are working with an explicitly lexical syllabus in your classrooms. Most syllabuses cover topic lexis. So in a unit on sport, for example, principled decisions will be taken about what sports to cover and what words connected with those sports should be included. But many of the most important and frequent words in the language are used in specific phrases in ways which are not always clearly related to the basic lexical meaning of the word. The word 'take', for example, is used in a range of phrases. We can take a bath or a shower; we can take an exam. It takes time to do something. You can take a quick decision or take account of something. On a journey we take a train or a bus or a taxi. In the busy day text above we noted some important uses of the word 'have'. It is very important to be aware of the power of the most frequent words in the language and to build these into our teaching strategies. It is important to teach with an awareness of lexis, both to get the best out of the classroom materials you have, and also to enable you to supplement those materials.

In Reader activity 9a (section 9.4.2 above) we identified a number of grammatical items from a spoken text which might reasonably be highlighted in form-focused activities. But in addition to covering the kind of grammatical items that are familiar from working with a structural syllabus we need to make sure we provide good coverage of the most frequent words and phrases in English.

In the 1970s and the early 1980s ELT syllabus designers were very attracted by the idea of a *notional* syllabus. The syllabus was described as 'notional' because it tried to list the notions or meanings that were seen as important for learners. Syllabus designers argued that if we could find what meanings people most frequently seek to encode in English, what they most often write and talk about, this would give us a good guide as to what should be included in language syllabuses. But notions or meanings are very abstract. How do we begin to quantify—to count—the meanings in a given stretch of language? A possible answer to this conundrum lay in the work of people like Michael West and the *General Service Wordlist* he produced in 1953. Although it is almost impossible to make a list of the most frequent meanings or notions expressed in English it is possible to make a list of the most frequent words in English—in fact nowadays, using computers, it is not only possible, it is quite easy.

One insight which West offered was that the most frequent words in the language do an awful lot of work. They occur again and again and again. So much so that a mere 700 words account for roughly 70 per cent of all the language, all the texts we hear and read and speak and write in a given day or week or month or year. If we take this further, then we find that the next 800 words in the frequency list account for another 10 per cent of all text. So taking together the most frequent 700 and the next 800, a total of the 1500 most frequent words, we account for 80 per cent of all text. Add another 1000 words, to make 2500, and we can account for 86 per cent of all text. To summarize:

The most frequent 700 words in the language make up 70 per cent of all text.
The most frequent 1500 words make up 80 per cent of all text.
The most frequent 2500 words make up 86 per cent of all text.

At first sight the figures are very surprising, but a look at the first twenty in the frequency list goes some way to explaining the figures:

the, of, and, to, a, in, that, I, it, was, is, he, for, on, you, with, as, be, had, this

The word 'the' on its own accounts for between 5 per cent and 6 per cent of all text. The word 'of' makes up almost 3 per cent of all text. So these two words between them make up around 8 per cent of text.

The problem with words like 'the' and 'of', however, is that by themselves they have no value. They are often called structure words because they don't mean anything until they begin to combine with other words. This means that we are not looking simply for the most frequent words but for the most frequent combinations in which they occur. Consider 'the' and 'of', for example. They are frequently found in phrases like 'the beginning of', 'the end of', 'the middle of', 'the front of', 'the back of'. So we need to highlight not simply the words, but the phrases in which they occur. Because these words are so frequent and occur in all kinds of texts it is likely that we will build up a pretty reliable picture of the way they behave by using the pedagogic corpus. So teachers will readily recognize the importance of structure words like 'the' and 'of'. But there are other high frequency words which are important for learners. How do we identify and deal with these?

9.5.2 How to teach lexically

If we are to give lexis its proper place in the syllabus we need to help students to identify and organize the most important words, phrases and patterns in the language.

Here are some steps you can take to help you achieve this goal:

1 Get hold of frequency lists and familiarize yourself with the most frequent words of the language. We have provided in Appendix 6 a list of the most frequent 200 words in spoken English, together with lists (in alphabetical order) of nouns, verbs, and adjectives found in the most frequent 700 words of English. These are all words that are worth highlighting when they occur in a text which learners process. When you are preparing a text for teaching check out your frequency lists to help you decide what words to focus on.

2 Think carefully about frequent words and ask yourself why they are so frequent. Why, for example, are 'time', 'hand' and 'point' among the most frequent nouns in English? Nowadays good dictionaries are based on careful corpus research and list the most frequent uses of important nouns like these.

The Oxford Advanced Learner's Dictionary lists the following phrases with 'time':

> on time, by the time, this time tomorrow, spare time, a waste of time, a long time ago, at one time, next time, this time, every time

The Macmillan English Dictionary lists the following phrases with 'hand':

> hand in hand, shake hands, give someone a hand, lend a hand, a good hand (of cards), (close/near) at hand, by hand, second hand, hands off, hands up, on hand, on the one hand … on the other hand

The Cambridge Advanced Learner's Dictionary lists the following phrases with 'point':

> The point is, to miss the point, (that's) a good point, that's not the point, I can see your point, beside the point, make a point of, freezing point, melting point, up to a point, what's the point?

3 If you do not have your frequency list to hand you can check your intuitions on word frequencies. Good dictionaries mark words according to frequency bands.

4 Find a grammar book which tells you about the way frequent words work. Thornbury's *Natural Grammar* provides an excellent picture of some of the most frequent words. Thornbury lists, for example, all the uses of 'take' referred to in section 9.4 above.

5 Find a grammar book which gives useful lists of words. Collins Cobuild *Intermediate English Grammar,* which is based on corpus evidence, provides good lists of, for example, verbs like 'book', 'buy', 'make', 'cook', and 'pour' which are commonly followed by an indirect object with 'for' as in 'He cooked dinner for the family' or 'She booked a taxi for the children'.

6 Don't waste time teaching really rare words. Just give an L1 equivalent and save time to work on more important words.

7 Some topic words can be learnt as lists or from pictures. Don't use up a lot of class time on, for example, the vocabulary for clothes. Let learners work on these for themselves.

8 Make learners aware of the importance of collocation and set them exercises which make them think about the importance of collocation. For example, the *Collins Cobuild Dictionary* lists the following collocations with 'strong':

> a strong personality, strong enough to, strong wind/current, strong words, strong action, strong language, a strong case against, a strong possibility, strong points, a strong team, a strong currency, strong drink, a strong colour, a strong taste

This provides input for an interesting exercise. Once learners have met the word 'strong' in text it would be useful to give learners a list of these collocations and ask them what words are used in the place of 'strong' in their language.

9 Encourage learners to search texts for

- useful phrases: there are, for example, a large number of essential phrases expressing basic meanings to do with time, place and quantity. Phrases like 'sort of', 'kind of', and so on, and 'things like that' (often called *vague language*), are all very common in spoken language. It is important for learners to begin to see the language as made up of phrases rather than single words;
- patterns with prepositions: prepositions play an important part in organizing language.
- patterns with non-finite verb forms (infinitive and '-ing' forms).

10 Recognize the importance of recall in language learning. A lot of language learning consists in simply learning useful words and phrases. These are useful in themselves, and they also provide learners with the raw material for developing the grammar.

11 Try to build up patterns systematically. Begin with the basic meanings of prepositions, for example. Then identify associated words, and finally systematize those words. Finally ask learners to identify in texts the patterns they have acquired.

12 When teaching pronunciation create examples incorporating common words and phrases rather than individual words.

13 Set dictionary exercises which make learners use dictionaries creatively so that they pay attention to collocation and to the grammatical patterns associated with words.

14 Encourage learners to keep a phrase book rather than a vocabulary book. It is important for them to build up units of language larger than a single word.

15 Encourage learners to do their own research and take responsibility for the language. One way of doing this is by encouraging them to explore the pedagogic corpus for themselves. When they ask you a question about language try to refer them to examples which will enable them to find an answer for themselves. Instead of answering questions yourself see if another student can provide an answer.

9.6 The process of syllabus design

The diagram (p.197) offers a summary of the syllabus design process as we have outlined it in this chapter. We begin with an assessment of learners' needs. What do they want to do with the language? These needs may be very specialized and relatively easy to determine. They need, for example, to follow a course in bakery, or they need to read medical research articles. Alternatively the needs may be diffuse and difficult to pin down—they need English for general social purposes. We also need to determine what topics learners will need to deal with. Again this is relatively easy with bakers or medical students, much more difficult with general purpose English.

Once we have determined needs and topics we can begin to specify target tasks. What can learners do in the classroom which will reflect or contribute to what they want to do with English outside the classroom? The answer to this question helps us to build up relevant task sequences. In some cases the task sequence will clearly involve texts. The medical students, for example, will need to work with written texts. In other cases we will find or create texts. If our general learners need to understand written directions, we will find samples of these directions. If they need to understand and tell personal anecdotes, we will find recordings of such anecdotes, or we will make appropriate recordings as we did with David Foll's 'Busy day'.

When we have a series of task sequences and associated texts we need to organize these into a syllabus. We can do this in part by assessing task difficulty, relying on our knowledge of our learners and our knowledge of what they can do. We may also consult a list of factors contributing to task difficulty such as that provided by Skehan (1998). We will also assess the difficulty of the associated texts in the light of our experience of working with learners at the appropriate level. This assessment of tasks and texts will enable us to organize task sequences into a viable teaching sequence. It will provide us with a task syllabus.

To move from a task syllabus to a language syllabus we need to analyse the texts we have collected, the pedagogic corpus, looking for grammatical features and frequent words and phrases which are worth highlighting. This will give us our language syllabus. This syllabus needs to be checked out against frequency lists identifying the most important words and phrases. This checking process may identify gaps which need to be filled.

Once we have assembled our syllabus and teaching materials we can go ahead and use them in the classroom. But this is not the end of the process. We need to monitor and refine materials. Sometimes this will involve redesigning tasks in line with the parameters set out in Chapter 8, to make

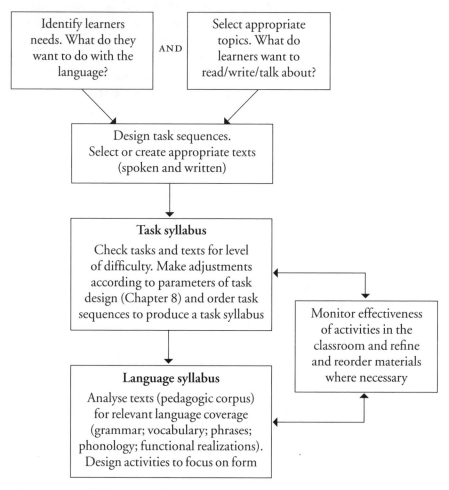

Figure 9.2 Syllabus design procedures

them easier or more challenging, or to make the task instructions clearer. Sometimes experience of teaching a course will lead us to reorder tasks. Something which caused more difficulty than we anticipated may be moved to a later stage in the course. We will assess not only the task sequences, but also the activities which focus on language form to make sure that they are effective in providing learners with appropriate insights.

The process of course and syllabus design is extremely complex and time-consuming. Ideally, for it to be successful, it needs to happen as part of a co-operative venture, with teaching colleagues involved at all levels of its design and piloting. We may find a satisfactory instrument at our first attempt, but, as Lorie Wood points out at the end of her draft Course Plan in Appendix 5, we will almost certainly be able to refine and improve it with experience.

In fact most of us already have a syllabus in the form of a coursebook. It is quite rare that teachers have to design a whole syllabus from scratch. Sometimes we need to plan short courses for particular groups which need to be designed specifically with the needs of the learners in mind. Most often what we need to do is add a syllabus strand to a coursebook that is already in use, so that it meets the needs of our students better. For example, a strand focusing on spontaneous spoken English or a task-based strand. The next and last chapter recognizes this and begins with a section on ways of combining and integrating TBT with existing coursebooks

9.7 *Follow-up activities*

1 Look through a coursebook you are familiar with and see how many examples you can find of the modal 'would'. Do these give a good picture of the word and its meanings and uses? Do the same thing with one or two other common words such as a preposition or a modal verb.
2 Look at the examples you have gathered in Reader activity 9a in section 9.4 above. How might you use these to make a form-focus activity for your learners, for example, by setting a gap-filling exercise?

Further reading

Nunan, D. 2004. *Task-based Language Teaching*. Cambridge: Cambridge University Press.
Chapter 2 looks at the grading of tasks and at syllabus design within the context of task-based learning and teaching.

10 HOW TO INTEGRATE TBT INTO COURSEBOOKS AND OTHER FREQUENTLY ASKED QUESTIONS

10.1 Introduction

We have been collecting questions about task-based teaching over the last ten or so years—from teachers all over the world whom we have met or got to know through workshops, seminars, and courses. Their questions have, in a very big way, helped us to shape this book.

We have also asked teachers who use tasks regularly and who are committed to TBT why their colleagues and other teachers they know don't use tasks in their lessons. What reasons do they give? What problems do they perceive with task-based learning and teaching? The mind map (Figure 10.1) gives an overview of their responses.

Many of these reasons have been given as reasons for not trying TBT or for giving up after a few attempts at using tasks. If you have read Chapter 1 and other chapters in this book, you should by now be able to give some advice on many of these problems.

READER ACTIVITY 10A

What advice would you give?

Look at Figure 10.1. Which of these 'problems' do you feel you could now help other teachers resolve?

Choose two or three that are common in your teaching context and list what advice you would give.

We asked the teachers who contributed tasks for this book for their advice and tips for teachers wishing to implement TBT. We then matched these to the problems perceived, and to other questions about TBT we had collected earlier, all of which form the basis of this chapter.

So this chapter pulls together much of the content of this book and develops it in a practical and, we hope, illuminating way, drawing on the advice given by our band of experienced task-based teachers whose bio-data appears at

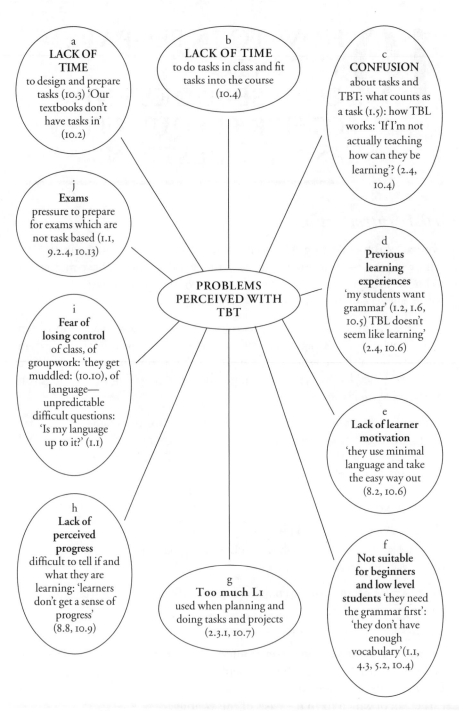

Figure 10.1 Problems perceived with task-based teaching

the back of this book. Some of the problems above have, we feel, been adequately covered in earlier chapters. Some questions will be answered quite briefly and will refer you back to sections in the book that respond to the question more fully. Others require longer answers. Since the biggest problem overall was 'lack of time for preparing and doing tasks', we shall start with one of the most common questions, giving a detailed response, and then go on, more briefly, to other questions.

10.2 How can I integrate tasks into my textbooks and save on planning time?

Reliance on a textbook minimizes preparation time. This section offers a range of solutions for teachers who are obliged to stick to their textbooks and don't have time to create their own tasks from scratch.

In the words of one of our teachers:

> Few textbooks present material in a TBL cycle, but often it only takes a little tweaking (e.g. adding a goal, or changing the order of activities) to produce a TBL lesson. You don't have to create from scratch, nor do you have to look for ready-made TBL packages.
> (James Hobbs, Japan)

So let us look at ways of doing just this.

10.2.1 Identifying tasks and activities that just need 'tweaking'

We looked through a wide range of popular coursebooks in preparation for this chapter and noted that many contained a fair number of tasks and task-like activities and some even contained a number of TBT lessons, but, with a few exceptions, these were not referred to as 'tasks'.

Some tasks appeared in lead-in, warm-up, starter, or preview sections, some in grammar and vocabulary sections, some in reading and listening sections, some in writing sections, and some in speaking sections. Tasks, it seems, often come in disguise. On the other hand, of course, there are sometimes activities in books that call themselves tasks, but are in fact form-focused practice or display exercises, like acting out a shopping dialogue in pairs. They may have meaning potential, but they are not primarily concerned with exchanging meaning.

Early on in a unit there are often listing tasks, matching tasks, ranking tasks, and sequencing tasks that are useful at the start of a task sequence as a way of introducing target vocabulary. Questionnaires and quizzes are popular, as are prediction tasks, and there are generally some chances for learners to talk about their own lives and share experiences, although these are often rather vague, and need tightening up.

These potential tasks go under a whole range of headings, as can be seen here:

It's your turn
Think... then compare ideas
Reach a decision

SPEAK OUT!   **Questions & answers**

With a partner

Listening challenge!

Figure 10.2 Tasks under other headings

Sometimes there are no headings at all, just an instruction like: 'In pairs', 'In groups', 'Discuss ...', 'Write a ...'.

So the first thing to do is identify what activities in your next coursebook unit have at least some of the characteristics of tasks. (See Chapter 1 (1.4) and Chapter 2 (2.1).) Appraise any potential tasks in the light of your students' needs—decide whether to adapt them in order to increase opportunities for spontaneous speaking, planned speaking, or writing of some kind. Then develop them into more effective tasks by applying the relevant parameters outlined in Chapter 8, for example by clarifying or adding a goal, or adding a post-task report stage.

Here are some ideas for what to look out for in different coursebook sections.

Topic 'lead-in' sections
The first page of a unit often starts with a topic and some points to be discussed in pairs or groups. In many cases, these only need a slight tweak to turn them into tasks that will generate more purposeful and more sustained interaction. Two examples follow. Both give several specific ideas for learners to talk about, which is good, but they could both be enriched. Can you think how?

A day out

 Work in pairs. Think about places near where you live. Where can people go for: an exciting, an interesting, a relaxing day out?

Figure 10.3 Face2Face Elementary: *page 66*

Here you could ask learners to give reasons for their choices, thus adding to their agenda. You might also like to specify that they must agree on one best place for each category, which is likely to prompt more discussion and make the goal clearer. As a post-task activity, get them to report to another pair or to the whole class, justifying their choice of place, and finally let the class vote on the best place for each category. So, finding the most popular place in each category becomes the final goal and gives the report a purpose.

> in groups ...
>
> When did you last stay out late? Where did you go, who with, and how did you get home? What's public transport like late at night where you live?

Figure 10.4 Natural English Intermediate: *page 103*

Because this involves recounting a personal experience, add a pre-task stage. Give learners a few minutes individual thinking time to recall and plan what to say beforehand, and they

- will feel more confident speaking,
- are likely to have more to say,
- won't be thinking what to say while others in their group are speaking, so
- they will listen to the others' ideas more intently.

You could also specify a goal—ask them to find out who stayed out the latest, and who had the easiest/most difficult journey home. Afterwards, ask these people to tell the class about their transport experiences and vote which was the easiest and/or worst. You could then hold a short class discussion on late-night public transport and possible improvements, a theme that comes up again later in the unit.

Alternatively you could adapt the theme slightly and ask them to think of a night out when they had a terrible time getting home. They could compare experiences and see who had the worst journey home.

So here we have tweaked the tasks by applying three parameters: adding a specific goal, pre-task planning time, and a post-task report.

Vocabulary-building sections
Vocabulary-building sections which often, but not always, precede reading and listening activities, sometimes contain useful sorting or matching tasks as preparation. Others contain activities that focus on form, getting learners to practise or display control of form. With a little thought, these could sometimes be upgraded to tasks, giving opportunities for genuine communication.

Example 3
Unit 13 of *New Headway Beginners* begins with a picture of George and Sadie, each wearing a shirt, a jacket and trousers, and shoes of different colours. The names of the eight colours themselves are printed in the appropriate colour and listed down one side. The three activities are:

STARTER   1 Look at the pictures of George and Sadie. Find the colours.

2 Complete the sentences with the colours.

1 George's jacket is **black**_____ . Sadie's jacket is _____ .
2 His trousers are _____ . Her trousers are _____ .
3 Her shirt is _____ . His shirt is _____ .
4 Her shoes are _____ . His shoes are _____ .

T 13.1 Listen and check. Practise the sentences.

3 What colours are your clothes today?

Figure 10.5 New Headway Beginners: *page 96*

READER ACTIVITY 1OB

Tweaking instructions

The three instructions in Example 3 all give learners a chance to match the colour words to clothes. Suggest ways you could supplement instructions 2 and 3 above so that learners can engage in more meaning-focused interactions using colour words.

Write your new instructions.

Commentary

We assume the teacher will have previously begun the lesson with some kind of introduction, for example, talking about the colours of the clothes she is wearing.

For instruction 2, you could

- do a preliminary teacher-led task getting learners to identify 'something white', 'something red' as fast as they can. This can be done either with the textbook pictures or pointing to things in the classroom; it provides rich exposure (especially if you talk about the objects as learners point to them) and requires minimal learner production.
- get learners to set a true/false quiz to give another pair. For example, 'Sadie's shirt is white'.

To increase the challenge, both these tasks could be done with books closed (or eyes shut) as a memory-challenge task. Or you could send two people out of the room and have the class (in pairs or as a whole) remember what they were wearing.

For instruction 3, rather than just saying the colours of their clothes today (which is, as it stands, simply a language display activity—everybody can already see what colours they are wearing and don't need telling), you could

- play a true/false game: 'Say two true things and one not true about the colours of your clothes'. The class identify which is false;
- get learners to find out who in the group is wearing the most colours. For example: 'In groups of four, list all the colours you are wearing. Which one of you has the most? Tell the class. Listen to the others to find out which person in the class has the most different colours on today' or 'Find out which group in the class has the most colours between them';
- do a teacher-led colour survey task to find out the most popular colour. 'Who is wearing something red? Hands up if you have something red on.' Possible responses might be: 'My skirt red or red jacket'. Recasting their replies ('Yes— that's a lovely red jacket—very stylish!') increases learner exposure to comprehensible input. Then count how many people are wearing this colour;
- play an identification game: describe someone by the colours they are wearing. For example, 'This person is wearing white, black, pink and grey. Who is it?' This could be done by learners in pairs looking round the class and deciding who to describe, or in larger groups of learners who take turns to describe one of the group.

Vocabulary Phrasal verbs

1 Work in groups. Tell the other students about your neighbours. Who are they? What are they like? Do you have any problems with them?

2 a) Read this letter and answer these questions
  1 What problem does Yvonne have?
  2 How has she tried to solve the problem?
  3 How has this problem changed her day-to-day life?
  4 How does she feel now?

b) Work in pairs. What advice can you give Yvonne?

NIGHTMARE NEIGHBOURS
I've lived in a rented flat for the last six months and until recently life has been very quiet and peaceful. But now a new couple have **moved in** next door and they are making my life impossible. The main problem is that they have parties . . .

[The letter continues for another 15 or so lines and contains ten examples of phrasal verbs which are focused on later]

Figure 10.6 Face2Face Pre-intermediate: *page 72*

Example 4
Unit 9 in *Face2Face Pre-intermediate* is called 'Life isn't perfect' and the theme is 'Common problems. Section 9c, 'In the neighbourhood', begins with a vocabulary section on phrasal verbs. There are six activities, to last about 45

minutes. Here are the first two—the next four are devoted to the practice of phrasal verbs themselves.

READER ACTIVITY 10C

Adapting activities

How might you adapt these two activities to maximize speaking or writing opportunities and give a more focused lead-in to the text? Write the instructions you would give.

Commentary

For activity 1, you could change the interaction patterns, give a more specific goal, and set a more detailed agenda. For example:

> Walk round and talk to as many people as possible about your neighbours (either your present ones or ones you have had earlier). Try to find at least two people with helpful neighbours (remember in what ways they are helpful) and two with problem neighbours (what problems?). You have eight minutes. Then go back to your seat and note down the details and prepare to tell the class the most interesting things you found out.

If you feel this would be too chaotic with your class, you could tell them to change partners every two (or more) minutes. Or simply have learners in fours, talking to each of the other three in turn for one or two minutes. You could also turn this into a survey to find out whether problem neighbours outnumber helpful neighbours or vice versa by adding either an oral report-back phase, or written summaries of group findings (displayed or passed round for others to read).

For activity 2, you could add a prediction task before the reading. For example:

> In pairs, consider the title 'Nightmare Neighbours' and list two or three things 'nightmare' neighbours might do and what effects these things may have. Suggest possible solutions for each scenario. Tell someone from another pair what you thought and add their ideas to your written list. Pass your lists round to find what ideas you had in common.

This would recycle some of the vocabulary from the first activity, expand their range of language experience and make the reading process more engaging— whose ideas will appear in the text? On the next coursebook page there is a listening activity where five people are interviewed about their neighbours, and learners listen and match pictures to the people. So the above prediction task also serves as good preparation for the listening.

You could also make the task agenda more specific: 'Think of three possible pieces of advice for Yvonne and give reasons why each piece of advice might or might not work'. This, too, could be written or spoken.

Skills lessons

Look carefully at the tape-scripts and texts in the unit, and see what kind of tasks you could do before them that would give learners a real purpose to listen to the recording or read the text. Chapter 3 gave many ideas for such tasks. There may already be some lead-in activities in the coursebook that just need a little tweaking, like the prediction task on 'Nightmare neighbours' above, and the one below, which is good example of a task sequence which integrates all four skills.

Parties

1 What sort of parties are these?

- housewarming
- leaving
- fancy dress
- 18th
- surprise
- Halloween

Masked Ball, Venice

2 What other types of party can you think of?

Alyson, Geoff & Rachel

3 Work with a partner. What do you think makes a good party? Write a list and agree on the three most important 'ingredients'.

4 ☐ 30 Listen to Alyson, Geoff and Rachel talking about the ingredients of a good party. Compare their ideas with yours.

5 Answer the questionnaire below. Then turn to page 142 and compare your score with a partner.

Figure 10.7 Inside Out Intermediate: *page 62*

This in fact is an example of a whole TBL lesson. Steps 1 and 2 are sensible pre-task preparation activities, and the teacher is left free to decide how to set them up—they could be done in pairs or groups. Step 3 gives a specific agenda for the main task and the outcome (a list of three important party 'ingredients') is clearly defined. Step 4, where learners listen with the purpose of comparing their own list with the ideas offered by the speakers, again has a clear outcome. Step 5, the questionnaire, is a highly interactive reading task. None of these need much tweaking. If, however, your learners need more pressure to focus on accuracy, you could add a planning and report-back stage after step 3, an evaluation of how far their ideas matched those in the recording after step 4. To get them to re-read the questionnaire, they could be asked to guess and then find out how their partner had responded to each item. As an extra writing task, they could then write (individually, silently, from memory) a short description of their partner's attitude to parties to give to their partner afterwards to check to see how well they remembered. To make it more fun, the teacher could collect all the descriptions in and pick some to read out loud—without giving the name— to see if the class can identify the person it is about.

Many coursebooks provide tasks to be done during the reading or listening stages; the questionnaire format is an excellent example of this. Other common tasks include sequencing jumbled key points or pictures or matching them to paragraphs, or comparing the facts in a summary or in a picture with the facts in the text or tape-script. *Inside Out Intermediate* has good examples of all these—see, for example, Unit 10, where the topic is 'Things to do …', the visual contains six different kinds of lists and the instruction is: 'Read the article on page 87 and match the four people to their list'. (Note they give more lists than people—including extras makes a matching task more challenging.)

Unit 11C in *Face2Face Pre-intermediate* contains two task sequences of three or four tasks each, one sequence based on a news recording, and one based on a written text. The first, on the topic of news items, has a set of three tasks: ranking four headlines according to interest value, sequencing the same headlines while listening to a news broadcast, then, from memory, matching eight pieces of more detailed information to the headlines. The second task sequence (about a pet kangaroo) starts with matching words to pictures and predicting the sequence of the pictures in telling the story, then reading the article to check the story. A second reading is encouraged with a subsequent true-false task. After some form-focused work, the final speaking task asks learners in groups to recall, list, and share interesting news items they have noticed during that week. Interestingly, as in all the examples above—none of these activities is referred to as a task, even though they are all focused on meaning.

If, in your textbook, there are no obvious tasks based around skills lessons, it would not take much time to plan a set of tasks, using ideas from Chapter 3, for example, predicting from the headline and first line of a text, guessing the sequence of jumbled key points, groups setting their own true/false quiz, or a set of questions.

Comprehension questions
These often have instructions like: 'Work in pairs. Ask and answer the questions.' as in *Cutting Edge Elementary*: 120–1. Some books suggest: 'Compare/check your answers with a partner'.

A simple way to generate more talk and thought is to get learners to justify their answer by saying what clues they found for each one. They can report back to the class the questions they disagreed about. Or turn it into a 'jigsaw' by giving each learner in a pair only half the questions and getting them to find out from each other the answers to the others (with evidence).

There are other ways to make comprehension questions more fun and engaging:

- cover the text, or put the questions on the board, and make learners guess or imagine (and tell each other, or write) possible answers before allowing them to read or listen. This can result in quite imaginative answers and funny class discussion. To make it more challenging, push for full answers with more detail, or make them explain their answers;
- set the questions as a memory challenge competition—cover the text after one fast reading. Done singly, then in pairs, then fours, this can generate lively discussion. (See Chapter 3 (3.7).)

10.2.2 Re-ordering activities

Textbook lessons that start with a focus on form mean that even when learners come on to a speaking activity they are still in the mind-set that is concerned with producing specified forms. We need to think how we can achieve an initial focus on meaning.

Do the grammar-based lesson last

In most cases the most important change we can make simply involves re-ordering textbook activities. For example, in a classic PPP cycle, where new language is introduced and presented and practised in a context, start with the final stage—the production stage—and turn this into a task; it might need a more specific goal adding, or some other tweaking. Keep textbooks closed, so that learners don't have a chance to get into the mental set of focusing on one specific grammatical form or function.

Brainstorm words and phrases and ideas related to the topic with the class (pre-task preparation). Get learners to do the task, plan what to say and report the results to the class (task cycle). After commenting or giving feed-back on the content of their task reports, go back to the textbook, saying 'Let's look more closely at some of the forms you might have used when doing your task', and do the form-focused exercises quickly. If you can remember what other language they used to express their own meanings (or if you have made a note of this in your notebook), highlight those patterns and expressions too—this gives value to their own efforts, and shows there is not just one correct way of expressing those meanings. Next lesson, or some time later, you might get them to repeat the task or do a similar one with a different partner.

Some trainee teachers once referred to this process as 'PPP upside-down' (J. Willis and D. Willis 1996) but, since it offers far more learning opportunities, maybe we should think of it as being the right way up.

Do the skills lessons first

Look for reading and listening activities in which there is generally little control of language. In most cases the skills lesson follows on from the form-focused work that has been done. Try switching things round and using skills lessons for tasks which prepare the way for form study in the future. Use some of the suggestions in Chapter 3 for text-based task sequences, and later, those in Chapter 6 for follow-up language and form-focused exercises based on the textbook texts.

10.2.3 Adding and integrating focused tasks

'Focused tasks' is a term coined by Ellis (2003) to describe tasks where specific language features are likely to occur naturally in the interaction or do occur in fairly large numbers in the text. With closed tasks like 'Spot the difference', language forms are easier to predict but even then, you can never predict precisely what language learners will use for the task. If you have time to record fluent or native speakers doing the task, you will at least get some idea of what language features may occur naturally. (See Cox 2005 for more on this.)

If a coursebook lesson begins with a presentation of new grammar, followed simply by practice exercises, you might like to add a task at the start that focuses on common meanings.

> Example 6
> Imagine the textbook lesson begins by looking at the use of verbs of liking and disliking, followed by the '-ing' form of the verb and goes on to say to learners:
>
> Make a list of three things you like and three things you don't like.
> Use these phrases:
>   I like/love/enjoy …ing.
>   I don't like/hate …ing.

Instead of this you could begin the lesson by telling them two or three things that you and other people in your family like/don't like doing. As you talk, ask if anyone in their family has any of the same likes and dislikes. This then becomes a teacher-led comparing task, giving rich exposure to relevant language and concepts and requiring full learner engagement with meaning but minimum learner production. Then set a task where they have to list their partner's likes and dislikes and go on to do a class survey. Beforehand, give learners some pre-task preparation time and help with any vocabulary they need. If you follow the task with a report phase culminating in the survey, you might, in the planning stage, reformulate any key phrases they want to use in their reports: 'He no like drive at night'. 'Oh, driving at night? Right, so he doesn't like driving at night. I don't like driving at night either.' They may not get it right at the report stage; they may simply not be ready to learn this yet. But the important thing is that they are focusing on telling you about their partners and getting their meanings across. Then after the task sequence, go back to the coursebook unit, finishing with the exercises that focus on form, and in addition, give more examples based on the meanings they were expressing during the task and report stages. Let them practise those too, and write them down.

Here are some more examples of focused tasks:

- Lana Loumpourdi (2005) found that getting learners to prepare questions for the personality questionnaire 'How brave are you?' based on hypothetical situations naturally generates questions in the second conditional such as: 'What would you do if an alien space ship landed in your back garden?'. When thinking up the four alternative options for each question they would write things like 'I'd/I would pack my suitcase as fast as I could'. They assembled questions and options from other pairs and then swapped questionnaires, did them, and worked out their scores. Much laughter ensued and much English was used, even by a group of boys who were normally reticent. Her other focused tasks included getting her learners to find out from each other the three biggest lies they had told last year (past simple revision); for past simple and continuous question practice she set up a crime scenario with detectives and witnesses.
- Yevgeny Slivkin designed a 'Fictitious marriage investigation' scenario to give practice with present tense forms in Russian. It is based on the fact that sometimes people who wish to obtain a green card to stay in the USA 'marry' someone who has US citizenship although they have no intention of ever staying together as a couple. Learners acting as immigration officials interview 'husband/wife' couples individually, asking questions about aspects of their daily lives, to investigate whether they really do know each other well enough to be married. This involves the couple in preparing a very solid case before the interview. If their interview answers do not match, and if they cannot plead their case, they will be deemed to be 'fake' couples who will end up being deported. (See Appendix 2.5 for full details.) It is much more fun than simply practising present tenses for daily routines. It could also be used for focusing on the past simple, by asking questions about how they met and the events leading up to their 'marriage'. This scenario is a variation of the 'Alibi' game—see Leaver and J. R. Willis 2004: 27 for another example, set in a military peace-keeping context.

Revision tasks
Focused tasks are useful for textbook revision, too. To revise textbook language: imperatives, food and drink vocabulary, countable/uncountable nouns, sequence connectors such as 'first', 'then', etc. Eva Kloster in Argentina got groups of 12–13-year-old students to create recipes that could be made in class, with no actual cooking. They wrote full recipes for things like 'Olympic cake' and 'Pyramid sandwich' and gave live demonstrations in

class followed by class tastings. It was a lot of fun. It also recycled language well, as, when preparing the writing and the presentation, learners were encouraged to go back to the textbook unit to make sure they got things right. The learners benefited from hearing the others use similar language and from reading their recipes.

10.3 How can we find time to design tasks and plan TBT lessons?

Any good lesson takes time to prepare. Planning TBT lessons takes no longer than planning any other kind of lesson once you have gained some TBT experience, especially if you use and adapt a coursebook—as we saw above. But here are some things you could try:

1 Collaboration
A lot of teachers, such as Eva in Argentina whose work we saw above, and others in the USA and Japan said that they work with their colleagues to plan their TBT, gather materials and work out good scenarios and projects. One teacher said the key is to create 'collaborative cultures':

> We are convinced that one of the main ingredients for our success has been working in a team which has always been supportive and encouraging. Working in teams is a must!

Claudia Bey, who chaired a Serbo-Croatian department in the USA, reports:

> Two colleagues and I created one 4-hour long TBT scenario for students who would be acting as peace-keeping forces in Bosnia. It was given during a 2-day immersion experience. The topic was 'Smuggling people'.

> We started with a feature article in *National Geographic*. They reported that one Bosnian trader who was involved in this type of business had been arrested. So, we knew that this was a real problem that our students might face in Bosnia.

> The two Serbian-Croatian teachers collected a number of articles to get the background knowledge, and based on that we created the scenario and all the other materials: background texts, phone calls, handwritten letters, interviews, overheard conversations, etc. Once we had the basic scenario, we put the students through the different tasks, as if they were really in a situation like that. The feedback was overwhelmingly positive: they found it very challenging to read the handwritten Cyrillic; they really enjoyed the telephone calls. They liked hearing colloquial language. It felt very real and authentic to them. They found the whole

experience interesting. We are still using this TBT scenario for all classes in the program, so the development time was not a problem.

2 Collecting texts
Finding suitable texts can take time. Whenever you read a suitable text, make a note of its source, copy it, and file it. You could also ask students to help. A group of upper intermediate students found interesting reading texts for a writing class, mainly from the web; they each supplied one text, and wrote a short review of it, to persuade other students their text was worth voting for. Students then read the reviews (not the texts) and—on a separate piece of paper—gave each a mark out of five, and thus we chose the most popular ten topics for the term. The ten texts were then sequenced, quick reading tasks and a range of writing tasks designed for each, and finally language work planned for the term based on the texts.

3 Collecting recordings
To save time, get your students to record. If you work somewhere where English is spoken, or near where speakers of English gather, students (in pairs, each with a recording device) can go out and interview people on topics they have prepared beforehand. They obviously have to explain their purpose and ask permission to record their interviews, but once recorded, they can replay, listen and choose sections to transcribe and later present their interview in class, supported by transcriptions. These can then be used for form-focused study.

Many teachers pointed out that once you have a good task or suitable text, you can use it again and again. It never gets boring, because in TBT lessons, the learners give so much of themselves that every time the results are different and you learn something new. So, as Claudia Bey and her colleagues found, it's worth some investment of time up front—you save time later.

10.4 How can I make time to do tasks in class?

The pressure of completing the coursebook or covering the language syllabus by the end of term can be quite daunting. But we need to think in terms of letting learners learn rather than trying to teach everything thoroughly. And rather than spending a lot of time teaching grammar and pronunciation aiming at native-like mastery (which we know they will never achieve), maybe we should spend more of that time allowing them to learn through using (or attempting to use) the language themselves. Unless they live in an English-speaking environment, it's only in class that they will get a chance to interact in English, and have the support of their teacher when planning and drafting what to say or write. While they are working in groups or pairs, you can give them some individual attention and respond to individual needs. This is a good use of class time.

And if you still need convincing, do this calculation for your students. Research on classroom interaction has shown that with no pair interaction, in a teacher-led classroom of 30 students, with 4 lessons a week over 36 weeks, each individual learner will, on average, only get one and one quarter hour's worth of speaking time a year (J. Willis 1996: 18). Ten minutes of pair interaction a lesson brings this up to 13 hours a year. Still not a great deal of speaking time—we need to aim for more—but at least they get some practice in managing their own interactions and experimenting with ways to get their meanings across.

READER ACTIVITY 10D

Calculating speaking time

Go through your next textbook unit and decide what activities you can spend less time doing in class, and what learners can do at home at their own pace, after just a little in-class preparation.

Then work out how much speaking time individual learners are likely to get in class over the next week. Multiply this up to get the figures for a year.

Here are some ways of making more efficient use of classroom time:

1 Ask learners to prepare topic- and task-related words at home
As we have already suggested, learners can do some preparation for the next lesson's task at home, so they will have already looked up words they might need and thought out what to say. They can list in their notebooks any queries they still have, and ask you in the first few minutes of the next lesson. This will save time at the pre-task stage.

2 Set grammar exercises for homework
This has the advantage of each learner being able to work at their own pace and to try to work things out for themselves. With low level learners, you might like to start each exercise in class, but ask them to complete the exercises at home, ready to show you in class next lesson. Train them to leave their books open on their desk when they arrive, so you can walk around and quickly check that everyone has done the exercises. If there is something they are not sure about, they can put a question mark or write a question to ask you in class. They can check each other's work, and then you can offer a short review session.

3 Do the listening/reading and follow-up activities at home
Nowadays most books come with a student CD or DVD, so listening as well as reading can be done at home (where they can listen or read as many times as they need to), and checked out in class quickly next lesson. Time the lesson so the pre-reading or pre-listening tasks which normally involve some speaking and reporting back (for example, prediction or sequencing and in

pairs or groups) are done in class, then they can do the rest of the reading/listening task cycle and any form-focused exercises based on the text at home or in their own time.

Here's an example of how this could work with a beginners class:

> Example 7
> Look back at the *New Headway Beginners* task on clothes and colours in Example 3 in 10.2.1. above.

To make time for the extra colour tasks:

- in the previous lesson, tell learners they will be talking about the colours of people's clothes next lesson. Give them a handout with a list of colour words and words for clothes to learn at home; check to see if these are recorded somewhere, or ask them to check pronunciation in the dictionary.
- after the tasks, set the listening and practising (T13.1) with their own CDs for their next homework. Ask them to time themselves at home to see how fast they can say all eight sentences. Next lesson, ask them to give you their times and ask a few people to read the sentences fast to the class. This kind of follow-up shows you are serious about homework practice (as well as being good practice in using numbers for timings).

4 Encourage independent vocabulary learning

Helping learners to learn topic words and phrases can take up a lot of class time and is not necessarily the best way of approaching something which ultimately depends on rote learning. Encourage learners to keep vocabulary notebooks, to write in new words and phrases and to revise their entries independently. It has been suggested (Meara 2001) that if learners really put their minds to learning words from word lists they can learn up to 50 new words in one hour—this will, however, depend on many factors, like the level of learners and similarities between the L1 and the target language. Nation (2001) reports that the most effective method is for learners to use small word cards with translations on the back; they flip through the pack to see how many they can recall, then shuffle and go through again. (If learners write in pencil they can erase the new word once they know it and re-use the cards.) This may seem old fashioned but it does seem to work. If the cards also contain one or two typical phrases or collocations containing the new word it might help learners use the word productively as well as providing a context to help recall. Expending cognitive effort also helps recall so you could give learners lists of words and phrases they will need for the next topic and encourage them to use classifying activities like putting words and phrases on to mind maps, or making odd-word-out quizzes. They can compare mind maps and do each others' quizzes quickly as a warm up in the next lesson.

It is estimated that a learner needs knowledge of some 2000 word families to be able to operate in a language independently (Bauer and Nation 1993). A word family is a word and its associated forms. For example the verb 'talk' would have in its family the inflected forms 'talks', 'talking', and 'talked', together with the noun 'talk' and the adjective 'talkative'. In theory, if Meara's figures are correct, this would involve 40 hours of independent study. So given half an hour of vocabulary study a day the target could be reached in 80 days, or sixteen weeks of study at five days a week. Of course things are not as simple as that. Beginners, who are not familiar with the sounds and shape of English words, would be most unlikely to reach the figure of fifty words an hour. If you forget a word, you have to relearn it. Then there is the fact that the ability to recognize a word and its L1 equivalent does not guarantee the ability to use that word. However, it would certainly help learners recognize more words when reading graded readers, which would reduce the frustration factor and increase enjoyment of reading, as well as giving them insights into uses of the new words.

To gain productive control, learners also need to experience these words and phrases in their natural settings (social chat, task-based interactions and texts), and revise them (preferably within 24 hours, then again within a week and then at longer intervals) in order to recall them. So a quick three-minute burst of direct vocabulary revision in every lesson, would save time spent teaching vocabulary in class. Marilyn Dahl in the UAE found her learners really enjoyed simple revision games such as, for example:

> Write down as many food words and phrases as you can in two minutes. Tell us how many you got. Now compare lists with a partner by reading them out loud, combine them, and count again.

The advantages of rapid independent learning of words and phrases include:

- it is something concrete and challenging for a learner to do;
- it can be rewarding and satisfying when they have reached their daily targets and find they can understand more when reading and listening;
- it is easily testable—learners can test each other (for example with their word cards) for two minutes at some point in each lesson;
- it would contribute heavily to learners reaching the take-off point of 2000 word families;
- it encourages learner independence.

So if the bulk of initial vocabulary learning can be done largely out of class, this saves class time for tasks that will recycle the new words, and illustrate them in context with their common collocations and patterns. Attention can also be drawn to them in the post-task, form-focused phase, when the basic words and phrases can be further built on and extended, and written into vocabulary notebooks/phrasebooks.

10.5 How can you change attitudes of students who aren't used to TBT?

Sometimes students tell you they just want to be taught grammar because they are worried they never get it right and they think that one day, magically, they will, if you teach it often enough. Most students will admit they would also like to be able to talk to people in English, so

- explain that they will only learn to talk by trying to talk;
- that by talking, and listening to people talking (and reading widely) they will naturally consolidate their grammar and acquire more;
- tell them plenty of people learn a foreign language without having any grammar lessons. (Prabhu's pupils just did tasks, no grammar lessons, and they acquired enough language to pass their grammar-based exams, and could communicate quite fluently. TBL helped them acquire naturally);
- choose some simple engaging tasks that are fun and have concrete outcomes, that they can prepare in advance and achieve with satisfaction and enjoyment;
- to start with, let them prepare in writing what they might want to say— this gives them 'discourse space' (Kelly and Gargagliano 2001);
- always end a TBT lesson with a focus on grammar and new words and expressions that have come up in the task. Learners can practise these and write them in their notebooks to revise at home. Next lesson go back to these and recap with some quick pair-practice of language from their notebooks. It's very much a question of 'packaging'—two short bursts of grammar a lesson with a task in between.

As we saw in Chapter 9 (9.2.5), Jason Moser's students had been very negative about their English before they started TBL, but most learners will 'come alive' once they realize that it is not just a question of grammar. When they can express themselves in English and do fun tasks, then their attitudes are more likely to change.

10.6 How can I motivate my students to do more than just the minimum?

The key, as we stressed Chapter 1, is the notion of engagement. Learners have to want to engage in meaning on their way to achieving an outcome. To guard against minimal responses, the advice in Chapter 8 (8.2) will help. There we suggested introducing interim goals, giving precise instructions, giving charts or tables to fill in, and pushing for more detailed output.

If learners have invested some of their own time prior to the speaking task in planning and thinking through what they can talk about, they are more likely to engage with the task when they do it. At least they will know some of the basic vocabulary and they are less likely to run out of things to say. Duane Kindt in Japan gets his students to prepare for conversation tasks using 'Students own conversation cards' (SOCCs) on a range of topics. These are illustrated cards that learners design and make for themselves at home, writing briefly about a specified number of points on the given topic that they will talk about in class. The cards act as cues for both learners in the pair and give a sense of security. There are self assessment and grading schemes and a feed-back stage. (See Duane Kindt's SOCC website for more detail.) His learners obviously benefited from SOCCs and soon realized they were able to hold a conversation in a social setting, which is in itself motivating.

There are other ways, too, of making tasks intrinsically motivating. A lot of teachers gave advice on this, based on their experience. Here it is, divided into broad topic areas.

Task design
- The way the task is presented visually has an enormous impact on production.
- We think personalization is the key. We have found that abstract topics that would motivate us to talk in a classroom do not always guarantee our students' interest. But talking about concrete, even mundane things can be surprisingly fruitful.
- Use tasks that require imagination, creativity (predict a story ending) or involve humour (your silliest/most embarrassing moment). These are great for group-work dynamic.

An example from Glen Poupore:

> Students were given background information about one episode of the sitcom *Friends*. Students created questions they thought would be answered by the end of the episode and later they provided their own answers. Students often come up with humorous questions as well as creative and humorous answers. Observing students on videotape as they do this task, the smiles and laughter are numerous; they are just plain having fun together and really enjoying the task.

Make the goals and real-life purposes very clear
Many teachers put this as their main or second most important piece of advice. Here are some things they suggested:

- Raise your students' motivation by telling them how interesting/exciting the activity will be (if it is!) and what the purpose of the activity is. Learners really appreciate knowing why they are doing an activity. Make sure you tell them one of the goals is to enable them to face this kind of situation in real life.

- Explain the real-life purpose of the task and make clear the contexts in which the language of the task would be relevant.
- Use TBT with online components. Such activities give students the chance to meet, interact, and engage in a fruitful conversation that would, hopefully, make an impact (little as it may be) on the way they view learning.
- Email opens up the possibility of international communication in English. Some textbooks actively encourage learners to find email pen-pals and write to them about the topic they are currently doing in class.

David Coulson recommends holding a regular 'English Day' (or give an English party with an agreed theme) to which you invite international students and other English speakers to come. (See Coulson 2005.) They will experience English in use in an international context, which can be motivating.

See Chapter 1 (1.4 (f)) and Chapter 7 for more on language and the real world.

Methods in class
Teachers' suggestions included:

- Move around and help: keep everyone involved; encourage participation.
- Don't be afraid to repeat activities. Student language often improves with the second or third go. This will give them confidence and help them feel good.
- After the activity, have your students realize how well they have performed in it. Even when there are problems to be overcome, there are always aspects of the task in which students have done well and by showing them that, you can raise their motivation and make them experience some sense of achievement.

Most of the tasks we have described so far have been based on co-operation. For variation and to raise motivation you could bring in an element of competition.

Draw a score chart on the board for each pair or team. Give points for any aspect of content or language—they don't have to be just for 'right' answers; for example, give points for interest value and detail in final reports or projects, new words or phrases used, good questions, clear answers, long responses, degree of participation, amount of target language spoken in groups (minus points for excessive L1 without permission, and plus points for little or no L1). You might need to agree each time what aspect(s) you will award points for. Be generous and give lots of points; make it fun but be as fair as possible.

10.7 How can we prevent overuse of L1 and encourage learners with the same L1 to use English during pair-work and project work?

Most teachers do not think it's a good idea to ban use of L1 outright. Beginner and low level learners have been known to suffer, feeling they have no way to contribute in class or communicate with their teacher. We used to feel that if we allowed L1 in an English lesson, it was the thin end of the wedge—learners would no longer try to express themselves in English—but now we recognize the advantages of using L1 in certain cases.

Some teachers of true beginners, like Aurelia García in Argentina (Chapter 2 (2.3.1)), Heidi Vande Voort Nam in Korea, and Annamaria Pinter (2006) in Hungary, get their students to do a similar task in their L1 to start with. This opens up the content area, lets them get ideas for what to say and/or strategies to do the task. Heidi explains:

> I begin activities in Korean, and then more advanced students supply the vocabulary or I do, so that they can do the same thing in English.

> As they then repeat the task with others, and later work towards some kind of report or presentation of findings, their use of English gradually increases. By the end of the year, use of L1 has normally dropped to a minimum.

But there are definitely other times when the mother tongue—or another common language—is useful:

- quick translation when an unknown word comes up—especially if it is a word not common enough to teach or spend time on guessing from context. Ask learners if they can translate the word for other students; if you speak their L1, you can check comprehension; with a mixed class, you will have to go with the student consensus—ask someone with a bilingual dictionary to help.
- generally it is best to do all the classroom organization and instruction-giving in English, as this creates a very real context and purpose for listening. But check they understand the task instructions by asking someone to say what they think they have to do in L1. If some students disagree, you might need to clarify. At a higher level, they can do this in English.
- make sure they know why using English as much as they can is beneficial: 'use it to learn it'.

Jason Moser in Japan reports:

> Whatever the task, L1 will emerge. There is no formula except solid classroom management. I think Japanese has a role to play, but I make it

clear where it should be avoided. During the report stage I think it is crucial for getting the students to work together to make a report. I lay out clearly when, where, and for what Japanese may be used. I can speak Japanese so I can tell when it is being used for learning and not. Most students, once they understand the rules, work within them.

Many teachers draw up a set of rules for when L1 is allowed to be used by the teacher and by learners. In fact, one good way forward is to let your students do this as a task, and then share ideas and agree on a final set of guidelines. You could also ask them to think of specific guidelines for L1 use during projects and pair-work. Encourage them to keep to these during group work by:

- displaying the rules or guidelines where all can see
- going round and monitoring, helping when they get stuck
- asking groups afterwards how many points out of five they would give themselves for sticking to English during the task—according to the guidelines.

Another task would be to ask students when and why they speak L1 in class, and help them overcome these particular hurdles. One teacher in Turkey (Eldridge 1996) recorded pair-work in his class of 13-year olds and found his students consistently used Turkish for interactive phrases that mark agenda points in interactions like 'Ok then, shall I start?' 'So, lets …', 'Fine, right, that's it then'. In fact they tended to switch to Turkish once off the main task agenda. If his students had been able to listen to recordings of native or fluent speakers doing a similar task, they could have noticed (with teacher guidance) how such meanings were expressed in English. Hobbs (2005: 149) provides a useful classification of interactive lexical phrases.

For more on aspects of spoken language that learners might need help with, see Chapter 7 (7.4).

10.8 How do we keep learners' interest during a post-task report stage?

Here are some suggestions for maintaining the interest of learners during the report stage:

- Ensure, when learners are planning their reports, that the instructions encourage them to include relevant detail which makes the reports more interesting.
- Before starting the report-back phase, make sure most of them have finished planning their reports, otherwise they will still be trying to improve their own report instead of listening to each other.

- Give them a purpose for listening to or reading each other's reports, i.e. note down three things that are similar to or different from their own reports/stories; or to take note of the facts to collate for a class survey.
- Tell them they have to listen so they can prepare and write two/three questions to ask the people reporting. (They could be graded on the quality of the content of their questions.)
- They can write two true facts and one false statement about each report they hear or read, to give as a quiz after the reports are finished.
- They can evaluate—i.e. give a grade and/or a comment for different aspects of each report: on the interest level and content/entertainment value/presentation—or complete a sentence on a slip of paper: 'What I liked particularly about X's report was …'.

To give a different view, Jason Moser reports:

> Ironically, it is the teacher-fronted reporting that I would say many students would rank as their favourite part of the sequence … because they get to share meaningful time with the teacher who is sharing stories and just showing interest in student lives.

10.9 How can we give learners a sense of their own progress?

Much of the language that students learn during TBT cycles is acquired subconsciously and learners are simply not aware of what they are learning and ways in which they are improving. The following techniques—already mentioned elsewhere in this book—have been found to help them perceive their progress.

- Make sure learners keep records in their notebooks of new words, phrases, and patterns from each lesson; spend ten minutes every few lessons going over these in class and get the class to quiz each other on them. Count up totals of words and phrases every month.
- Get learners to repeat the task once or twice with new partners, and point out in what ways they have improved by the end.
- Every so often, get learners to record, transcribe their task interaction, then correct and improve it, and finally do the same (or similar) task again later. Save some early recordings and transcriptions so they can compare them with those they do at the end of term. (You could get different pairs of learners to record each time, so each task is being recorded by one or two pairs each lesson.)
- Make learners keep a portfolio of all written reports and all transcriptions (of tasks and interviews done) so they can see how much they have accumulated and improved over a term.

- Ask a visitor (not necessarily a teacher) to come into class on a regular basis to talk to learners in English and answer their questions about topics they have covered since the last visit. The visitor can also go round and watch and listen while learners are repeating tasks that they have done before with a different partner (see Lopes 2004) and join in. At the end of the class, the visitor can give the class some feedback about what they enjoyed hearing about, and comment on the progress learners have made. If grades for oral work are needed, this is a chance for the class teacher to sit at the back, listen, and jot down points for each learner contribution.

10.10 How can we control and keep discipline in large or difficult classes?

Patrick Kiernan advises:

> Using tasks means that the teachers have a different role from the traditional one where the teacher is the focus throughout. It is easy to be concerned about discipline and even the most well-organized speaking tasks are noisy. However, in reality, well-designed and well-staged tasks are motivating and give students a feeling of satisfaction. It is difficult for students to fall asleep during a task and if they are not participating it will be easy to see. Explain the task very carefully and also make sure they know how using tasks can help them learn English ….

If you have large classes and fixed desks, and/or students who tend to get out of control easily, introduce set routines for different activity types and make sure they know what the rules are. A set of class rules can be proposed in pairs then agreed on by the class as a target task in itself. It can be shared, refined and drawn up into a document or poster that is kept on display.

Start with teacher-led tasks that require some kind of a written or drawn response from each student, for example, listen and draw, or underline, or sequence. Get them to check answers in pairs to reduce your marking load, but go round the class as they are doing this.

Train them to work in pairs with the student next to them, then to repeat the task or report to the student behind/in front of them. Number rows, so the odd numbers turn round, the even numbers stay facing forward. To start with, practise doing this fast and make it fun. Practise making fours in the same way—pairs turn to face another pair. A teacher I once observed in Teheran teaching 120 learners (sitting three to a wooden desk made for two, in a classroom over a noisy bazaar) had a bell she rang when students needed to change activities, or to stop talking and listen. There was no way she could monitor 40 groups of three during each task, but at least three quarters of them were speaking far more English than they would have done in a teacher-led class. And the 40 pieces of group writing reporting the task results were quicker to mark than 120 individual scripts.

In big classes, it is easier and quicker to get round to monitor groups of four than to monitor twice the number of pairs. But when you have groups of more than two, make sure each person has a role, and check they know what their role is: 'Hands up all secretaries; hands up all reporters'; see Chapter 8 (8.6). It's useful to have a group leader, too, whose role it is to keep the group on the task agenda and using English, and who can raise a hand once they have finished or if they get stuck. A group of teachers in Thailand and the USA have devised 'Team English' which 'uses team and member identification through colors and numbers while at the same time incorporating principles of cooperative learning, an approach to education in which students work together to achieve a common objective'. For example, the teacher might call out: 'Red team number 5—can you ask us your quiz question?' or 'All number 4s, hands up, you will be the spokesperson for your team'. (For their web-based article on large classes, see Further reading at the end of this chapter.)

Try to teach from the back of the class sometimes; at least spend more time at the back when monitoring group work.

Finally, a tip we got from Esther Ramani, a teacher in India where classes can be up to 70 or 80: every week, get all learners to move forward one row. The front row goes to the back. It is easier for learners nearer the front to hear, understand and concentrate. You can also encourage students to mix up a bit as they move forward or back. This means they will be in different pairs, at least for reporting, and they will learn different things from different people.

10.11 One-to-one classes

Teaching in a one-to-one situation means that you can tailor the course very precisely to that learner's needs and interests, and work with the data that they bring with them. For example, Beatrix Burghardt (teaching Hungarian) got her student (a diplomat) to bring in a first draft of a Christmas speech he would have to make at the American Embassy; it showed he was conversant with formal Hungarian, but it needed extending, so they worked on the content together. Another teacher in Ireland persuaded her very shy Japanese student (a businessman) to join a golf club; he brought in brochures of local golf courses to compare and select from, and practised talking about where he played golf in Japan.

However, it is more difficult to think of ways to create a natural situation in a class of two that requires more formal or prestige spoken language use, like the report stage in a larger class. There are two ways round this—finding an outside audience and using a recording device.

1 Outside audience
- If you teach more than one student on a one-to-one basis, try to find a time they can overlap for a spell on a regular basis; then they can tell each other—across a table, to give some formality—what they have been doing, and compare learning experiences.
- If you work with other one-to-one teachers you could exchange students on a formal basis for half an hour at regular intervals.

2 Making recordings
- Listen to your student talking to you in class on a prepared topic; push for detail where appropriate. You then make a recording of yourself telling them whatever you can remember about it. ('So what you said was …') Play it back in class and ask them to check the content. (You could deliberately leave gaps or get a few facts wrong.) By doing this, you are reformulating in standard English the meanings the student was trying to express—a valuable resource for the learner to listen to.
- At home, the student listens to the recording you made in class and tries to transcribe bits they find interesting language-wise, to talk about in class next day. For a later lesson, they could make their own recording of the same story, presentation or speech at home, and play it back to you in class.

The very act of recording (and knowing it will be played back) pushes the speaker to think of more effective ways of expressing something—a natural way to impose a focus on language.

10.12 How can you do tasks with learners of mixed ability/on different levels, and ensure all students can do the task?

For teachers working in a lock-step presentation-style methodology, teaching one target grammar item to a mixed class, mixed ability classes pose a very difficult problem: some learners will know it already and be bored, a few might be just ready to learn it, while others—not yet ready—will be bewildered. A task-based approach where the focus is on meaning means that all students have a chance to do the task within their own capabilities—so it is far less of a problem. It is however essential that all students understand from the start what each stage of the task entails.

With TBT, learners are able to work at their own level, and there are times when you can go round helping the weaker ones. When grouping students, use two ways—sometimes pairing weak with strong, so the weak learner is supported and the stronger one learns through helping; and sometimes put strong ones together and let them get on by themselves, while you spend more time with the weak ones. Weaker learners on their own together have more chance to speak out, and often gain confidence by being able to help another person.

When setting up group work, share the roles round so students get practice at skills they are less good at, with support of the group. Make sure the best students do not dominate—make them chairperson.

You will never get all learners to do the task equally well or to reach the same language level. But you should aim at all learners feeling they have improved from where they started and done their share of the task to the best of their efforts. If they feel they have achieved something worthwhile and have come to enjoy using their English, then you, as teacher, have done the best you can.

10.13 If we take up TBT, what exams are there that are truly task-based?

We wanted an expert opinion on this so we asked Roger Hawkey, currently working as a testing consultant, to answer this question for us. He explains:

Well, nearly all ESOL exams from the well-known international exam providers are nowadays based on the theory of communicative language ability. The rationale for task-based language teaching as outlined in Chapter 1 is equally applicable for language testing. The task has become the basic element in the design of most main language tests. This means that the exams try to test candidates' capacity to receive and produce the target language appropriately in authentic communication.

So, if your students need to take an external exam to gain a widely-recognized certificate of their target-language level, they will find that the exams mentioned later try to:

- test one, some or all of the language *skills* (reading, writing, listening and speaking) at a specified *level*—useful for international recognition if the level is linked to the *Common European Framework* (*CEF*)
- use *test tasks* which are like the communication activities the test-takers meet outside the classroom (e.g. reply to an email, understand a lecture, join a conversation)
- assess with *marks* or *grades* based on how well test-takers meet the overall language demands of the tasks
- use communicative *assessment criteria* (for example, appropriacy, fluency, etc.) in descriptions of the levels concerned.

But, you, as a TBL teacher, will want to judge for yourself how truly task-based the various exams are, compared, for example with the *internal tests* you may have been using or the *local tests* available to you. You will be wise to look carefully at the information materials of the exam providers. These are more comprehensive and detailed than they used to be because testers know it is good testing practice to try to tell test users what they need and want to know.

So, go to the *test provider websites*, and look, especially, for information on: who the test is intended for, what it tests, through what kinds of tasks? how it is delivered (pencil and paper? computer?), how it is marked and certificated? is it *modular?* (i.e. candidates can take a test in whichever skill or skills they need, at the level(s) most suitable for them), are the exams scheduled (for example, twice a year) or are they offered whenever needed? and so on. Much easier for you to make your decisions, of course, if *sample test papers* are provided.

Hunt around the following websites (and others on the net):

- www.cambridgeesol.org.uk: for their general English exams at all CEF levels, business English exams, IELTS test for candidates needing an English language qualification for future studies or work in an English-medium country
- www.trinitycollege.com.uk: for their Spoken Grade Examinations, 12 grades, grouped into four stages of language development, and their Integrated Skills in English exam, which has a portfolio element
- www.ETS.org: for their exams to meet requirements for admission to colleges, universities, and other organisations or companies.

10.14　Teacher's tips for implementing TBT

To end this book, we hand over to the voices of our band of practising teachers who have already contributed so many ideas to this book. What follows is a collation of their most useful tips for teachers intending to implement TBT for the first time.

Teachers' tips for Task-based Teaching

Give clear instructions

Prepare your task well before you set it – think through each stage carefully – how to organize it and what instructions to give at what points.

Make sure all the students know what to do.

Explain, explain, explain the end goal and the type of work expected. Students (in Asia) tend to want to just answer questions "correctly". I've found that with some types of task, I shouldn't number the steps or students will answer them point-by-point and not try anything creative.

INTRODUCING TBT WITH CLASSES NOT USED TO IT

- Start from the experiences your pupils already have.
- To begin with, try a short simple task – one with a definite goal.
- Explain the purpose of each task, and at the end, summarize language goals.
- Start practical.

INVOLVE YOUR LEARNERS

- Talk to your students – they know best what they want.
- Involve them in the selection of topic areas and even in the design of a task.
- Look for feed-back from them on how they liked the task e.g. ask them for two things they liked and one suggestion.

Accuracy and correction

Allow learners to make mistakes - it's all part of the fluency process.

Resist the urge to correct errors the moment you hear them. Hold back!

Correct supportively at the end, don't interrupt a learner in flow.

Jot down a few common errors you hear during the task cycle. In the final form-focus phase, or even in the next lesson when you've had a chance to plan better, write the phrases on the board, gapping the place where the error occurred. Ask the class to complete them in pairs. (But do remember there are lots of patterns that are late acquired, like third person singular so it's better to treat these very quickly and concentrate on common phrases and useful collocations.)

BE FLEXIBLE

If a task is going really well, and all students are engaged, let it go on—but stop in time to complete the task and bring things together positively at the end of the lesson. If you don't have time for a full report in the same class, you can set a written report of what they discussed for homework.

Be prepared to tweak the task as it progresses.

If things go wrong, think on your feet – and don't be afraid to stop the task and be creative – think of another way of doing it.

BE POSITIVE

Ensure all learners realize their creativity and their participation are valued.

At a form-focused feed-back stage, don't just correct mistakes, but concentrate on the positive; you could end with some of the good expressions you heard, or new phrases which were correctly spoken or written, and practise those with the whole class.

Look at the glass as half full not half empty. Do not think of your students as 'objects to be taught' but as partners from whom you can also learn about life. For me that is one of the basics of a task-based approach.

DON'T FORGET THE GRAMMAR

TBT does not mean you have to leave forms completely aside. The task will naturally involve a combination of structures, words, and meanings, which you can draw together and focus on afterwards.

Identify useful language from the text or task recording and prepare form-focused activities in advance for doing after the task. Then you know how much time to leave for this stage, and what to focus on at planning stage.

CHALLENGE YOUR STUDENTS!

- Don't underestimate students' desire to be challenged. Students – even children – often know more than you think.
- Don't intervene too much when students are doing the task. Set it up and step out of it. Let them do it on their own.

Don't give up

- If a task doesn't work first time, reflect on what went wrong, (maybe ask your students or colleagues for their suggestions) adapt it and try again.
- Learn from your mistakes. Always ask how you could make a bad task better, and a good task great.

To get started with TBT

- Learn by doing: i.e. try out a simple task, add a planning and report phase, and see how it goes.
- Don't be afraid to give up control. The students need you to facilitate and support them...not hold their hand every step of the way. Students will be autonomous if you let them be.

Figure 10.8 Ten tips for implementing TBT

And finally, in the words of two other teachers:

> From PPP to TBL is a difficult change to make because it implies doing away with years of traditional training and methodology history, which, though less than ideal, has for decades provided a secure frame where teachers can stand. There's only one answer to that: 'risking is winning'; and once the first experience has been successful, you realize that there's another way of teaching; and that this new way is, among other things, much more motivating and enjoyable for both students and teachers.'

DO NOT GIVE UP —IT REALLY WORKS.

We sincerely hope it works for you and your learners too. Try it and see.

Further reading

On getting students to record tasks:

Kindt, D. *'Turning up the heat': Energizing Conversation with Cassette Recorders.*
http://www.jalt-publications.org/tlt/articles/2000/06/kindt
Kindt, D. http://www.nufs.ac.jp/~kindt/pages/SOCCs.html
On getting students to prepare for conversation tasks using Students Own Conversation Cards (SOCCs).

For accounts given by teachers of the way they implemented and explored TBT with their classes in different countries and at different levels:

Edwards, C. and **J. Willis.** 2005. *Teachers Exploring Tasks.* Palgrave Macmillan Oxford.

For full coverage of the research concerning TBT and TBL:

Ellis, R. 2003. *Task-based Language Learning and Teaching.* Oxford: Oxford University Press.
Ellis, R. (ed.). 2005. *Planning and Task performance in a Second Language.* Amsterdam: John Benjamin.

For more on vocabulary learning:

Meara, P. 1995. 'The importance of an early emphasis on L2 vocabulary'. *The Language Teacher.* http://www.jalt-publications.org/tlt/files/95/feb/meara.html.
Nation, P. and **R. Waring.** *Vocabulary Size, Text Coverage And Word Lists.* http://www1.harenet.ne.jp/~waring/papers/cup.html
Beaton, A., M. Gruneberg, and **N. Ellis.** 1995. 'Retention of foreign vocabulary learned using the key-word method: a ten year follow-up'. *Second Language Research* 11/2: 112–20.

For ways to manage very large classes:

MacDonald, M. and Z. Thiravithul. *Team English for Large Classes.*
http://www.onestopenglish.com/teacher_support/methodology/archive/cl
assroom-management/large_classes.htm

Coursebooks featured in Chapter 10

Cunningham, S. and P. Moore with F. Eales. 2005. *New Cutting Edge Elementary.* Student's Book. London: Longman: 120–1.
Gairns, R. and S. Redman. 2002. *Natural English Intermediate.* Student's Book. Oxford: Oxford University Press: 103.
Kay, S. and V. Jones. 2000. *Inside Out Intermediate.* Student's Book. Oxford: Heinemann Macmillan: 62.
Redston, C. and G. Cunningham. 2005. *Face2Face Elementary.* Student's Book. Cambridge: Cambridge University Press: 66.
Redston, C. and G. Cunningham. 2005. *Face2Face Pre-intermediate.* Student's Book. Cambridge: Cambridge University Press: 72, 88.
Soars, J. and L. Soars. 2000. *New Headway English Course Beginners.* Student's Book. Oxford: Oxford University Press: 96.

Appendices

APPENDIX 1
SAMPLE TASK-BASED LESSONS

Here are seven sample tasks submitted to us by teachers around the world who are committed to TBT. The tasks are arranged in alphabetical order by surname of contributor.

Appendix 1.1: Earthquake safety

Teacher Yvonne Beaudry

Context Motivated adults, low intermediate, private language school, Tokyo.

Topic Earthquake safety; this task can be adapted to other natural disasters.

Background This was the third of a three-lesson unit to be taught by several teachers to different classes. It followed intensive reading and news-based authentic listening lessons with vocabulary work.

Task sequence
1 The class discussed natural disasters, brainstormed vocabulary (floods, wildfire, Richter scale, shelter), and shared personal experiences. (10–15 minutes)
2 Small groups discussed questions on earthquake preparedness and survival and transferred this information to a chart. The columns of the chart were divided into 'before', 'during' and 'after' stages of an earthquake (see p. 79). The cells of the chart are small to force note-taking instead of sentence writing. (20 minutes)
3 I distributed authentic pamphlets from the Red Cross and other organizations. Different groups received different stages of information. Each group compared the official information to the information in their charts and decided what information needed local adaptation. (20–30 minutes)
4 Students reviewed some phrases for giving directions and paired up to practise finding the emergency exit blindfolded. This provided a 'task break' in a long lesson and was practical – electricity sometimes fails during a quake. (10 minutes)

5 A jigsaw task. Groups with different stages of authentic information shared their information and added to their charts. (30 minutes)

6 Follow up included listing items to include in an earthquake kit (15 minutes), and reading stories of politics and earthquakes, e.g. how building code violations caused many accidents in Taiwan's 1999 quake, the long period that people lived in tent cities after the Kobe earthquake and international rescue co-operation.

Evaluation   Students reported that doing this activity in English made them focus on an important issue that was easy to ignore in Japanese.

Some students reported that the emergency exit activity was the highlight.

Yvonne's notes for teachers

Warm-up questions and trivia

Discuss the following questions:

• Natural disasters – what are they? (cyclone, tornado, earthquake, tidal wave, locusts, avalanche, floods, volcanoes, landslides, wildfire)
• Which natural disasters occur in Japan? Where/When?
• Have you ever experienced one?
• What was the world's biggest earthquake?
• What major earthquakes have occurred in the world in the last ten years?
• What is the Richter scale? How does it relate to the Japanese system?

Discussion

Discuss the following questions:

• What did you learn about earthquake safety in school?
• Have you ever been to a mock earthquake (the shaking trailer)?
• Where is the nearest refuge to your home/work/school/institution?
• If you don't know the above, it is homework.
• Where is the emergency exit in this building? Could you get there from this room if the lights went out and there was smoke?
• Try it with your eyes closed.
• Where is the safest place to be in an earthquake if you are in these places: in a house, on a high floor of a building, at your workplace, in a subway station, on the street, in your car?

Information sharing

1 Distribute the worksheet 'Earthquake safety' (see p. 79) and have students fill in the top row in small groups. For 'Before an Earthquake' they should consider a general state of preparedness. Take 'After an Earthquake' to mean up to a week after. For 'During ...' they should consider whatever various scenarios they can think of.

2 Have a short whole class discussion for groups to compare information.

3 Distribute the worksheet 'Earthquake Safety Information'. Have different students or groups read different sections and exchange information. A supplementary sheet for more advanced classes is available.

4 Have the students add to the second row of the 'Earthquake safety' worksheet. Besides just adding information, is there anything they need to delete or change? For example, most people in Japan think a helmet is essential but most other earthquake prone countries say it is pointless— by the time you get it, the main need for it is over.
Information from the Red Cross
http://www.redcross.org/services/disaster/0,1082,0_568_,00.html
and the Los Angels Fire Department
http://www.lafd.org/eqindex.htm#menutop

5 Have students make a list of what should be in an earthquake kit, personalizing it as needed (diapers, medicine, bilingual dictionary, …). Distribute the worksheet 'Earthquake kit'. Did they get many of the items? Do they think all the items are important? Which ones apply only to house or to apartment dwellers?

6 Hand out questions from the worksheet 'Earthquake tales'. Use with caution. If any seem unsuitable for your class, talk about feelings and fears instead—'The Big One' seems inevitable in Tokyo, are you scared?

Homework suggestions

Writing
• Follow-up on one of the topics from 'Earthquake tales'.
• Collect some survivors' stories from large earthquakes. Retell them in your own words.

Vocabulary

Encourage students to keep up their Vocabulary Notebooks.

Appendix 1.2: Text puzzle: Profits and media

Teacher Craig Johnston

Context First year college students in Japan studying mass media (i.e. a content course).

Topic The influence of the profit motive on news as reported by the media.

Background A mixed ability class with a very wide range of levels but the average was somewhere around low intermediate.

Task stages
1 See Worksheet below. Each paragraph of the article was broken into segments: clauses or even smaller units.

2 These segments were presented to the students in mixed order and the students' job (in mixed-ability pairs) was to recreate the original paragraphs. (There was no inter-paragraph mixing of segments.)

3 When students felt they were finished, they were presented with the original and asked to 'compare and repair'.

4 Focus on form: Students were asked to identify 'chunks' of language in the article. The stronger students found quite a lot, for example:
X have a lot of control over Y
some of the (negative consequences/problems) that result
mass media
harming the environment
losing advertising revenue
the ((current) economic) system

Evaluation I find this kind of task to be very effective for a few reasons:

1 It gives students a reason to engage with the text—they really wanted to figure it out for themselves and they stayed very focused.

2 The act of comparing (and repairing) with the 'official version' provides confirmation of comprehension and, where necessary, red flags signalling miscomprehension.

3 I also like it because it allows me to highlight and review certain forms without needing to get into lengthy explanations of grammar points. For example, if I want to draw attention to cause and effect, I parse the text in such a way that students have to wrestle with the placement of segments containing '*As a result...*' or '*Since....*'. Different parsing strategies can be used to focus attention on collocation, patterns, rhetorical devices, discourse features, etc.

4 The above are achieved in a student-centred manner. I don't have to spend much time explaining. (With such a mix of abilities in the class, my explanations are in danger of leaving half the class bored and the other half confused.)

WORKSHEET

Profits and media, Part I

Each paragraph in the article below is mixed up. Arrange the sections of each paragraph to recreate the original version.

Example:

a then I had breakfast. At 7:30 I

b I woke up early this morning. I had a shower and

c left for work.

Answer: b, a, c

Introduction

a the mass media are corporations too.

b At the end of that article, I noted that

c Today and next week we'll look at some of the problems that result when mass media become giant corporations,

d In last week's article we learned about some of the negative consequences of the power of large corporations.

e when profit dictates what is news and what is not news.

Where is the Watchdog?

f affecting the direction of medical research, avoiding taxes, and teaching children to be materialistic. So,

g There are at least three reasons:

h are they silent?

i We learned last week that the current economic system is doing serious damage in our world.

j why do the media so rarely criticize the economic system? After all, the media should be a watchdog, protecting us—why

k Multinational corporations are harming the environment, keeping worker pay extremely low in some countries,

Reason 1

l and they don't want it to change. Therefore,

m Corporations like the current economic system

n that media company risks alienating corporations and losing advertising revenue.

o if a media company strongly or frequently criticizes the economic system

Reason 2

p from the current economic system.

q If, for example, governments made new laws that required corporations to pay higher taxes,

r Naturally therefore,

s those new laws would hurt media companies.

t Media companies are corporations and they benefit

u media companies do not want the economic system to change.

Reason 3

v a lot of control over their media 'children'. Consequently,

w even larger corporations, and these 'parent' corporations have

x journalists often feel pressured to avoid writing stories that will anger the parent company.

y Large media companies are often owned by

Appendix 1.3: Family values

Teacher Shaun Manning

Context About 20 mixed level Korean university students aged 19–30. Students are not separated by level so range of ability is from near-native speaker to non-speaker.

Topic Family life in Asia. This was the first lesson of a 3-lesson series.

Background English program is a graduation requirement.

Objectives To introduce the topic; to evaluate and modify expressions of opinion.

Target task Compare the values of your group to those of others and try to find a matching group.
1 Students had to read a list of slightly controversial statements (see below) and decide if they agreed or not with each one.
2 They then had to work together to rewrite the sentences into a form that they all could agree on (i.e. reach a consensus on a revised sentence for each item on the list).
3 A spokesperson read out their team's version of the sentences and other teams listened and noted how they had been altered.
4 Teams then decided which team is closest in 'family values' to theirs.
5 Language focus was on the altering of the controversial statements in the light of the meanings that learners wanted to express—changing words like 'should' to 'might want to…' or 'get permission before marriage' to 'get advice before marriage.'—this was done *during* the task itself, with the help of the teacher.

These are the statements used in the task:
1 Children should only leave home after they are married.
2 Old people should be encouraged to stay in old people's homes rather than with the family.
3 People should not have more than two children.
4 Children should always obey their parents.
5 You should always get your parents' permission before getting married.
6 Children should pay rent to their parents if they are at home and have a job.
7 You should always be ready to help a member of the family.
8 The members of a family should live in the same area so that it is possible for them to visit each other.
9 Family life is less important in the modern world that it was in the past.
10 The government should do more to help families. (E.g. give daycare, medical care and money to parents.)

Some typical team answers:
1 Children should leave home when they can take care of themselves.
2 Old people should be encouraged to stay with their family.
3 It's a personal choice, etc.

Evaluation
1 Students liked the topic and the task provided plenty of laughter and interactivity.
2 Groups were able to reach a consensus on the items.
3 The informal nature of the linguistic focus helped them express what they wanted to say, rather than only work on changing modals (for example). However, it could have been done more formally.
4 I had planned it as a 20-minute activity; but because they were 'flying' in their groups, I let them keep going—it took the entire period. (50 mins.)

Appendix 1.4: Guess what animal this is

Teacher Theron Muller

Context Low intermediate first-year students, 18–19 years old, at a women's junior college in Japan.

Topic Animals

Target task Guessing game: students describe an animal then other group members guess what animal it is. This is then repeated but using an animal cartoon character.
1 I gave them a written example and they guessed the animal (a snake).
2 They each, as individuals, chose an animal and wrote out their description, using dictionaries and asking others in their group if they were stuck for words.
3 In groups of 5 or 6, with their desks in circles, they read out their descriptions.
4 They took brief notes about what animals and key words their other group members used.
5 We repeated the activity using animal cartoon characters, such as Mickey Mouse.

Evaluation I was really surprised how the dynamic changed as they started reading their descriptions: from thoughtful to enthusiastic and laughing. During the reflection time at the end of the lesson, when prompted to 'Write about what we did today' one student responded, 'We studied about animals today. "Animal quiz" is fun for me. But cartoon character is difficult for me'. Another wrote: 'We did game very enjoy. We choose many animal and character'.

Sample learner data

M. N.	R. M.	M. M.
Most people think it's big animal	It heals us.	This animal good tree climber.
It have long nose	It memorize trick.	It has a tail.
It can't run quickly	For example: shake hands and sit	It like banana.
It live in Africa very many	It can't speak.	
It eat grass	It is runs fast.	(Monkey)
(Elephant)	(Dog)	

Samples of two learners' notes of key points

Kanae	dog	like running
Rena	dog	shake hand
Miho	monkey	run quickly
Chie	elephant	long nose
Mai	panda	black and white

Kanae	dog cute	likes running
Rena	dog	shake hands
Chie	elephant	big ear and long nose
Mai	elephant	it can't run fast/big ear
Mai	panda	It has two colors/wite and brack

Appendix 1.5: 'Moulin Rouge' movie trailer comparison

Teacher Glen Poupore

Context South Korean teacher trainees on a speaking and writing skills course at MATESOL level.

Topic The DVD for the movie *Moulin Rouge* with Nicole Kidman and Ewan McGregor. The DVD contains two different movie trailers for the movie: one was designed for a North American audience and the other for a Japanese audience. The trailers are similar but also quite different in terms of what is shown, the music being played, and the overall mood of the trailer. Each trailer is about two minutes long.

Tasks 1 To watch the two trailers and to note down as many differences as they can. Students see the trailers twice, then in pairs they make a list of differences.

2 To speculate and explain why there are such differences between the two trailers. This can lead to a good discussion about cultural differences.

Language study Teacher provides the script for the trailers with some challenging vocabulary underlined. Students try to guess the meaning by using the context (and without using their dictionary).

Evaluation Movie trailers are short in dialogue with lots of visual support that make them easily usable with different levels. The movie was popular, it has sexy movie stars, and it is quite bright and colorful which makes it visually stimulating. Finding differences adds a level of challenge and interest. The cultural element is also interesting to the students.

Follow-up task (which could be given in a later class)
Separate students into those who have seen the movie and those who haven't. Students watch the movie trailers again and, in pairs, following the Guidelines (below), write a brief story of what they think will happen in the story (or what they remembered happening—taking into account the trailer).

Guidelines

Include
1 the setting (where the story takes place),
2 who is in the story (at least four characters),
3 the main plot of the story, and
4 how the story ends.

Appendix 1.6: Junk we carry around with us

Teacher Sandee Thompson

Context 12 intermediate students from a variety of Asian nations and two from Quebec. Age range was 23–60. Halifax, Canada.

Pre-task (Priming) phase I set the context by bringing in my bag and having students guess the contents. I then removed items from the bag and asked them to categorize them in some way that made sense to them (e.g. things that had scent, things that made a noise, money, rectangular shapes).

Task phase Students did the same task with the contents of their own book bags and talked about it with their partners.
Listening: students heard a tape of me doing the same task with a colleague. They were asked to take note of any differences that were apparent between the recording and their own discourse.

Language focus phase: students returned to their pairs and made notes of the differences they had noticed (e.g. native speakers tend to comment on the contents the other person removes, tend to paraphrase what the speaker says and often turn precise numbers in to quantifiers and vice versa).

Task repetition: they redid the task with a different partner and this time took note of what their partner said as they unloaded the contents.

Report phase: Students briefly reported their findings to the class. They also mentioned what they had noticed about the native speaker's interaction.

Form focus: From this lesson comes an analysis of quantifiers. We put a chart on the board and I elicit the quantifiers they used. These could be: a few (pens), a couple of (paperclips), a number of (lipsticks), a bunch (of coins). They then come up to the board and write in 'actual numbers' that correspond with the quantifiers—'2 or 3' for a few, '2' for a couple, '10' etc. for a number of, and so on. I also use a guided discovery task I created to provide them with extra language work. They listen to the native speaker talking on tape, fill in an identical chart with 'quantifiers' and 'actual numbers', and then compare it to what they did in order to explore how they are used in natural speech.

Evaluation The students enjoyed the task because they were sharing a part of themselves with their partner and because it provided the opportunity for a laugh (the things that we cart around with us for months on end without being aware of!).

Students liked being asked what they had noticed and enjoyed comparing what they did with what native speakers did. My keener students incorporated much of what the native speakers had done and the weaker students picked up what they could. In some cases, this was not much but it allowed them the opportunity to do the task a second time, which helped their confidence.

Variation Later I recorded a male colleague doing the same task to see if there were any differences in the way he did it from the way my original colleague (a woman) had done it. There weren't. But it gave me a chance to use both recordings with the class and ask them to compare the contents of his bag and her bag, and to use both for 'noticing' activities (listening for useful phrases and comments, etc.).

Appendix 1.7: Giving directions

Teacher Sandee Thompson

Context Beginners class in Halifax, Nova Scotia, Canada; mixed nationalities, age range 18–27.

Pre-task (Priming) phase I gave the students a small map of Halifax and asked them to tell their partner how to get to their home from school.

Task phase I gave students a sheet with instructions on how to get to my house and asked them to read the map, find the places mentioned and trace the route, following my written directions.

Planning and task repetition: students were asked to look at my directions, pick out phrases and language they might find useful, and then make notes about directions to their own home. They then redid the task when they felt ready.

Report phase: students were asked to give directions to their partner's home to the other groups and then the students in class put a push pin in that spot on the map and pinned the directions to that area of the map as well.

Form focus: students studied the written directions again and identified specific phrases of location, verbs giving directions, etc. Then we had a lesson focusing on the imperatives and prepositional phrases (turn right at the lights, etc).

Follow-up: I tested their knowledge by having them give me directions out of the room and down to the teacher's room.

Evaluation It was successful in more ways than one; in addition to becoming more confident in giving directions, the learners discovered they lived quite close to each other. After that, they started spending time with each other and waiting at the bus stop together.

APPENDIX 2
SAMPLE PROJECTS AND
SCENARIOS

Appendix 2.1: A new cafeteria

Teacher Aurelia García

Project briefing You want to open a new cafeteria and you own the premises in the corner of C. Gil and Irigoyen Streets ('ex-Mega Deportes'). In order to be successful you need to carry out some market research in the area to find out prospective customers' preferences. Work in groups of 4 or 5.

1 Design the questions for the survey you will carry out in the different bars/pubs in the area.
2 Carry out the survey.
3 Analyse the answers you get. Present this to the class.
4 Think up a creative marketing strategy which will ensure your success. Write this up briefly and display it for the class. Compare your ideas.
5 Produce a menu for your cafeteria. Include logo, slogan, prices, and any other necessary information. Display your menu. Vote to choose the best one.

Appendix 2.2: Radio talk show: Healthy teens?

Teacher Aurelia García

Project briefing Teens seem to have heard it all before. For as long as they can remember, parents, teachers, perhaps even doctors, have been telling them to eat vegetables, limit sweets, and drink milk.

Now, this advice takes on new meaning for a lot of very different reasons: How can they control their weight to put on muscle instead of fat? What's a healthy weight for them? How can they squeeze in a good, quick meal after school? All good questions which will find an answer in your talk show.

Think of …

- name of the programme
- possible guests
- commercials
- audience phone calls

Broadcast your programme.

Background and context This task was carried out as part of the teachers' training course, and also as part of the curriculum of a pre-intermediate group of teens. This is a group of only nine students around 13–14 years old. We use *Enterprise 2* as coursebook and in Unit 6: 'Food, glorious food', I proposed this project. I wrote different roles on slips of papers and we put them in a bag and they just picked out a role. They presented the talk show live. Unfortunately, I haven't got the technological resources to record them, which would be fantastic!

Teacher evaluation It's nice to see how they surprised each other at seeing how they have developed a character or designed a commercial, without the others even noticing this silent and hard (secret) work, which has been taking place for 2 weeks. The fact is that they get so involved in their own tasks within the project, that they forget about their partners. They laugh and enjoy the process and applaud themselves a lot.

While the task cycle is being developed the kids cover the contents proposed in the textbook unit. In the class after the presentation, they have to sit for an exam which in general terms had very good results.

Acknowledgements Aurelia's tasks were initially part of a TT scheme, and put together by the Instituto de Ciencias de la Educación para la Investigación Educativa (ICEII).
The teachers were: Dr Vilma Pruzzo de Di Pego, María Graciela Di Franco, Aurelia García, Eva Kloster, Jorgelina Rodriguez, Griselda Gulgliara, Regina Alfonso.

Appendix 2.3: Scientific presentation: Atmosphere and weather

Teacher Lorie Wood

Context Upper intermediate adults, working at a ship repair facility on a US Naval Base in Japan.

Project time Two weeks (20 classroom hours).

Topic Atmospheric pressure, 'wild' weather, fog and mist.

Stages
1 *Preparation:* The class was put into groups of three to create presentations. Each group worked on some aspect of the main topic. They selected their own specific topic, studied the target vocabulary from the textbook and became familiar with the content of their topic.
2 *Planning:* Students did Internet research on their chosen topics and developed a presentation. They had to provide information on the topic, and also create a scientific experiment that demonstrated the phenomenon they were explaining.

3 *Presentation:* All groups gave a power point presentation, a full explanation and a demonstration using their experiment. In the experiment (p. 97) 'mist' was heated in the bottle. This showed up clearly against the black paper. The presentations were followed up with a question and answer session.

Evaluation This class was quite nervous during this project as it was their first. I had used an experiment in the classroom while I introduced the target vocabulary from the textbook. Even though they were hesitant initially, they really seemed to enjoy themselves while they worked on their project. In fact, afterwards, they asked me when they would be doing another project. The only problem was a scheduling conflict; we didn't have enough time. We really needed about one more day, so that students were really confident before the presentations.

Appendix 2.4: Creating a newspaper

Teacher Lorie Wood

Context Advanced adults.

Project time 40 classroom hours over one month.

Background Students were studying vocabulary frequently used in newspapers: editorial, interview, news, feature, etc.

Project Each student created their own newspaper. They had to
- choose a native speaker to interview for a feature story;
- write a true news article;
- write an editorial on a global issue;
- write a letter to the editor on a base issue; and
- write an amusement review.

In preparation, they had to
- read a variety of newspapers and magazines;
- collect samples of each of the above types of articles, plus a sports article, advertisement, comic strip, political cartoon, a column, and a news article that described a situation in which someone was 'charged with' a crime ('charged with' was one of our target expressions).

Procedures
1 Students set up the interview and then developed their questions, and started to collect their articles. We compared and discussed the various writing styles.
2 Interview stages: a local reporter came and gave a presentation on conducting interviews, and answered questions. After this they practised their interview skills with each other in preparation for the actual interview. The interview was conducted and recorded. Next, they transcribed their interviews. During this time, we focused on the blended

sounds of native speech and cleared up misunderstandings. This was very insightful for students. Additionally, we had reflective discussions about the interview process.

3 Students started writing and revising as needed.

4 A second guest speaker, the editor of the base newspaper, came and discussed journalism and newspaper formats.

5 Students then created a design for their newspaper, incorporating the collected samples with their own stories. Students also had to write a sentence describing why they chose the particular articles they had collected and incorporate that into their page designs.

6 The newspapers were printed and distributed.

7 We then read the newspapers and had a wonderful discussion on the entire project, the topics in the articles, etc.

Evaluation The final projects were excellent. The outcome exceeded my expectations, and the students had a tremendous sense of accomplishment. When I first introduced the project, they honestly felt it was impossible, but through the process, not only did they find they could do it, but they could do it well, even easily.

Appendix 2.5: Fictitious marriage scenario

Teacher Yevgeny Slivkin

Context This task was carried out by American learners of Russian.

Background Sometimes people who wish to obtain a green card and stay in the USA marry someone who has US citizenship, even though they have no intention of staying together permanently as a married couple. These arrangements are called 'fictitious marriages'. Young Russian people who come to the US on student visas do this sometimes, since there are a lot of their former compatriots who have obtained US citizenship and who live in this country legally and they are willing to help.

The US Immigration and Naturalization Service tries to reveal these fictitious marriages, interviewing alleged spouses separately, asking them different kinds of cunning questions about each other to which only real spouses would be likely to know the answers. These could be questions about every day habits, gastronomical preferences, interests, hobbies, manners and so on. Before these interviews 'spouses' try to agree on as many things as possible in order to avoid discrepancies in the course of the interview.

Instructions Today our role-play situation will be the following:

Sveta and Vova, Kira and Misha—you will be two Russian couples suspected of fake marriages.

Roman and Vanya—you are immigration officials who will be conducting an interview in Russian.

Sveta and Vova; Kira and Misha—your task is to talk to each other in order to get prepared for this interview. You have to decide where and how you came to know each other and tell each other about your daily habits so that you will give the same answers when interviewed separately.

Roman and Vanya—your task is to come up with interview questions which will allow you to check on whether their marriages are genuine or fake.

Then you will conduct the interview and decide whether Vova and Misha should be deported from the country or not.

Procedures Ideally it takes a double conversation lesson to implement the whole scenario. During the first hour the two pairs of students who played the roles of the fake spouses prepared for their interview in the classroom. The two students who played the roles of the immigration officials prepared their questions outside of the classroom (in my office). I circulated between the classroom and the office, monitoring and helping them all, and sometimes giving them hints about what they should expect to be asked or to hear.

The 'officials' were allowed to have all their questions in written form during the interview but were encouraged not to read, but to ask them naturally. The 'fake spouses' were allowed to make notes in the course of preparation for the interview, but they were not allowed to use them during the interview. So, during the interview, they often became confused, gave wrong answers, and the 'officials' caught them on some discrepancies.

The interview was conducted during the first 20–25 minutes of the second hour. A 'husband' and a 'wife' from different couples were interviewed at the same time in different corners of the classroom. (The first interview actually could be conducted in the last 15–20 minutes of the first hour, if the preparatory work is complete.)

During the last 20 minutes, the 'officials' confronted the 'fake spouses' with discrepancies in their answers and asked for explanations. This is the most amusing and enjoyable part, since the 'spouses' tried to creatively extricate themselves from difficult situations, saying things like: 'Oh, my wife/my husband likes to buy new furniture/move furniture in the sitting room all the time, so I do not remember where exactly the sofa is located'; 'I can't tell you which side of the bed my wife/husband sleeps on, since she/he usually keeps tossing and turning all night', and so on.

I've staged this scenario three times, and each time one of the 'fake spouses' was deported, much to his or her annoyance.

Evaluation They really had a lot of fun with this activity. It was the first time in my teaching career that I saw students who did not want to leave the classroom for the break!

Variation The whole scenario could of course be squeezed into a one-hour lesson, but the number of topics for the questions should be limited, and the interviews would be much shorter.

APPENDIX 3
TRANSCRIPTS OF TASK
RECORDINGS

Appendix 3.1: Topic: Problem-page advice

Transcript contributed by David Cox

A Well, Christina, what advice would you give this woman?

C Well, I don't know, her ..., she seems to be having a lot of trouble with her daughter. I would say to her though that maybe she shouldn't be too pushy,

A mmm ...

C because her daughter could really react to that and just become really angry and ... you know ...

A Yeah. Go even further.

C Yeah, yeah.

A I think that, erm, she shouldn't, it's hard not to worry but I don't think she should get too worried about it because I think that a lot of times teenagers go through this phase and you know it's sort of something they have to learn their own independence and once they feel themselves then they're able to take their parents back into their lives.

C Yeah, exactly. I think that's ...

A Speaking from experience.

C No, I think you're right. Yeah. Often parents they just want to hold on to their kids as long as they can and they don't realize the child wants to break away and have friends that the parents don't necessarily have to know about or ...

A Right.

C Yeah.

A Yeah, becoming an adult.

C Yes, definitely, but just wait until she's past those teenage years, she'll come back.

A Yeah, and I mean, you know, just being as supportive as they can. You know, saying that, you know, that we're there for you, and erm that's I think about the best they can do, just make it clear that you love and support your child ...

c … your child in as many ways as you can, definitely, yep, good, I think those would work.

For a recording of the same task done by different people, see Cox 2005:183–4.

Appendix 3.2: Topic: Logic problem

Transcript from J. Willis and D. Willis 1988: Transcripts 158b

DF Okay?

BG Yes

DF well, two clues to help you. One of them went to London to visit her mother. There is only one woman so that must be Mary. Okay?

BG Right, So Mary went to London—

DF So it's Mary and mother. John bought a computer but not at Manchester, therefore it must be—

BG John must have gone to Birmingham.

DF Birmingham. Computer. And who's the other one? Peter.

BG must have gone to Manchester.

DF Manchester, to see—to go to the theatre. Okay?

BG Yes.

Appendix 3.3: Topic: Catherine: Working from home

Transcript from Gairns and Redman 2002

E So, do you like working from home?

c Oh yes, the great advantage is that I can work when I want to, (Right) and I can stop when I want to eat, and, well, eat when I want to, really, it's very good if you have a family and children. (Mm) Erm, also you don't waste time travelling to and fro from work …

E Ah, that's very good, yeah.

c So you have that extra, extra time, but the main disadvantage is that, well, you don't have that social contact that you get in an office …

E … or the friends … yeah.

c … or the fellow workers, yeah, erm … and it's harder to get away from work, it's always, if you've given a part of your house over to it, it's always there, you know, when you pass by the office, you see your computer (Yes, yes.) It's harder to escape and it does take up a lot of room in your house as well.

E Sure.

c That's the main disadvantage.

APPENDIX 4 (Workshop Handout) DESIGNING AND USING COMMUNICATIVE TASKS

Aim To design a sequence of different types of task that will generate *free language use* and lead to an *outcome* that can be shared with others.

Your topic ....

Seven types of task
1 **Listing: brainstorming and/or fact finding** e.g. things, qualities, people, places, features, things to do, reasons.
2 **Ordering and sorting: sequencing, ranking, classifying** e.g. sequencing story pictures, ranking according to cost, popularity, etc.
3 **Matching** e.g. listen and identify, listen and do (TPR), match phrases/descriptions to pictures, match directions to maps.
4 **Comparing: finding similarities or differences** e.g. comparing ways of greeting or local systems, playing 'Spot the Difference', contrasting two seasons.
5 **Problem-solving: logic puzzles, real-life problems, case studies, incomplete texts** e.g. logic problems, giving advice, proposing and evaluating solutions, predicting a story ending.
6 **Projects and creative tasks** e.g. doing and reporting a survey, producing a class newspaper, planning a radio show.
7 **Sharing personal experiences: storytelling, anecdotes, reminiscences, opinions, reactions** e.g. early schooldays, terrible journeys, embarrassing moments, soap opera scenes, personality quizzes.

Willis, D. and J. Willis 2007. *Doing Task-based Teaching*. OUP.

Planning a task-based lesson

1 Try out your task(s) with someone else. Refine your task instructions and write them down.
2 If possible, record two fluent speakers doing the task(s) (1–2 minutes each), and select and transcribe extracts to use in class.
3 Following the TBT framework below, plan each phase. Decide at what point(s) to use the recording(s).

TBT framework

Pre-task priming activities/mini-tasks
Task   **Planning a report**   **Reporting back**
Form focus Identify useful words, phrases and patterns from the texts/recordings. Systematize them: classify into semantic, functional, notional or structural categories.   Devise analysis and practice activities.
Task repetition and/or evaluation

Willis, D. and J. Willis. 2007. *Doing Task-Based Teaching*. OUP.

APPENDIX 5
SAMPLE TASK-BASED COURSE PLAN

English and global issues (draft course outline)
by Lorie Wood

Background

The 'English and global issues' unit plan was developed from students' requests to explore global topics and to pursue that exploration in English. Research for the unit uncovered the following textbooks: *You, Me and the World* and *Topics for Global Citizenship* by David Peaty (2004, 2005). Many of the activities in this unit were developed from ideas and topics presented in these texts.

Additionally, this unit plan was designed with the specific language needs and interests of students at the US Navy Ship Repair Facility (SRF) in Yokosuka, Japan. It was given to them as a handout at the start of their six-month (10-hours-a-week) course. However, it can easily be adapted to suit any student population.

Topics, tasks and useful websites for English and global issues

1 Environmental preservation/conservation
a Watch the EcoSurfer video and discuss.
   Identify areas of concern from the video and personal observations. List their causes and their potential consequences.
b Consider current natural environment policies and take positions for debate.
c Take photos of environmental issues and/or problems near your home or on the base, describe the situation and make a brief proposal for correcting the problem.
d Discuss whether this website below is really about environmental issues.
   www.sunnier.com/environment
e Watch news video about New York's garbage policies, discuss and debate.
f Guest speaker: US Navy chemist, presentation with Q&A following.

2 *Ecotourism*

a Investigate the following websites to understand the concept of ecotourism:

www.ecotourism.org

www.goipeace.or.jp

b Design a trip that upholds the Ecotourism Principles, and prepare a presentation.

c Identify the relevance ecotourism has for Japan.

d Describe, in an editorial format, how ecotourism can contribute to world peace.

e Describe your opinions in an open discussion forum (a 'Conversation Café') on sightseeing and its possible ecological disadvantages.

3 *New technology*

a Identify one technological advancement that could make a significant impact on one or more of the global issues we are studying. See the website below for an example of one of the many new technologies changing the world:

www.kyoceramita.com.au/files/1/eWoodLauch.pdf

b Identify any kind of technology not currently employed by SRF that could improve current practices by making them more ecologically friendly. Create a proposal for submission to the Captain.

c Discuss EcoBusiness. Use the Internet to investigate what EcoBusiness is and identify five ecobusinesses that sell a product that you routinely buy from a 'non' ecobusiness. Create a brochure for one of those businesses to be shared with your classmates, followed by a 'Conversation Café' discussion.

4 *Water conservation*

a Discuss current practices, international concerns, potential consequences, what can be done, what can you do in a 'Conversation Café' format.

b New technology video—watch and discuss.

5 *Global warming*

a Investigate and discuss the causes and impacts of global warming, alternatives for energy, and whether or not global warming is fact or fiction.

b Watch 'The day after tomorrow,' and discuss. Prepare for a 'Could this happen?' debate.

Consider the following in your group preparation. The websites below may also be helpful.

Aspects currently discussed in regard to global warming:

a Destruction of the ozone layer

b Acid rain

c Reduction of tropical forests
d Reduction in the diversity of wildlife
e Marine pollution
f Toxic waste going beyond national borders
g Desertification
h Pollution emanating from developing nations

www.globalwarming.org/science_archive.htm
www.nrdc.org/globalwarming
www.nrdc.org/air/default.asp
www.nrdc.org/cities/recycling/gnyc.asp

6 The homeless and poverty

a Look online and find statistics on homelessness for three different countries. In the homeless statistics, how many children are homeless? For those countries, identify resources for the homeless. Compare your findings with those of your classmates. In an open forum, determine which of the countries investigated have the greatest percentage of homeless people. Develop and share opinions about why this country has such a severe problem.

b Discussion: how do people become homeless? What stereotypes do we have of the homeless? What would we do if we suddenly found ourselves unemployed and unable to find work for 1 month, for 6 months, for 1 year, 2, 5?

c Find the poverty statistics for Japan, the US, and one other country. Discuss the fact that the minimum wage cannot pay for housing. Solutions?

d What is Heifer International? How is it helping the world fight poverty and hunger? Using the internet, find another organization that is trying to make a difference in the world and prepare a brief presentation that details its mission.

7 World peace/Nobel Peace Prize winners

Discussion: What does world peace mean to you? How do you think this could be accomplished? What could you do? What could Japan/US do?
Identify Nobel Peace Prize winners and their contributions. Choose one that in your mind has made the greatest contribution to peace. Prepare a presentation.

8 Volunteering

a Investigate different volunteer organizations and find one that interests you. Describe the organization to your peers and tell why you'd like to help this organization either by volunteering or some other way.

b Set up a volunteering 'conference' and prepare a recruitment presentation/booth for your volunteer organization.

9 Making a difference

a Investigate how 'real' people have made differences. What can you do to make a difference? What will you do to make a difference?

b Create a group proposal to Capt. Taylor outlining some of the ideas that SRF or another command could implement to make a difference in any of the areas that we have discussed in this unit. Develop a realistic recommendation for SRF and/or other commands. Write it up as a formal proposal and submit it to Capt. Taylor.

NOTES: We will be frequently working in the computer lab because there will be times when you want to do research to prepare for discussion and varied materials that I would like you to read. To keep this course ecologically friendly, I prefer that you read materials online rather than print them out.

One last task: Please read various articles in English or Japanese and summarize one in English each week. Submit on Fridays. In addition, please provide the original articles regardless of whether they're in English or Japanese. Thanks!

---

*Lorie's comments on this draft

'I have had so little time since I became a teacher that most things never go beyond the draft form. I tend to work with the drafts, jotting notes as I go along, but never formalize them. So this is still a draft—I don't know that it could ever be a final product as it needs to be revised and updated with new issues, technology, websites etc., and tailored to the needs of each specific group of students.'

'I am now back in the USA and have been and will continue using parts of it with a much broader community of students. In fact, I have adapted the environmental conservation and preservation aspect as part of an Earth Day focus for a group of 6–10 year olds to be done in 7 hours. I am also currently using the material on homelessness as an ongoing 'global awareness raising' course for a local group of teens (native and nonnative speakers) who meet for an hour once a week. The topics are universal, and the resources for customizing and personalizing them for whatever age group or language level are readily available. The key is to always incorporate a task that is appropriate for the student.'

APPENDIX 6
WORD FREQUENCY LISTS

The 200 most frequent words in English

in order of frequency (read down the columns, from the left)

the	get	where	part	against
be	more	after	little	home
of	when	back	late	early
and	can	right	child	something
to	up	should	life	small
a	out	even	old	service
in	who	how	seem	begin
that	about	most	end	per
have	see	because	state	party
it	time	find	government	hold
I	know	don't	same	one
for	other	man	case	all
on	take	down	woman	if
you	some	much	point	their
he	them	good	call	what
as	like	want	system	so
with	him	day	ask	could
this	its	between	yes	than
at	think	need	again	people
by	into	many	world	me
but	use	mean	group	your
his	then	our	hand	now
not	my	own	include	before
from	year	tell	set	leave
they	work	three	course	through
do	only	us	high	thing
she	come	still	interest	long
or	two	last	Mr	far
which	give	here	follow	might
an	just	too	company	each
we	look	feel	never	under
her	new	must	turn	number
there	may	house	while	however
say	any	off	try	another
will	over	great	form	why
go	also	put	show	start
would	first	both	area	keep
no	very	place	write	open
make	way	change	problem	school
well	such	become	provide	away

Nouns in the most frequent 700 words

in alphabetical order

account	cut	hand	model	project
action	date	head	moment	property
activity	day	health	money	quality
age	deal	help	month	question
agreement	death	history	morning	range
air	decision	home	mother	rate
amount	demand	hope	movement	reason
application	department	hour	music	record
area	design	house	name	relation
arm	detail	idea	nature	report
art	development	individual	night	research
authority	difference	industry	note	rest
bank	director	influence	nothing	result
base	door	information	number	role
basis	drink	interest	office	rule
bed	education	issue	officer	rule
behaviour	effect	job	page	scheme
benefit	end	kind	paper	school
bill	event	king	parent	section
body	evidence	labour	part	sense
book	example	land	party	service
boy	experience	language	patient	share
business	eye	law	pattern	shop
car	face	letter	peace	side
care	fact	level	people	sign
case	family	life	performance	situation
cause	father	light	period	society
centre	feature	limit	picture	son
century	field	line	place	sort
chapter	figure	list	plan	sound
child	film	load	plant	source
church	firm	lot	point	staff
city	food	love	police	stage
claim	food	man	policy	state
class	foot	management	position	step
club	front	manager	pound	story
colour	fund	mark	power	street
committee	future	market	practice	structure
community	game	material	president	student
computer	garden	matter	price	style
condition	girl	measure	problem	subject
control	god	method	process	system
cost	government	million	product	table
country	group	mind	production	tax
course	half	minute	programme	teacher

term	trade	value	war	woman
test	type	view	water	work
theory	union	voice	way	worker
thing	unit	walk	wife	world
time	university	wall	window	year

Verbs in the most frequent 700 words

in alphabetical order

accept	control	hope	pay	speak
achieve	cost	increase	play	spend
add	could	interest	please	stand
agree	cover	involve	produce	start
allow	create	join	provide	stay
answer	cut	keep	put	stop
appear	decide	kill	raise	study
apply	demand	know	reach	suggest
approach	describe	lead	receive	supply
attempt	design	learn	reduce	support
be	develop	leave	regard	suppose
bear	die	let	relate	take
become	do	lie	remain	talk
begin	draw	like	remember	tell
believe	drive	live	represent	thank
break	eat	look	require	think
bring	establish	lose	return	try
build	exist	love	rule	turn
buy	expect	make	run	understand
call	explain	matter	say	use
can	fail	may	see	visit
care	fall	mean	seek	wait
carry	feel	meet	seem	walk
cause	find	might	sell	want
change	force	mind	send	watch
charge	get	move	serve	wear
choose	give	must	set	will
claim	go	need	shall	win
close	grow	notice	share	wish
come	happen	open	should	work
concern	have	order	show	would
consider	hear	own	sit	write
contain	help	pass	sound	
continue	hold			

Adjectives in the most frequent 700 words

in alphabetical order

big	fine	less	open	similar
black	free	light	personal	simple
central	general	little	poor	single
certain	good	long	private	small
close	great	main	public	special
common	hard	national	recent	strong
complete	high	necessary	red	sure
different	important	old	round	white
early	large	only	same	wide
easy	last		short	young
far	late			

TEACHERS WHO CONTRIBUTED TASKS AND ADVICE TO THIS BOOK

Alicia Mora van Altena is from Argentina and works at Yale University in the USA. She has taught Spanish at college level since 1987 and before that she taught in Argentina at secondary and college levels for twenty-one years.

Maggie Baigent is British and teaches students of all levels and faculties at Bologna University, Italy. She has also worked in Egypt and Spain, and contributed to the Oxford University Press series *Clockwise* and *Natural English*.

Yvonne Beaudry, from Canada, teaches high school in Japan. She has previously worked in Sri Lanka, Indonesia, and Singapore as a volunteer, teacher, and curriculum developer; she is currently doing an MSc TESOL.

Claudia Bey (USA, German) works at the Defense Language Institute in the USA, which teaches languages to military personnel to be stationed overseas, such as the UN peacekeeping forces, for whom she designed the task in this book.

Dale Brown is British and works for GEOS Corporation in Japan where he develops English teaching and learning materials for a wide range of learners.

Beatrix Burghardt, Hungarian by birth, works as language coordinator for the Department of Central Eurasian Studies at Indiana University, Bloomington, USA, where she teaches Hungarian to diplomats at introductory and intermediate levels.

Joann Chernen is Canadian. She teaches ESL in the Professional and Career English Department at Vancouver Community College and communication skills for foreign-trained pharmacists at the University of British Columbia. She has also worked in Japan.

Bella Anna Cohen, Russian by origin, is now a US citizen. After teaching English in Europe and Chicago she moved to the Defense Language Institute as Russian specialist, program manager, OPI tester, and Diagnostic Assessment Specialist.

Rosane Correia is Brazilian and has been teaching EFL to Brazilian students at different levels. She also works as a branch supervisor for Centro Cultural Brasil Estados Unidos in Campinas, Brazil.

David Coulson is British and has taught Japanese learners of all ages and levels for many years. He now teaches communication classes to undergraduates at Niigata Women's College and is developing ways of teaching storytelling.

Marilyn Dahl, Canadian, works for The Higher Colleges of Technology in the United Arab Emirates, teaching English at various levels to young Emirati men. She previously taught ESL in Canada and the USA.

Aurelia M. García is from Argentina. She teaches English in a high school and a private language school in La Pampa. She also teaches Didactics and Practice at UNLPam and is an active member of an educational research team.

Roger Hawkey, from Britain, has many years' experience in English language teaching projects in Africa, Asia, and Europe. He is now a consultant on test impact and also supervises doctoral students in that area of research.

James Hobbs is from Britain and has lived in Japan since 1991, teaching high school, adult, and university classes. He is currently a full-time lecturer at Iwate Medical University.

Simon Humphries is British and is currently teaching English to engineering students at Kinki University Technical College in Japan. He has also taught French in the UK and completed a distance Masters in TESOL with Aston University.

Bob Jones is from Britain and has been teaching English in Japan since 1990. He now runs his own small school in Gifu Prefecture. Before going to Japan, he taught in Spain, Sweden, Malaysia, and the UK.

Michael Kelly is an English instructor from the USA who has been working in Japan for 10 years. He had a ESL column called Mikey's ABC in the Kobe Shinbun and now runs his own school in Akashi, Hyogo, Japan.

Patrick Kiernan is British and works at Tokyo Denki University, Japan, teaching English to engineering majors. He has worked in Japan for over 15 years and has taught students from beginner to advanced, and to all ages.

Celia Eva Kloster is from Argentina where she teaches English (all levels) at several high schools and at a private language school. She is an active member of an educational research team at the University of La Pampa.

Maria Leedham is British and works at Oxford University, UK, teaching undergraduate and postgraduate students. She previously taught in Japan and is on the editorial board of *The East Asian Learner*.

Lamprini (Lana) Loumpourdi is Greek and teaches teenagers and adults (intermediate and advanced) at a private language institution in Greece. She has also taught beginners and given seminars on testing to postgraduates at Aristotle University.

Shaun Manning is Canadian and teaches methodology at Hanguk University of Foreign Studies Graduate School of TESOL in Seoul, South Korea. He has developed online business English and task-based learning EFL programs.

Tim Marchand currently runs a Smith's School of English franchise in Kyoto, Japan. Originally from Britain, he has lived in Japan since 1998 where he has also taught English to business, high school and university classes.

Jason Moser, from Canada, is head of curriculum at the Osaka Shoin Women's University in Japan where over 20 Japanese and native-speaker instructors have successfully introduced task-based English teaching into their classrooms.

Theron Muller, an American, is co-owner of Noah Learning Center, a small English school in Nagano, Japan. He teaches students of all ages and levels, including various college classes.

Simon Mumford is British and works at The University of Economics, Izmir, Turkey, teaching the English preparatory year. He has also taught on summer courses in UK.

Glen Poupore, from Canada, teaches in Korea on the Konkuk-Illinois TESOL Program, a graduate school with students from intermediate to advanced level. He previously taught English to undergraduates in Konkuk University.

Yevgeny A. Slivkin is originally from Russia. After teaching Russian language and literature at three universities in the USA, he now teaches at the Defense Language Institute in California, where they run intensive language courses.

Sandee Thompson is Canadian and is the Director of Studies and a CELTA tutor at the International Language Institute in Halifax, Nova Scotia, Canada. She has taught EFL at various levels for over 13 years.

Heidi Vande Voort Nam, American, has been teaching English in South Korea since 1997. She currently teaches in the Department of English Education at Chongshin University.

Sandra A. G. Wiecek is a Brazilian EFL teacher at CEL-LEP, a large language institute in São Paulo, Brazil. She is currently teaching basic and intermediate levels and is interested in affective learning.

Lorie Wood taught English at a US Naval Base in Japan for seven years, using a range of project-based materials. She is now back in the USA where she runs 'The Learning Park', a home-stay language school.

Yasuro Tanaka is Japanese and teaches upper secondary students ages 16–18 at Funabashi High School, Funabashi City near Tokyo. He has been teaching in Japan for 24 years.

Aiden dela Cruz-Yeh is Filipino/Taiwanese and works at Wen Zao Ursuline College of Foreign Languages, Taiwan, teaching language and culture and intermediate and advanced EFL.

REFERENCES

Bachman, L. and **A. Palmer.** 1996. *Language Testing in Practice.* Oxford: Oxford University Press.

Bauer, L. and **I. S. P. Nation.** 1993. 'Word families'. *International Journal of Lexicography* 6/4: 253–79.

Breen, M. 1987. 'Contemporary paradigms in syllabus design: (Parts 1 and 2)'. *Language Teaching* 20: 91–2 and 157–74.

Bygate, M. 2001. 'Effects of task repetition on the structure and control of oral language' in **M. Bygate, P. Skehan,** and **M. Swain** (eds.). *Researching Pedagogic Tasks: Second Language Learning, Teaching and Testing.* Harlow: Longman

Carter, R. A. and **M. J. McCarthy.** 1995. 'Grammar and the spoken language'. *Applied Linguistics* 16/2: 141–58.

Corder, S. P. 1967. 'The significance of learner errors'. *International Review of Applied Linguistics* 5: 160–70.

Corder, S. P. 1973. *Introducing Applied Linguistics.* Harmondsworth: Penguin.

Coulson, D. 2005. 'Collaborative tasks for cross-cultural communication' in **C. Edwards** and **J. Willis** (eds.). *Teachers Exploring Tasks in ELT.* Oxford: Palgrave Macmillan.

Council of Europe. 2001. *Common European Framework of Reference for Languages: Learning, Teaching, Assessment.* Cambridge: Cambridge University Press.

Cox, D. 2005. 'Can we predict language items for open tasks?' in **C. Edwards** and **J. Willis** (eds.). *Teachers Exploring Tasks in ELT.* Oxford: Palgrave Macmillan.

Cullen, B. 1988. 'Brainstorming before Speaking Tasks'. *The Internet TESL Journal* Vol. 4/7.

Davis, P. and **M. Rinvolucri.** 1988. *Dictation: New Methods, New Possibilities.* Cambridge: Cambridge University Press.

Djapoura, A. 2005. 'The effects of pre-task planning time on task-based performance' in **C. Edwards** and **J. Willis** (eds.). *Teachers Exploring Tasks in ELT*. Oxford: Palgrave Macmillan.

Edwards, C. and **J. Willis** (eds.). 2005. *Teachers Exploring Tasks in ELT*. Oxford: Palgrave Macmillan

Eldridge, J. 1996. 'Code switching in a Turkish secondary school'. *ELT Journal* 50/4: 303–11.

Ellis, R. 2003. *Task-based Language Learning and Teaching*. Oxford: Oxford University Press.

Ellis, R. (ed.). 2005. *Planning and Task performance in a Second Language*. Amsterdam: John Benjamin's Publishing Company.

Ellis, M. and **C. Johnson**. 1994. *Teaching Business English*. Oxford: Oxford University Press.

Essig, W. 2005. 'Story-telling: effects of planning, repetition and context' in **C. Edwards** and **J. Willis** (eds.). *Teachers Exploring Tasks in ELT*. Oxford: Palgrave Macmillan.

Foster, P. 1996. 'Doing the task better: how planning time influences students' performance' in **J. Willis** and **D. Willis** (eds.). *Challenge and Change in Language Teaching*. Oxford: Heinemann.

Foster, P. and **P. Skehan**. 1996. 'The influence of planning on performance in task-based learning'. *Studies in Second Language Acquisition* 18: 299–324.

Fuchs, M., M. Bonner, and **M. Westheimer.** 1994. *Focus on Grammar*. Harlow: Longman.

Gairns, R. and **S. Redman.** 2002. *Natural English Intermediate*. Student's Book. Oxford: Oxford University Press.

Hobbs, J. 2005. 'Interactive lexical phrases in pair interview tasks' in **C. Edwards** and **J. Willis** (eds.). *Teachers Exploring Tasks in ELT*. Oxford: Palgrave Macmillan.

Jabbour, G. 1997. *Corpus Linguistics, Contextual Collocation and ESP Syllabus Creation: a Text-analysis Approach to the Study of Medical Research Articles*. PhD thesis. University of Birmingham.

Johnston, C. 2005. 'Fighting fossilisation: language at the task versus report stages' in **C. Edwards** and **J. Willis** (eds.). *Teachers Exploring Tasks in ELT*. Oxford: Palgrave Macmillan.

Kelly, C. and **A. Gargagliano.** 2001. *Writing From Within*. Cambridge: Cambridge University Press.

Kelly, C. and **A. Gargagliano.** 2004. *Writing From Within: Introductory.* Cambridge: Cambridge University Press.

Leaver, B. and **J. R. Willis** (eds.). 2004. *Task-based Instruction in Foreign Language Education: Practices and Programs.* Washington D.C.: Georgetown University Press.

Leedham, M. 2005. 'Exam-oriented tasks: transcripts, turn-taking and backchannelling' in **C. Edwards** and **J. Willis** (eds.). *Teachers Exploring Tasks in ELT.* Oxford: Palgrave Macmillan.

Lightbown, P. and **N. Spada.** 2006. *How Languages are Learned* (Third edition). Oxford: Oxford University Press.

Long, M. 1988. 'Instructed interlanguage development' in **L. Beebe** (ed.). *Issues in Second Language Acquisition: Multiple Perspectives.* Rowley, Mass.: Newbury House.

Long, M. and **G. Crookes.** 1992. 'Three approaches to task-based syllabus design'. *TESOL Quarterly* 26/1: 27–56.

Lopes, J. 2004. 'Introducing TBI for teaching English in Brazil: learning how to leap the hurdles' in **B. Leaver** and **J. R. Willis** (eds.). *Task-based Instruction in Foreign Language Education: Practices and Programs.* Washington D.C.: Georgetown University Press.

Loumpourdi, L. 2005. 'Developing from PPP to TBL: a focused grammar task' in **C. Edwards** and **J. Willis** (eds.). *Teachers Exploring Tasks in ELT.* Oxford: Palgrave Macmillan.

Lynch, T. and **J. Maclean.** 2001. 'A case of exercising: effects of immediate task repetition on learners' performance' in **M. Bygate, P. Skehan,** and **M. Swain** (eds.). *Researching Pedagogic Tasks: Second Language Learning, Teaching and Testing.* Harlow: Longman.

Lys, F. 2004. 'Using web technology to promote writing, analytical thinking and creative expression in German' in **B. Leaver** and **J. R. Willis** (eds.). *Task-based Instruction in Foreign Language Education: Practices and Programs.* Washington D.C.: Georgetown University Press.

McCarthy, M., J. McCarten, and **H. Sandiford.** 2005. *Touchstone 1.* Cambridge: Cambridge University Press.

Meara, P. 1995/2001. 'The importance of an early emphasis on L2 vocabulary'. *The Language Teacher.* http://www.jalt-publications.org/tlt/files/95/feb/meara.html.

Mehnert, U. 1998. 'The effects of different lengths of time for planning on second language performance'. *Studies in Second Language Acquisition* 20: 83–108.

Nation, P. 2001. *Learning Vocabulary in Another Language.* Cambridge: Cambridge University Press.

Nunan, D. 1989. *Designing Tasks for the Communicative Classroom.* Cambridge: Cambridge University Press.

Nunan, D. 1995. *Atlas: Learning-centred Communication.* Boston: Heinle and Heinle.

Nunan, D. 2004. *Task-based Language Teaching.* Cambridge: Cambridge University Press.

Peaty, D. 2004. *You, Me and the World.* Tokyo: Kinseido Publishing Co. Ltd.

Peaty, D. 2005. *Topics for Global Citizenship.* Tokyo: Kinseido Publishing Co. Ltd.

Pica, T., R. Kanagy, and **J. Falodin.** 1993. 'Choosing and using communication tasks for second language instruction and research' in **G. Crookes** and **S. Gass** (eds.). *Tasks and Language Learning: Integrating Theory and Practice.* Rowley, Mass.: Multilingual Matters Ltd.

Pinter, A. 2006. *Teaching Young Language Learners.* Oxford: Oxford University Press.

Prabhu, N. S. 1987. *Second Language Pedagogy.* Oxford: Oxford University Press.

Schmidt, R. 1990. 'The role of consciousness in second language learning'. *Applied Linguistics* 11/2: 129–58.

Selinker, L. 1972. 'Interlanguage'. *International Review of Applied Linguistics* 10: 209–31.

Sinclair, J. and **M. Coulthard.** 1975. 'Towards an analysis of discourse' in **M. Coulthard** (ed.). *Advances in Spoken Discourse Analysis.* London and New York: Routledge.

Skehan, P. 1998. *A Cognitive Approach to Language Learning.* Oxford: Oxford University Press.

Stevens, V. 2004. 'Webhead communities: writing tasks interleaved with synchronous online communication and web page development' in **B. Leaver** and **J. R. Willis** (eds.). *Task-based Instruction in Foreign Language Education: Practices and Programs.* Washington D.C.: Georgetown University Press.

Storch, N. 2002. 'Patterns of interaction in ESL pair work'. *Language Learning* 52/1: 119–58.

Sweeney, S. 2004. *The Effect of a Project Based Methodology on English Language Learning and Performance amongst Elementary Level Arab Students.* MSc Dissertation, Aston University, Birmingham.

West, M. 1953. *A General Service List of English Words.* London: Longman, Green and Company.

Willis, D. 2003. *Rules, Patterns and Words: Grammar and Lexis in English Language Teaching.* Cambridge: Cambridge University Press.

Willis, J. 1996. *A Framework for Task-based Learning.* Harlow: Longman Pearson Education.

Willis, D. and J. Willis. 1987. 'Varied activities for variable language'. *ELT Journal* 41/1: 12–18.

Willis, D. and J. Willis. 2001. 'Task-based language learning' in R. Carter and D. Nunan (eds.). *The Cambridge Guide to Teaching English to Speakers of Other Languages.* Cambridge: Cambridge University Press.

Willis, J. and D. Willis. 1988. *Collins Cobuild English Course Level 1* (Transcripts). London: Collins ELT.

Willis, J. and D. Willis (eds.). 1996. *Challenge and Change in Language Teaching.* Oxford: Heinemann Macmillan.

READER ACTIVITIES

INDEX